Tony Blair:

The Man Who Lost

His Smile

Tony Blair:
The Man Who Lost His Smile

Leo Abse

ROBSON BOOKS

First published under the title *Tony Blair: The Man Behind the Smile* in 1996, and as an updated edition in 2001.

This new and updated edition entitled *Tony Blair: The Man Who Lost His Smile* first published in Great Britain in 2003 by Robson Books, The Chrysalis Building, Bramley Road, London, W10 6SP

An imprint of Chrysalis Books Group plc

British Library Cataloguing in Publication Data
A catalogue record for this title is available from the British Library.

ISBN 1 86105 698 2

Typeset by SX Composing DTP, Rayleigh, Essex
Printed by Creative Print and Design, Ebbw Vale

Critical acclaim for *Tony Blair: The Man Behind the Smile*:

'A highly controversial but splendidly written book by one of Labour's great socialist reformers. Abse's pithy observations, combined with his unapologetic criticism of New Labour may not suit the faint-hearted, but it should the rest of us.' Mark Seddon, *Tribune*

'Age does not weary the exoticisms of Abse's tirades . . . fine raillery . . . touched by genius.' Matthew Parris, *The Times*

'. . . an extraordinary book . . . Leo Abse is a heretic . . . a howl of pain and fury . . . an angry disavowal of New Labour and all its works . . . gives expression to opinions that many within the Labour Party may hold but few would dare to express.' Julia Langdon, *Glasgow Herald*

'. . . entertainingly sinister analysis.' *Independent on Sunday*

'A devastating and disturbing portrait of a man who could be our next Prime Minister.' David Hughes, *Daily Mail*

'A ruthless appraisal of New Labour. A savage denunciation of the Leader . . . At a time when sycophancy is the rage in Labour circles this extremely eccentric book is well worth a read.' Tariq Ali, *Punch*

'Abse has the courage to express what many fear: that a Labour Government under the leadership of Blair is likely to be hesitant and ineffective.' Anthony Storr, *Sunday Times*

'. . . [a] powerful philippic.' Anthony Howard, *The Times*

'Abse's book . . . now seems extraordinarily prescient in its forecast of "government by dream which will collide with reality" and of a leadership "exuding the debased charisma of our popstars and fashion models".' Peter Dunn, *New Statesman*

Also by Leo Abse:

Private Member:
A Psychoanalytically-oriented
Study of Contemporary Politics

Margaret, Daughter of Beatrice:
A Politician's Psycho-biography of Margaret Thatcher

Wotan, My Enemy:
Can Britain Live with the Germans in the European Union?

Fellatio, Masochism, Politics and Love

To Ania Czepulkowska
In Love

First of all, you must learn the constitution of man and the modifications which it has undergone, for originally it was different from what it is now. In the first place there were three sexes, not, as with us, two, male and female; the third partook of the nature of both the others and has vanished, though its name survives. The hermaphrodite was a distinct sex in form as well as in name, with the characteristics of both male and female, but now the name alone remains, and that solely as a term of abuse . . . Each of us then is the mere broken tally of a man, the result of a bisection which has reduced us to a condition like that of a flatfish, and each of us is perpetually in search of a corresponding tally.

Plato's Symposium

Contents

Acknowledgements

This psychobiography, with all its updatings and additions to the second edition of *The Man Behind the Smile*, could not have been produced without the aid of my indefatigable amanuensis Frances Hawkins; only by her constant invigilation, preliminary editing and counselling, has the work been completed.

Friends are much needed to incite and encourage an octogenarian to persist in writing. Without in any way committing them to agreeing with the contents of this polemic, I would wish again to thank them, and others, for the support they continued to give me. Some responsibility for this edition therefore falls upon: Gillon Aitken, literary agent; Reva Berstock, psychoanalyst; Michael Bloch, biographer; Rabbi Sidney Brichto; George Bull, biographer and translator; Alan Cameron, publisher; Stuart Cameron, administrator; Paul Cavadino, penologist; Laura Coy, travel consultant; Stephen Cretney of All Souls; Michael Foot, Renaissance Man; Geoffrey Goodman, editor and biographer; Jürgen-Michael Gottinger, management consultant; Bert Greatrex, my classmate; John Gritten, biographer; David Hughes, political editor; Hardy Jones, educationist; Brett Kahr, psychotherapist and composer; Fred Kendall, publisher; Julia Langdon, biographer; Charles Leeming, solicitor; Graham Little, political scientist; Harry Lloyd, retired magistrates' clerk; Richard Martin, economist; Colin Merton, Savile Club Librarian; Eddie Mogridge, builder; Christopher Morgan, religious correspondent; David Parfitt, painter; Dacre Punt, designer; Jeremy Robson, publisher; Andrew Ross, botanist; Martin Rowson, cartoonist; Ivan Sadka, solicitor; Peter Soar, solicitor; Mike Steele, lobby correspondent; Brian Thompson, headmaster; Richard Tilleard-Coles, psychiatrist; George Warburg, banker; Ernest Woolf, psychoanalyst.

I am, too, as ever, grateful for the help and stimulation given me by my psychoanalyst elder brother Wilfred, my poet younger brother Dannie, my historian son Tobias and my daughter Bathsheba Morabito.

I am much indebted to George Lewith and Vidurath Mayadunne, whose friendship and medical skills have helped me to overcome some of the disabilities caused by my stroke in 2002. And, not least, I give my thanks to my physician Stephen Hirst who, to the dismay of my enemies, continues to keep me alive.

I would wish in this work to record, as in my previous books, my indebtedness to the Torfaen Labour Party and the electors of the Eastern Valley of Gwent who, for thirty years, with considerable forbearance, gave me the opportunity to observe, participate in, and endure, the strange life, sometimes ennobling, sometimes demeaning, which is the lot of the children of the Mother of Parliaments.

John Smith:
The Lost
Leader

On 12 May 1994 the Leader of Her Majesty's Opposition, the Right Honourable John Smith, lost his gamble. A heart attack he had endured had made him aware of his vulnerability, but he was not content to amble along as a respected backwoods Edinburgh lawyer. His ambition was greater, as was his capacity; he took the fateful risk, and plunged back into politics. When death cruelly mocked his daring, the whole nation mourned. The British Labour movement stood bereft. In the Commons John Smith's peers huddled together, comforting each other in their desolation, and vowed they would not engage in a bitter fratricidal struggle for the succession; the precepts of their lost leader governed them. They believed, as the nation believed, that a good man had been taken from them; and that perception was correct, for there was a singular lack of dissimulation in John Smith. Unlike most politicians, his public image and his private life were wholly congruent.

I encountered him, and learned of him, during the bitter devolution debates that in 1978 and 1979 took place in and out of Parliament when, yielding to aggressive nationalist clamour, a weak Labour government, struggling to remain in power with a precarious majority that could be endangered by nationalist MPs, sought to impose upon Wales and Scotland a form of government to which Wales was overwhelmingly hostile, and one to which many in Scotland were indifferent. Party devolution issues, as again in 1996, arouse rare political passions. John Smith, on the front bench, was one of the two main government spokesmen attempting to steer through a devolution bill, one to which I was wholly opposed. In a parliamentary ploy, I sponsored, with considerable support, what is termed a 'reasoned amendment' to the bill, and thus succeeded in wresting from the government, as a precondition to implementation of the devolution proposals, that first they had to be approved by way of a referendum by the electorate of Wales and Scotland. It was during that referendum campaign that I came into direct conflict with John Smith; and even as with one's enemies we often learn to understand them more than those we love, for love can be blind, so in political disputes, we sometimes can measure opponents more objectively than allies. I did not find John Smith wanting.

The catalyst which brought me nearer to the man was a televised Oxford Union debate when he, together with Emlyn Hooson, now a Liberal peer, put the case for devolution and I, together with Leon Brittan, opposed the motion. Although I suspect, and hope, the Oxford Union is altered and that the undergraduates now are less politically precocious and less precious, in the 1970s it was an anachronism; the youngsters role-played *Brideshead Revisited* parts, Edwardian postures were affected, carefully prepared impromptu interventions were *de rigueur*, and a painfully self-conscious style and strained wit gained disproportionate approval. I had often been invited to speak at the Oxford and Cambridge Unions and, although I had been much disconcerted on my first attendance by the responses, I was familiar with their absurd and highly mannered nonsense and had long since made the necessary adjustment, had accepted the prevailing idiom, and consequently many times enjoyed a good dinner and an evening out away from the tedium of the Commons. But this devolution debate was not fun; it was for real. The referendum polling date was near – St David's Day 1979 – and a substantial section of the electorate, certainly in Wales, was viewing the programme. It was not possible, however, simply to use the occasion to speak over the heads of the undergraduates to the voters; reverberations coming from within the audience would resound through the screen and a negative or positive response by the youngsters could play a part in influencing the votes of the viewers. It was necessary, therefore, to tailor one's contribution in the short time available to two disparate groups; and laughter and high seriousness had to be conjoined.

I was comfortable in my contribution, and all went very well; but the debate for the pro-devolutionists was a disaster. John Smith was disadvantaged by his professional legal training, and even more by a speaking style developed during his arduous student debates at Glasgow University, traditionally conducted with an earnestness and intensity frowned upon in the Oxford Union, where frivolity and irony were overvalued. Thus ill-equipped, Smith could not adapt, and although his earnest, heavy-handed, studiously prepared piece would have passed well enough in a court or in Glasgow, coming from the ambience of the Union it was a catastrophe; and, of course, he possessed the sensibility, even before he completed his speech, to know that he had failed.

The following morning we did not travel back to London together and for a while he avoided me in the lobbies of Westminster. But when, many months later, in an important Commons debate he made a devastating attack upon the Tories, who wilted as, with fact and logic, he assailed them, I congratulated him; he was half embarrassed by my praise and immediately ruefully recalled his dissonant Oxford speech. But, more revealingly, he began criticising the speech I was deservedly praising; he commenced categorising its omissions and its flaws, all of which in fact were, at most, peccadilloes. He was not seeking from me disclaimers, reassurances that they were of no importance; on the contrary, he wanted corroboration from me that his self-criticisms were totally valid.

This was unusual behaviour. Among MPs after a debate there is only too often a sickening display of hypocritical mutual congratulation between participants, each telling the other how splendidly he has performed; but John Smith wanted no such massaging. And, because he knew I would be cruelly objective, I was to find that from time to time, after a speech, he would sometimes approach me shyly, not asking but waiting for my assessment. Always, however, no matter how good I said his content and presentation had been, still he insisted on their inadequacy; becoming aware of the pattern, I recall once telling him to cease punishing himself, but it was to no avail. The perfectionist was in the grip of a condition described by the French poet Mallarmé as the 'malady of the ideal'. The coronary he was to suffer was not the cause of his death; that thrombosis was but a symptom of that fateful malady.

His affliction was his compulsive search for the ideal; and that ideal had been set for him by his card-carrying Labour Party headmaster father whose school he had attended. There he was expected to get it right even when other children were out of their depth: 'It was always "Why weren't you top of the class?" In the end it was easier just to be top of the class,' he once said. And always his father's injunction governed him as he walked up, as was his wont, to the top of mountains or when he sought perfection in the attainments of himself and in himself. His quest for perfection brought many benefits for the Labour Party as the shoddy glitz and superficiality of the Kinnock era gave way to John Smith's painstaking insistence upon well-thought-out policies and careful political stratagems informed by high standards and moral values. To some at the top of his party, this was an unwelcome approach. There are politicians for whom stillness is death and who, to survive, must forever live in a frenzy of excitement. They cannot tolerate delay and, presenting their inchoate notions in language as vague as their content, inflict upon us premature and faulty decision-making; they insist tomorrow is today and anyone who challenges their novel calendar is dubbed a 'yesterday man'. John Smith, in private Labour political circles, was so labelled by the self-styled modernisers surrounding Tony Blair, who peddled the tale that the resistant Smith was stubborn, arrogant and impervious to change.

That tension should have arisen between Smith and Blair was predictable; the one had genuine and profound roots in community, in the little Scottish fishing village where he had lived out his childhood, and knew and understood the value of continuity, and indeed had revelled in writing a history of his own settled family from the eighteenth century onwards; the other was essentially a gypsy, the son of a man who held strong but ever-vacillating political views, sometimes communist, sometimes High Tory, as he wandered, dragging his family with him even to the Antipodes, forever burdened with the irrational guilt of the illegitimate and forever concealing his ambiguous lineage from his own family. Smith was a man with roots; Blair is rootless. That their attitudes to the traditions of the Labour Party should have differed was a consequence; the one respected those traditions, the other irreverently dismissed them.

Smith felt, as a country village lad with the sea in his ears, 'the very pulse of the machine' and loathed disruption in the elemental, in the determined patterns within life. Abortion repelled him and, unlike the majority of his party, he consistently voted against those seeking to relax the existing laws. His abhorrence was principled; it gave him no political advantage. He represented a constituency with only a small number of Roman Catholics; he was certainly not yielding to lobby pressures. Despite all my persuasions, he supported Enoch Powell's 1985 bill which would have criminalised research on embryos. In vain did I plead with Smith to desist in his support, telling him that abortion ended life but that *in vitro* fertilisation created life and gave the infertile the boon of parenthood. He was unconvinced and voted against my amendments to Powell's bill. In the end I was able to wreck that bill only by filibustering, making hours-long speeches that sabotaged Powell's parliamentary timetable.

But such stances by Smith gave overzealous Blairites full opportunity to misrepresent him as rigidly conservative, lacking the will to make the necessary changes in party and national policies. That, however, was not the appraisement made by a large section of the public. Taking another view, many increasingly responded to one who they saw as making a serious effort to meet the nation's problems, and one who, at last, possessed gravitas; it was unexciting politics but it was honest and deserved respect. The private man, refusing to be precipitate and striving over-conscientiously to remove blemishes from all the policies he hoped one day to implement, was paying a heavy price for the approval that he was slowly but increasingly gaining from the public; for in his pursuit of such policies he was severely handicapped, weighed down with guilt as he was that, by his honest presentation of the tax implications of Labour's policies during the 1992 General Election, he had let himself and his party down, and had contributed to the subsequent defeat. He felt he had not lived up to the standards he had set himself as a political strategist.

The mood that scorched John Smith, his recurring sense of dissatisfaction with himself however great his actual achievement, is recognisably a theme running through Freud's earliest papers and which continued into his last work. Freud regarded dissatisfaction as endemic to the human condition: 'There is always something lacking for complete ... satisfaction; *en attendant toujours quelque chose qui ne venait point* [always waiting for something which never comes].' Total contentment is denied to mankind; at the most, the happiness that comes from satisfaction of needs 'is from its nature only possible as an episodic phenomenon'. This disposition, Freud believed, was genetically determined and, reductively, he commented: 'However strange it may sound we must reckon with the possibility that something in the nature of the sexual instinct is unfavourable to the realisation of complete satisfaction.' Those who impose upon themselves excessively high ideals and targets in their restless search for fulfilment are denying biology; they are attempting to abolish the distance between their ego and their ego-ideal, but no matter how much they strain themselves, they are in danger of plunging fatally into what is an unbridgeable ravine. And so, to our loss, it happened to John Smith.

According to opinion polls taken in the months before his death, 72 per cent of the electorate believed 'he looked to be like a man with high moral standards and with the air of a family doctor or bank manager'. Nevertheless, by March 1994 the MORI pollsters were still able to interpret their statistics to disparage John Smith. They reported: 'John Smith has failed to inspire the voters; his rating remains evenly balanced with 38 per cent of the public in favour and against.' John Smith, however, patiently fought on and when he died Labour was reported to have a lead over the Tories of 21 per cent. After John Smith's death, believing such a lead was unsustainable – certainly until some new leadership had over time established itself – the Labour Party displayed scrupulous and rare political tact. Some, with more intimate knowledge of the capacities of the possible contenders, claimed that Robin Cook, with his past commitment to the Labour movement, his extraordinarily high intelligence and piercing debating skills, was best fitted to the challenging task; but the physical disadvantages from which he suffers bore heavily upon him and he disqualified himself. A public debauched by meretricious television, conditioned to demand the photogenic, to mistake image for content, would probably have ill received such a leader. Gordon Brown, another possible contender of ability, was privately becoming locked in a struggle with Blair; but, exacting the price that in any future Labour government he would, in effect, be joint premier, he conceded, albeit smouldering with anger, to the man he thought was inferior. With the field thus limited, Blair was poised to be a front-runner; and, although Labour Party activists were sceptical and 47 per cent of the party members did not vote for this untried, untested man, the new method of election of a Labour leader, founded on the one man one vote principle and with many more than ever before participating, gave the crown to Blair.

And then came the astonishing consequence. By a political chemistry unable to be adequately analysed by all the confounded conventional commentators, the unknown Blair, within weeks, achieved a result which all the painstaking work of John Smith had failed to bring about; and it occurred despite the polls telling us that at that time an increased optimism about the economic outlook was abroad. While in May 1994, in answer to the question who would make the best prime minister, 31 per cent declared for John Smith, in August 1994, 45 per cent declared for Blair. The Gallup polls showed that Labour commanded more widespread support than any party in Gallup's 57-year history and the Labour lead over the Conservatives was, by a wide margin, the largest either of the major parties had ever enjoyed over the other. Anthony King presented the Gallup poll figures and emphasised: 'Far more voters declare that Blair would make the best prime minister than ever thought that of John Smith, though his standing was high.' By the end of August the MORI poll revealed not only that the election of Blair as leader had resulted in a shift of middle-class and southern voters behind the Labour Party but also that a big shift in voting intentions had taken place among women throughout the country.

Some of the perplexed political commentators sought to dismiss this sea change in public opinion as a temporary infatuation; the 'honeymoon' period would soon be over. A very few others, more insightful, hazarded a guess that, as had occurred in other European countries – such as Italy, where the death of the communist leader Berlinguer had resulted in the subsequent gain of political support by his party – the reparative guilt that could bring about such occurrences would fade once the mourning period for John Smith was over. Such prognostications proved spurious; time has shown that the phenomenon of Blair cannot be so explained. And since the divisions and sleaze of the government were in place at John Smith's death, Blair's sudden and immediate leap into electoral popularity cannot be attributed to Tory follies. By the date of the May 1997 General Election, the polls were showing that, in contrast to Major, Blair was overwhelmingly regarded as being a stronger leader, a man with better ideas and more in touch with ordinary people.

What then was the magic at work that enabled an almost unknown political figure to gain and sustain such popularity from May 1994 onwards? Despite widespread disenchantment with the performance of the two Labour governments among Labour and trade union activists, notwithstanding a visceral dislike towards him displayed by so many informed commentators and distinguished academics, and although more than one million took to the streets to protest against his Iraq war, which occasioned two unprecedented parliamentary revolts and the resignations from Cabinet of Robin Cook and Clare Short, still the opinion polls show that however sulkily the electors now abstain or register their votes, Blair remains, albeit precariously, in the ascendant. Has he been exercising during all these years the qualities of a charismatic leader? We have had our Thatcher but we are more accustomed to noting charismatic leadership in other lands: Gandhi in India, Hitler in Germany, Mandela in South Africa. We live in a more temperate political climate, inhospitable to exotics. Nevertheless, in my political lifetime I have witnessed two leaders in the Labour movement, Hugh Gaitskell and Aneurin Bevan, possessed of a charisma that hosts of followers found irresistible. And I have seen one Labour figure, George Thomas, Viscount Tonypandy, a primary schoolmaster lacking gravitas and with seemingly few qualifications, exercise an astonishing and rare charisma, which enabled him not only to capture his electorate and the Royal Family but to seduce a tough House of Commons, which yielded to his charm and made him Speaker. Is Blair of a similar order, and are the resonances which, until recently, he has teased out of a large section of the electorate, attributable to the same elusive qualities, the same bewildering fugitive traits, that enabled Gaitskell, Bevan and Thomas to cast their spells? Is his triumph in becoming and remaining Prime Minister in two successive administrations primarily due then to an ineluctable factor, and in attempting to capture and anatomise it, are we chasing a will-o'-the-wisp? 'There are,' Henri Peyre once wrote, 'three subjects on which no wise man should ever attempt to write: love, genius and leadership. Of the three, the last is the most mysterious and the most unpredictably and capriciously feminine.' The advice of the famed French cultural critic may be sage, but fools sometimes successfully step in where wise men fear to tread.

Charisma I: Hugh Gaitskell

The term 'charisma' was once used to describe the endowment of a leader blest or chosen by the gods. It was the quality and circumstance that we find described by the unknown founding father of Western history, long before Herodotus, in the Old Testament's Book of Samuel, where we learn of the emergence of a man upon whom the spirit of the Lord had fallen, King David – the magic poet-warrior, lover of Bathsheba and of Jonathan, the man 'wise in speech and handsome' – whom Christianity claims as the progenitor of Christ. The term in its original but not modern sense lingers on in the Anglican Renewal services of the Church of England, in the Non-conformist Elim Pentecostal Church and among the self-declared charismatics who, although not necessarily possessing charisma, believed they were chosen by God and have sometimes, as political leaders, played a significant historical role in the last century: the demagogic and neurotic Theodor Herzl, whose shadow still falls across democratic Israel, was possessed of messianic delusions prompted by a dream that God had chosen him to lead his people; and the United States's President Nixon, all of whose siblings were stricken fatally with tuberculosis, believed himself to have been selected by divine intervention. Today, however, shoddy journalists have debased the term in both its original and its modern sense; promiscuously they bestow the rare attribute upon media

15

'celebrities'. Such glib labelling will certainly not enable us to divine the constituents of the thaumatological qualities attributed to Tony Blair by many of his supporters and by not a few of his opponents.

Now, using as our clinical material the past Labour leaders Gaitskell, Bevan and Thomas, who enthralled so many, we must be armed with the findings of the two modern disciplines, political sociology and psychoanalysis, which have explored the phenomenon of charismatic leadership. To metabolise those findings, and then to ask whether, when applied to Blair, they validate or negate the claim that he is possessed of such leadership, may be a tough intellectual exercise, but it is an inescapable one; it may lead us into strange byways, but I do not believe that there is any other way to decode the vocabulary and grammar of the unspoken tongue of charisma, and consequently to learn whether Blair is genuinely in command of that outlandish language.

In political sociology we find the term charisma is austerely employed; its definition was provided by Max Weber, one of the founders of modern sociology, and the passing of the years has in no way subverted his description of the phenomenon. Max Weber saw charisma, in its relation to political power, as an extraordinary quality possessed by a person thought to give him a unique magical power. The man who possesses genuine charisma exercises a domination different from legal and traditional domination, for his power of command is extra-ordinary. Legal and traditional domination can become quasi-permanent structures that provide for everyday community life. But in changing times, such structures may become ill-adapted to the satisfaction of community needs. Weber believed, therefore, that in times of difficulties the 'natural' leader may be neither the usual official nor the master whose authority is based on the sanctity of tradition, but rather the man who is believed to possess extraordinary gifts of body and mind.

From this sociological point of view, such leaders may be prophets or heroes, magicians or demagogues; but as long as they dominate by virtue of charisma, the relationship of leader and followers is of the same general type. For better or worse, charismatic leadership is especially in demand in times of war and its increased incidence in such seasons often carries revolutionary implications incompatible with traditional authority. On the other hand, the appeal of charisma may also be used to support traditional authority and, for example, to oppose necessary adaptational change.

Weber maintained that charismatic leadership of an extreme type occurs frequently in emergencies and is then associated with a collective excitement in which masses of people surrender themselves to an 'heroic' leader. The leader dominates by virtue of a quality inaccessible to others and incompatible with the rules of thought and action that may govern everyday life. The people can then turn away from established rules and submit to the unprecedented order that the leader proclaims. In this way, an inward reorganisation of outlook and experience of themselves can be effected by masses of people. Such processes of inner disorganisation, already begun in the period of stress, succeeded by reorganisation, are in contrast with the more superficial adaptations that occur apart from charismatic leadership – when people adapt themselves to a major change in legal rules without at the same time internalising the ideas and feelings behind it. Clearly charismatic leadership involves a high degree of commitment on the part of the followers, well beyond that involved in other types of domination.

To Max Weber's concepts, based on his empirical and historical studies, some psychoanalysts insist on adding an additional qualification before they are prepared to label a leader as genuinely charismatic. Since a charismatic leader, they affirm, needs his followers as much as the actor needs his audience, such a leader will have the capacity, in this interdependence, to maintain the cohesion of his group of followers by keeping aggressiveness in suspense and diverting it towards out-groups. Gandhi and Mandela, as charismatic leaders, had their out-groups grimly provided, the one in British imperialists, the other in the South African whites; and Hitler created his own out-group in the Jews. Within our domestic scene, in the Labour Party, Gaitskell and Bevan bound their followers together by fiercely attacking, with considerable verve, not only Tories, but also opponents within their own party; and because they were engaged in a civil war, each leader targeting the same people within the Labour Party, seeking to enlist them to their own group, the battle, by British political standards, was a bloody one.

By the time, as a result of a 1958 by-election, I entered Parliament, Bevan had conceded defeat; but although he had deserted his own cause, the spell he had cast remained in place, and his followers held firmly to their belief in unilateral disarmament. The party's failure to come to terms with the ultimate violence, the hydrogen bomb, was tearing it asunder. The very minute I entered the Chamber to be sworn in as a new member, I was made depressingly aware by Gaitskell that I had gained entry into a battleground, not a united parliamentary party. Flanked by two South Wales colleagues, one of whom was my friend George Thomas, later Viscount Tonypandy, I had made my obeisance, moving from the bar of the House at slow pace and bowing three times to the Speaker. Then, after being sworn in before an observing House and receiving a kindly welcome from the Speaker, I moved, as I had been instructed by the attending Whips, behind the Speaker's chair. By convention, the Leader of the Party then leaves the Opposition front bench and also stands behind the Speaker's chair to greet the newly arrived member. Gaitskell's greeting was a frigid one; he gave me a wan smile, a less than half-hearted handshake, and a few perfunctory muttered words too strangled even to be heard. I felt his antagonism.

Gaitskell's reaction brought home to me the seriousness with which he took my identification with the Campaign for Nuclear Disarmament in Wales, which had caused the press to label me as an anti-Gaitskellite. A few years earlier, as the chairman of the Cardiff City parties, I had received Gaitskell on his visits to the principality and, with the local MP, Jim Callaghan, had dined him and his wife. Callaghan always wanted me to act as host since he has a permanently stiff elbow joint which prevents him from reaching to his pocket and he knew I would pick up the restaurant bill. On such occasions Gaitskell had vainly endeavoured to beguile me, hoping to convince me of the error of my ways; but Callaghan, after I had led his constituency to reprimand him for his presumptuous endeavour to expel Bevan from the Labour Party – the action of a gnat seeking to drive an elephant from his stamping grounds – knew better than to make the attempt.

However, Gaitskell's vexation that I had gained entry to the Commons had a particular origin: it had frustrated a ploy played by Gaitskell and Callaghan to bring into the House a powerful steel union boss who was a strong Gaitskell supporter. Gaitskell promoted the elevation of my undistinguished predecessor to the Lords and so created a vacancy in the safe seat of Pontypool, then regarded as a steel constituency; and with a little manipulation they believed the local party could be persuaded to adopt their favourite. Events proved otherwise. Welsh political life is ever convoluted, and its zest and vitality are to be found in the conspiracies and stealth that must precede every decision; nothing could be less tolerable than a prosaic and predictable straightforward result. Once it was known by the initiates that the Gaitskellite-dominated National Executive of the Labour Party was manoeuvring to have a compliant MP representing the constituency, the fate of the steel boss was sealed. The local party, despite pressures, stubbornly refused even to place him on their short list, and the success of those supporting my candidature was thus assured. It was not surprising to me, therefore, that Gaitskell, at Westminster, received me with less than enthusiasm.

Although I found Gaitskell antipathetic, there is no doubt that he fascinated many people. When I was with him I was always aware in particular of his caressing voice, which was extraordinarily seductive. In most other species it is the male which possesses the bodily characteristics that are the biological bases of charm used in the service of sexual union. But even if man is one of what Darwin called the anomalous cases, in which there has been an almost complete transfer of secondary orientation to the female, the male is not left totally bereft – and Gaitskell could certainly bewitch the birds in the trees; for not only men but women too would quickly fall under his spell. He possessed at least some of the qualities of a genuinely charismatic leader, for the charm which is the main asset of a charismatic leader, at once both weapon and armour, is one which conveys not only his magic power but also his delicate need for love and protection, and such protection was passionately offered to Gaitskell by what the political commentators of the time rightly described as his praetorian guard.

But it was more than my political stances that created the gulf between us. His whole political culture and, in particular, the style of leadership that grew out of that culture were alien to me. In the year I was elected, the Wykehamist, with an arrogance unsuccessfully masked in an excruciating and sickly display of saintliness, patronisingly declared:

We, as middleclass socialists, have got to have a profound humility. Though it's a funny way of putting it, we've got to know that we lead them because they can't do it without us, with our abilities, and yet we must feel humble to working people.

Fortunately for me, I came from South Wales, where, in my youth, outside a small band in Cardiff, there was, in effect, no middle class. The coal-owners, the capitalists, the big land-owners, the steel magnates, were all absentee landlords. It is true that in the valleys of South Wales there would be a clustering together of the local doctor, the mines manager, the solicitor, the forge manager and some comfortably off shop-keepers who, since no local aristocracy existed, would play-act as lords and ladies; but these members of the petit bourgeoisie dissociated themselves completely from the overwhelmingly solid proletarian majority that threateningly surrounded them. They certainly provided no leadership or expertise to the workers.

And those workers, without the 'abilities' of Wykehamists, and doing without middle-class mentors, created a trade union and labour movement possessed of a rare political sophistication. It was within that working-class culture that I had learned my political craft. I had therefore been tutored in irreverence, sceptical of the largesse bestowed by middle-class reformers; their contributions were not sacramental, and were not necessarily part of my canon. I was already alerted. I approved, but did not need, the warning given by Nye Bevan when, in 1938, he mocked the hauteur of reforming experts:

> The people are excluded from forming judgement on various matters of public interest on the ground that expert knowledge is required, and that of course the people cannot possess . . . The debunking of the expert is an important stage in the history of democratic communities because democracy involves the assertion of the common against the special interest . . . The first weapon in the worker's armoury must be a strongly developed bump of irreverence. He must insist on the secular nature of all knowledge.

But not all sections of the British Labour movement possessed the intellectual insolence of the Welsh; the majority, in an act of collective surrender, rapturously submitted to Gaitskell's elitism and charm. In some ways Gaitskell's command, like that possessed by other charismatic leaders, resembled that of a hypnotist – using awe and love, a father-like authority and infallibility, and yet a caressing maternal tone which evokes the image of a mother wooing her child to sleep with a lullaby. Gaitskell's attractive voice was that of the woman successfully encapsulated within him. A charismatic leader is at once both father and mother and thus fulfils the eternal wish which man expresses in the myth that male and female were originally one. But such a leader's own inner balance can be precarious, for he must at all costs prevent his active domineering drives from being overcome by his more submissive, feminine and seductive tendencies. Gaitskell's constant struggle to enforce party discipline was a symptom of his own inner disorder, and the impolitic rigidity with which he tried to impose changes upon the party's constitution and to alter Clause Four of that constitution revealed his lack of inner freedom.

This gave Gaitskell the appearance of operating mechanically and insensitively, and led Nye Bevan to hint, devastatingly, that he was a 'desiccated calculating machine'. But, for once, Nye's characteristically concrete imagery was confusing, for Gaitskell, paradoxically, was a deeply emotional man. He had found the power of the hydrogen bomb far too alluring, for he needed to identify with a powerful father image in order to protect himself from the threat of his own passivity. Perhaps some of that passivity arose from his identification with the Asian nurse who tended him for a short but decisive time in Burma, when he was an infant; certainly her influence was so strong that Gaitskell romantically and nobly imposed upon an uneasy Labour Party a totally unrealistic policy towards black immigrants that, electorally, was to make Labour pay a heavy toll for many years. That nurse was probably only one of a number of early influences that shaped the acquiescence within his character; and his need to ward off this disposition was to have important political consequences.

There will certainly be those who would prefer to dismiss the speculation that Gaitskell's extraordinary and unexpected passion for dancing and rock music perhaps provides clues to his constant need to be overassertive; it was certainly an odd interest for someone who presented so high-minded and severe a public persona. The dance, we must recall, is said to have its origins in the imitative movements by the tribe of the totem animal; that totem animal was the god/father of the primal horde who, in myth or fact, was killed and devoured by rebellious sons. Perhaps Gaitskell, in a show of innocent fun, could mask its totemistic intimations; it may be legitimate to ask if his interest was an acting out of some buried Oedipal rebellion. Could it be that the identification with the totem god/father that moved the dancing guilty repentant sons of the tribal horde was echoed in Gaitskell's participation in the dance and the rock of his day? And is there a concordance between the extravagant identification within the tribal dance with the slain father and the evident identification with an over-assertive father that was embossed on Gaitskell's personality? Be this as it may, what is indisputable, except by the purblind, is that Gaitskell's need to imitate a heavy-handed father, to play so affirmatively the role of leader, was psychologically over-determined. His projection of this psychological need on to the Labour Party debates, particularly on the issue of Britain's retention of the H-bomb, acted as a detonator, and thus when I arrived in the House of Commons, the Parliamentary Labour Party was torn and bleeding.

His need was the source of his obsessional traits that exacerbated the internecine party conflict on the bomb issue and were to prove disastrous for the party. His determined aim to emancipate the Labour movement from its traditional orthodox ideology was pursued with the fanaticism of a heretic. There are always dangers in any movement which is bound together by a common philosophy. The phase of childhood development in which the child alternates between dependence on his mother and the assertion of his own autonomy so often finds echoes in adult life; if the parent group with whom the individual is identified insists upon his total subjugation then some, to survive, must assert independence. Gaitskell's obsession required that party lines must be firmly laid down; but papal edicts lead to schisms. Under Gaitskell the rule books of the party had to be redrawn, no comma omitted and no 't' left uncrossed, lest the new holy writ should be ill-defined. His intelligence and, even more, his charm enabled him to assert his authority but his fatal obsessional flaw meant that he had to fight every battle, never to concede an inch, to 'fight, fight and fight again'; in practice, of course, this meant he won every battle but the last. He himself was never to be prime minister and if he had not died when he did it is, in my view, unlikely that Labour would have gained sufficient unity to be able to govern in the 1960s.

However, during his ascendancy over the Labour Party, there is no doubt that Gaitskell fascinated some of the most intelligent of Labour MPs; some were extravagantly in love with him. The one-time Home Secretary Frank Soskice, with whom, as he at my request piloted in the Lords some of my social reforming bills, I formed a close friendship, once told me, months after the event, that Gaitskell's death had extinguished all his joy in politics. And Bill Rodgers (now Lord Rodgers), with whom, despite his political vicissitudes, I have always maintained a friendship, used all his considerable organisational skills to protect Gaitskell from assault; and, like Roy Jenkins, who in May 1996 during a television interview frankly declared he had loved Gaitskell, continued to resent any posthumous depreciation of his hero.

The taunt that Gaitskell had around him a 'magic circle', the so-called Hampstead group, was well founded, for every leader possessing charisma does use magic, the hermaphrodite quality that enthrals his followers, for they, like all of us, unconsciously yearn to be both man and woman at the same time. The moods of the leader, sometimes alternating, sometimes operating simultaneously, can have a fatal fascination when he displays both his male and female qualities, provoking awe and solace as he switches from awesome authority father to tender mother; his fascinated followers can swoon into submission. As in all human relationships, the phenomenon of interchange of roles comes into existence, even as between man and woman and, indeed, even more markedly, in homosexual relationships. One partner can play the part of father, mother or child to the other, who, by identification or displacement, can also represent father, mother or child; and so, in like fashion, a double-triangular play can arise between the charismatic leader and his followers who, even while they submit to him, can also care for and protect him.

When Gaitskell waved his wand, he enchanted not only Wykehamists and Oxbridge men; tough trade union leaders fiercely protected him, and some of the most belligerent trade union MPs were his stoutest supporters. The support they gave him, when they ensured in the leadership election of December 1955 that he received twice as many votes as Nye Bevan, continued until his death. This unstinting approval of his policies was strangely toned; at his behest, the bellicose could become wondrously docile, and the obeisance yielded to him often came from the brightest among trade union MPs. I never ceased to wonder at Gaitskell's command over men like the redoubtable Charles Panell, an elderly, tough trade union MP, with a personal biography so different from his, a man saved only by lack of formal education from the fate of becoming a brilliant lawyer or disputatious historian. Docile towards Gaitskell, his rage at private Parliamentary Labour Party meetings against those of us who refused to join the genuflexions to his idol was incandescent.

Such irrational motivation between leaders and led does not

necessarily mean that charismatic leadership must inevitably lead to disaster. Provided a sense of reality and devotion to social aims are superordinate in the relationship, and provided the leader does not become intoxicated with power, the consequences can be benign. But charisma is a dangerous gift to possess. If the contending elements within the psychic life of the possessor are too precariously poised, and the inner balance between the active domineering and seductive strivings is felt to be at risk, then the charismatic leader can attempt to impose on others, as well as on himself, an excessive discipline; that is his only way to stay erect. Gaitskell's charisma had brought him the leadership of the Labour Party, but the authoritarian, intolerant and rigid style of leadership which he needed to maintain his own intactness was to deny him victory in the 1959 General Election. The country saw a party which had been divided by his provocations and was not prepared to give Labour its confidence.

When, a few years later, Gaitskell died at the young age of 57 there was much dispute over the nature of his enigmatic illness; but I would speculate that the answer to the mystery lies away from the varying medical diagnoses that have been proffered. In part, we encompass our own deaths. Gaitskell was no 'desiccated calculating machine', but he could give rise to a perception of himself as unbending and unremitting; in fact, the carapace he developed, although tough enough to protect him from external assault, was too frail to protect him from himself. Psyche and soma are rarely apart, and an internal psychic fracture or haemorrhage can and does find physical expression. Charisma, for some carriers, can be a fatal disease.

Charisma II:
Aneurin Bevan

There was no more compelling orator in Britain than the stutterer Aneurin Bevan. His was a remarkable lineage. From Moses to Demosthenes to Churchill, the eloquent stutterers have always been the most violent of men. God punished the stammering Moses for his ungovernable rage by refusing to permit this greatest leader of men to ever reach the Promised Land. Nye Bevan was to share a similar fate.

His oral aggression was feared by foe and friend alike. But he was no wild iconoclast; even his most destructive attacks on authority were ever accompanied by imaginative balms and soothing reparations. For this turbulent man, who once, with insight, described himself in a revealing private letter as 'so ill-balanced a vessel', yearned for calm, for peaceful havens and for what he so frequently called 'the serene society'. He loathed his own dis-ease, and his passionate and successful creation of the National Health Service was a marvellous bid by a man to heal himself by healing the nation.

When in my teens, sometimes I acted as chairman of Bevan's public meetings in Cardiff. The intergenerational rivalries that today are so ugly a feature of the competitive political scene in and out of Westminster had no place in the old South Wales Labour movement. Youngsters were encouraged to carry the torch; responsibility was thrust upon them, not grudgingly conceded, and it was considered fit that a committed young man should have the honour to preside over the large gatherings that, in those pre-television days, Nye Bevan's presence assured. For me, those occasions when I sat beside Nye were not necessarily easy moments. The awaiting audience was never listless; it was seized with expectancy, and the pitch of the chairman's introductory remarks had to chime with the mood that enveloped the hall. A prologue, devoid of histrionics, but never so prosaic that it diminished the occasion, was demanded. And, during the towering orator's inspirational address, always a morality tale, always part-sermon, the text was to be carefully scanned, even as, simultaneously, I had to resist the magic of the wizard lest all detachment be lost and no reserve was available to control and bless the mass audience when, in the immediate aftermath of the speech, reluctantly it came out of the spell to face again the drudgery of the mundane.

Too young to have witnessed Bevan, Professor Dai Smith, in his remarkable study of the relationship between the South Wales culture and Bevan's unique contribution to British politics, has studied a film of Bevan in the 1950s which showed him:

leaning forward, half-engaged in an over the garden wall conspiracy with his audience, disinclined to harangue where the whisper will have the listener striving to be in on the act. The gestures he makes are small-scale and friendly. The pauses are those of the metronomic master of timing, his tone is sweet and reasonable, confiding and bemused. There is the swoop, of body and of meaning, into a demotic mode that removes the platform between speaker and assembled until he has deflated pretensions and restored the arcane to the democracy, and all without descent into populist know-nothingness.

The extraordinary choreography which accompanied Bevan's delivery contained, however, one gesture which I feared. When he warmed up and the Welsh *hwyl* began, when the voice lost all its sweetness and mounted to a feminine falsetto, he would repeatedly take out his handkerchief from his breast pocket and wipe it deliberately across his mouth. Then I would squirm uneasily in my seat and wonder whether Nye would be success-ful in smothering the forbidden words, while the reporters below would expectantly hold their pencils and, looking up at the platform, hopefully await another indiscretion.

Unhappily, too frequently, he did not fail them, for his oral aggression sometimes could not only inflict havoc upon his opponents but, as with his notorious anti-Tory 'vermin' speech, could recoil upon his party and his colleagues. His handker-chief gesture was a symbolic attempt to stifle his own aggression, for he feared it himself; but the block in his speech betrayed in starker fashion that fear of his own violence. In part his stammer was an unconscious attempt to regulate his intemperate attacks.

But it was that falsetto voice emerging from that huge man which told of his diversity. None can doubt his identification with his forceful mother. He emblazoned, in his feminine identification, the ethos of what young political pups now patronisingly describe as 'Old Labour', for that party was essen-tially mother-orientated. It was the welfare party, maternally concerned, the comforter, the nurse, the bountiful. The great divide between that party, which gave Britain the welfare state and the National Health Service, and the Tories, was that the Conservatives were essentially father-orientated, basically authoritarian in mood, believing in an elite, at ease in a structured fag system and only restless with their Whips when, as in John Major's case, the leader fails to provide the dominance which they crave and which Thatcher, the phallic woman garbed in hermaphrodite finery, a father surrogate, did provide.

But a price is often paid by a male mother-orientated orator: his passionate oratory can seduce his audiences, but, lacking sufficient emphases, when called upon to face an individual woman he fumbles. His private hesitations and problems then may become enmeshed in the public domain. There, an aggressive, masterful and compelling display of eloquence, over-determining the essential femininity of the speaker and compensating for the private personal inadequacy, can, as with Nye Bevan, be speedily followed by imaginative and healing reparation. Often, however, the rhetoric of the sexually inadequate can have catastrophic results, as that great orator Adolf Hitler, whose speeches took millions to hell, only too chasteningly demonstrated. Despite Hitler's masculine show of uniforms, big boots and spurs, he certainly did no more than fumble in private with the pathetic Geli, his half-sister's daughter, who shot herself; and Eva Braun, though she tried to shoot herself for love of Hitler, never found before or after the episode a fully potent lover. But consolation for private impotence may be found in the sense of multi-potency to be derived from the highly charged intro-active group situation of the huge public meeting, where the oratory of the orator can bring temporary balm to his deeply wounded self-esteem, and bring him the full response that he has found himself incapable of prompting from an individual woman. Public but not private orgasms can thus be achieved.

Hitler's macho display as he bound his huge homoerotic assemblies to him was a masquerade; essentially he was the great seducer. And although in Nye Bevan's case the consequences were as benign as Hitler's were malignant, his goal when facing a large audience of men was also to achieve a consummation. Four-letter words were shunned in his days and sexual intercourse was described, coyly, as 'an act of intimacy'; that was the euphemism Bevan himself borrowed when he made explicit the technique he was using to captivate his listeners. The audience of the political speaker, he wrote:

> will never give their hearts and minds to him if he appears alien either by manner, matter or by the remoteness of his

illustrations. If he is strange there will be no intimacy and intimacy based on mutual sympathy is the essence of successful advocacy. He must therefore belong to those whom he is trying to persuade, belong in the profoundest sense of the term.

And by 'belonging' Bevan, at least unconsciously, was revealing that in his speech-making he was engaged in a wooing that went far beyond that of a class warrior identifying with his class. He rightly insisted that he was using the term in the most profound sense. He was not seeking the token votes of his audiences; he was seeking their hearts. 'The first function of a political leader,' he once wrote, 'is advocacy. It is he who must make articulate the wants, the frustrations and the aspirations of the masses. Their hearts must be moved by his words, and so his words must be attuned to their realities.'

It was to the hearts of men rather than women that he made his appeal; this was the need of his habitude as of his temperament, for he was following his earliest practice when all his speeches had been addressed to totally homogeneous audiences composed entirely of miners. And, as he began, so he persisted, never haranguing or commanding; his conquests were made more subtly with a feminine guile. He could, and did, play the coquette and, never brusquely but with immensely teasing foreplay, simultaneously brought himself and his audience, after so much intellectual romping and laughter, to a joyous climax.

The encapsulation of the mother, which played so considerable a determinant in Bevan's disposition, was, within the culture of South Wales, no idiosyncrasy. 'Mam' in the valleys had her own privileged domain in the home, where, in the Bevan household, Phoebe Bevan regally presided; although women overwhelmingly voted as their fathers and husbands, and did not overtly enter in any way into the union and political life of their townships, their influence was singularly pervasive.

These cultural factors must be taken into account before reductively attributing Bevan's markedly feminine orientation simply to imperfectly resolved Oedipal situations. Nevertheless it is impossible not to infer that the little Nye's secret relationship with his mother must have been intense, and that the corollary of such an attachment – the fear that punishment would come from the father if the secret was uncovered – gives us the clue to understanding the dynamic behind so many of Bevan's political stances.

Nye Bevan's father, in reality, was a gentle dreamy man, a most unlikely contender for the role of the destroyer who would eliminate a son suspected of clandestine incestuous desires; but the clinicians have long since taught us of how amidst the ambivalences afflicting the infant during the agonising Oedipus rite of passage, so often imperfectly negotiated, monsters can be fantasised that will haunt the adult throughout his life. Even as the ambivalences and oscillations of mood of the infant can lead to him both wanting and fearing to become the father's lover, so too, among the possibilities that have in the end to be renounced in the real world although never totally extinguished in the unconscious, is the desire to possess the mother which brings the ultimate fear of violence, of castration, to be inflicted by the father.

All through his political life Nye Bevan, fearing that buried desire may provoke elimination, sought to pre-empt the threat; he defended himself against the anticipated retaliation of authority by launching repeated attacks upon authoritarian figures and institutions. His stammer had protected him from the consequences of the outbursts he would otherwise have made against his fecund father, who had, as children jealously in love with their mother often prefer to imagine, forced his wife to have ten children; but as soon as he could find a substitute father against whom he could release his violence, then the stammer was insufficient to inhibit it and with physical violence he fell upon his hapless headmaster. When I was young, I heard first-hand in Nye's home town legendary stories of his fights with the unfortunate man; and anyone who heard, as I have, Nye talk privately of schoolmasters and formal education would not forget the extravagances of his attacks, and could hardly fail to appreciate how powerful was the violence he carried as a child. Fortunately for our society that violence was later to be transmuted, with devastating effects, into oral attacks upon the evils of capitalism.

He was, of course, an orator for his pre-television time, when immediacy was demanded, when the artificiality of over-prepared speeches was rightly suspect, when more than sound-bites was required; it was the time when spontaneity was all, when meditation and brooding may have preceded the speech but then would come the grand impromptu with the vitality of the unconscious propelling the orator. Now the autocue takes over the speaker, and the politicians are reduced to the role of second-rate actors. They become what Nye Bevan, once stressing the distinction between political speakers and actors, described as 'fundamentally mimes subordinated to their parts in a performance'; and as performing actors, of course, they require decor, stage lighting, cosmetic treatments, designer advice, Sheffield razzmatazz. Those of us belonging to Old Labour took our agitations to the streets, spoke on our soapboxes and makeshift podiums in the parks, plinths and ramshackle halls of our towns, with no props, no amplifiers; we depended on our passions, our language and our authenticity to establish a rapport with those we sought to convince. If our freedom from constraint meant that we often made intellectual errors, they at least belonged to us; the shameless vicariousness of our present-day politicians was no part of our communication.

With Bevan his communication did not, however, necessarily reach women. Certainly in Wales, on his own pitch, within a culture well accustomed to the denunciations and diatribes of the *Offeiriads* and lay preachers of the chapels, eloquence was not rare and therefore was not overvalued; they were familiar with the pulpit histrionics of preachers who, with voices nicely tuned to crack with grief and passion, harangued racked congregations. So women left their menfolk to their high-flown talk, and let them soar to the stars in their lodges while they at home kept their feet well on the ground. In crises and strikes their loyalty was absolute and supportive; but Mams treated their men as chattering little boys and did not always regard their talk with high seriousness. And indeed the Welsh mothers had good cause to be sceptical of rodomontade. When I became the Member of Parliament for Nye's neighbouring constituency, I saw how ironic it was that the grim conditions of the tumbledown hospitals and housing in the valleys of Monmouthshire, a county that had enjoyed, in Nye Bevan, a Member who had commanded the Ministries of Health and of Housing, had contributed to an infant mortality rate which was one of the worst in the kingdom; and indignant that there was in my constituency a slothful acceptance of these unnecessary deaths, my earliest and not unsuccessful campaigns were demands for remedial responses. But Nye Bevan could hardly be regarded as a great constituency Member. There were strange ambivalences on Nye's part to his birthplace; and just as all of us show an impatience towards the foibles of an elderly mother that we would willingly indulge in other old ladies, so Nye in many ways showed more concern for the nation than his own area. Tredegar and Ebbw Vale were too constricting, as had been his assertive mother; and Nye went soaring among the stars rather than foraging around the coal tips. In any event, Bevan's uncompromising radicalism and demand for change were, and not only for women in Wales, too revolutionary for a generation of women more sceptical and conservative and much more resistant to any upheaval, whatever promised betterment might be attained by the result.

But most men listening to Bevan were certainly beguiled by his hermaphrodite qualities. The raillery against, and the deflation of, unthinking authority, charged with violence but tempered by the solace and hope that in the most delicate and feminine of tones he brought them, were often irresistible and they succumbed, for with men he was at ease, even as with women he was often more awkward; his bumpy childless marriage to the spirited and handsome Jennie Lee had, I think, a brother-and-sister quality, and his domestic arrangements that led to his mother-in-law, with whom the couple lived, looking after them like children, no doubt corroborated the marital mood. Unlike Gaitskell, Bevan was no womaniser; what I believe he always wanted from women was the admiration that, in sibling rivalry in an overcrowded household, he had sought from his harassed mother and which, until her early death, he had gained from his sister Margaret May.

There was an occasion, precipitated by Nye, which explicitly spelled out to me this particular need. It occurred long before I came into the Commons. Shortly after I had become a solicitor and had, as a young man, opened my law practice in Cardiff, I received a message from Nye Bevan. He wished me to give an interview to an American woman academic who was with him in his nearby constituency of Ebbw Vale. She had, by his arrangement, been for a week with Harold Wilson observing his constituency, and then had been invited by Nye to join him for a similar time. The background to the granting of these facilities to the American was that she was engaged in writing a work on 'Bevanism' and, naively, had visited the Gaitskellite-manned Labour Party headquarters at Transport House, where she was rebuffed in her enquiries, and was told that she was attempting to scrutinise a phenomenon which did not exist. Undeterred, she had bearded Nye Bevan in the Commons and he had encouraged her to pursue her study. It would assist if, now that she had spent time with the left-wing leaders, she met someone articulate at the grass roots, and would I please oblige during the day she intended to spend in Cardiff? That day I was in the courts defending a murderer and did not relish the prospect of being distracted by some high-minded, grim but no doubt worthy American woman academic. I explained my difficulties but yielded, agreeing, unenthusiastically, to see her for a very short time during the court's lunch-time adjournment.

Her arrival made me curse my spurning the serendipity bestowed upon me by Bevan. To my surprise, she was an extraordinarily pretty young woman endowed with the arresting dark appearance of her Macedonian ancestors, and far removed from the stereotype of the aggressive and opinionated American woman academic that, in my misogyny, I had anticipated. Graceful, disconcertingly direct and full of generous laughter, which made her sharp mind more acceptable and much less abrasive, with our shared interests I responded to her as any young man would. B was not content with a short interview and decided to pursue her 'studies' for a while in Cardiff, and, fortunately for me, I was the object of the study. We became lovers and spent a holiday together before she went back to the States with the intention of returning, her thesis completed, in six months' time; our relationship was not meant to be ephemeral. The artist whom I was to meet before B's return had, however, other ideas; she became my wife, and so I was saved from the terrifying fate of having a politically ambitious spouse.

It was some thirty years before I was to see B again. An American matron accompanying Harold Wilson in the Commons broke away from him to speak to me. To my discredit, I fear recognition on my part came slowly. But ever since their first meeting, Wilson, I discovered, had remained in touch with B, meeting her when he was in the States and when, very occasionally, she came to Britain. Perhaps it was not surprising; she had been a dazzling young woman, and Wilson, always more talk than passion, evidently retained some romantic attachment, as ill-defined as when she had first met him.

But with Nye Bevan it had been otherwise; and she had never renewed the original acquaintance. He had liked the attention of the admiring young woman but his response to her had been one of Victorian propriety; I believe that was occasioned not by discipline but disinclination.

He was, in fact, more comfortable with a woman within a formal framework. He could not easily give what he felt he had never received, for Bevan, surprising as it may seem, despite all the acclamation and myriad acquaintances, was essentially a lonely man. He always carried an acute sense of deprivation, insisting 'so few people have given me anything'. Reared in a household teeming with competitive siblings, he evidently felt that he had not received his fair share of mother-love. Doubtless displacement of those feelings led him to empathise with all those born into a disadvantaged class, but it also meant that his relationship with women was hesitant, for, initially, he had, like all at the breast, wanted boundless love and this he felt had been cruelly denied him. The reciprocity for which he yearned was to be of a different order; it was established with his male audiences and with the extraordinarily delicate relationships he could, very exceptionally, establish with an admired male friend.

A footnote in a letter in 1930 from Nye Bevan to John Strachey, the great political educator to my generation, a man whose friendship I was later privileged to enjoy, is indeed revelatory:

You are very good to me, John. It hurts me a little that you give so much and I can give you nothing in return. So few people have given me anything that I feel a little strange and bewildered.

I count on our friendship as the one thing of value that membership of Parliament has given me. And yet as this friendship grows and becomes more and more part of me, I find myself becoming fearful. I am so conscious of

bringing to our relationship nothing of value, and therefore am frightened of trusting so much of my affection in
so ill-balanced a vessel.

Please forgive me for exposing so shy a feeling to the
peril of words. It is your generous nature that moves me to
speak even though I know that speech will bruise you
where it could caress.

Nye certainly knew speech could caress as well as abuse; that
is what was felt by his audiences as he enfolded them while
attacking his and their enemies. The same mood that bathed his
relationship with Strachey enveloped his public meetings. The
screaming 'outing' by today's small group of disturbed gays,
unable to come to terms with their destiny and wanting to
minimise their felt guilts by unloading their burdens on others
who prefer the privacy of their sexual orientation, has
lamentably contributed to a wider acting out of the homosexual
component that Freud has insisted is part of all our natures, but
that can often be so benignly sublimated. Even as the
homosexual component in a man's nature can play so enriching
a role with a woman, helping him to understand and so form a
deeper relationship with her, so too, as so evidently with Bevan,
it can intellectually light up a male friendship and, through
understanding and sympathy, bring succour and hope to
political congregations.

The prurient and the philistine may wilfully regard an
exploration of the qualities of charisma that leads to an
acknowledgement of the hermaphrodite disposition of the
political leader as an advertisement of such a leader's overt
bisexuality. Such a misinterpretation fails to acknowledge that
the hermaphrodite quality gives to leader and led the advantage
of understanding and of being understood, that the issue is one
of hermeneutics not homosexuality, not of sex but of sensibility.

But the prim and the timid are in one respect right in
suspecting a scandal, for the hermaphrodite leader uses his

charisma to provoke a metaphysical scandal. Not for him an adjustment to 'reality' or the espousal of policies that reduce him to a seismograph, passively responding to the blinkered prejudices contained in the latest opinion poll. He is not anchored to the present, for he is determined to shape the future; and that requires him, when he speaks to the masses, to use the heretical grammar of Isaiah and the prophets of Israel, the enforcement of the future tense, the extension of language over time.

Such talk, of course, is dangerous. It can lead to awesome follies, like a belief, acted upon, in the 'thousand years Reich'; but it can also lead to the fulfilment, at least in part, of the dreams of Martin Luther King, who shared his vision with America: 'I have a dream that one day this nation will rise up, live out the true meaning of its creed: we hold these truths to be self-evident, that all men are created equal.' Such visionary metaphysical scandals cannot only defy time but, we know, as we witnessed the ingathering of Jews from Iraq, Ethiopia and Georgia to a new State of Israel, and the creation of Mandela's South Africa, that they can too defy geography. Bevan's millenarianism was of that ilk; he was possessed of a vision of socialist Britain. He did not regard 'the vision thing' as a commodity to be hired from public relations firms.

Far from being shackled to an anachronistic past, Bevan's opposition to the acquisitive revisionism of Gaitskell was not the bathos of nostalgia or the pathos of sentiment; it lay in his dream of a richer, more generous future. Doubtless, within his interpretation of the history of the working class, to which in his speeches he repeatedly returned, he found some assurance of a possible political destiny for Britain's workers; but there was no Marxist assumption of inevitability. The past pointed the direction to the future – he was most certainly not a 'here and now' man – but the lesson he took from history was that the future could be shaped by the living, human will. This hero of Old Labour was not resistant to change; he was no dinosaur, and contemporary modernisers, so eager to jettison their party's traditions as detritus, need to note the distinction he drew between opportunism and a readiness to change, between political rewards and political achievements:

> The student of politics must . . . seek neither universality nor immortality for his ideas and for the institution through which he hopes to express them. What he must seek are integrity and vitality. His Holy Grail is the living truth, knowing that being alive the truth must change. If he does not cherish integrity then he will see in the change an excuse for opportunism, and will exchange the inspiration of the pioneer for the reward of the lackey.

Now, however, the citadels of socialism that Bevan attempted to defend have been spattered with the graffiti of these self-acclaimed modernists; their sprawl, their slogans, their poverty-stricken language, are so often the efforts of immature children fulminating against the founding fathers. They mock the socialist veterans as quaint, as anachronisms; but how fuliginous is their abuse. Devoid of fierce confrontment, of the élan, of the magic that are the possessions of the charismatic, their precious sound-bites are mere nibbles; how miserably muted are their cautious responses to the contemporary human predicament. The words offered – justice, communality – become increasingly abstract, desperately governed by a bid for consensus; at all costs conflict must be avoided. The old socialist Utopia was to be achieved by struggle, by class warfare, but that is now deemed distasteful. Violent language must be eschewed, the concrete imagery of a Bevan declared embarrassing; petty bourgeois southern English gentility is the mode. Gone is the understanding that no orator can change the world without verbal violence, for, like Bevan, he has always depended upon his aggression; indeed, the aetiology of his rhetorical capacity reveals his oratory as a defence against his dangerous rages. Did not Freud teach us that civilisation began when man first hurled abuse not spears?

And so now we find ourselves not inspired but dispirited as we are offered words, words that are worn, threadbare, filed down; words that are the carcasses of words, phantom words; and too many of the modernisers, aping their Tory contemporaries, in between their elocution lessons, drearily chew and regurgitate the sound of them between their jaws. Their rehearsals are far removed from the ruminations of Bevan before he made a speech. He did not sit at the feet of any university professor of rhetoric but no politician in my lifetime more successfully achieved, as he often did, the Ciceronian union of wisdom and eloquence that teaches, delights and moves men to virtuous living; intuitively Bevan acknowledged the exalted world that Cicero assigned to rhetoric, a word now used so carelessly and, usually, pejoratively. For Cicero, as for Bevan, the orator's life was a discipline undertaken with all the seriousness of a semi-religious vocation. The skills of the rhetorician, which in late antiquity were the very basis of diplomatic, military and administrative careers, are the skills which Bevan sought to acquire. He would not have demurred from Cicero's instruction:

One needs a grounded knowledge of the most varied things, so as not to rattle off meaningless words for others to mock at. One needs to shape one's discourse, not only culling but collocating effectively. One needs to read others' motives, to the very depths of human nature, since tickling or soothing anxieties is the test of a speaker's impact and technique. One should have at hand, as well, poise and the play of wit, an educated bearing, swift short ways of deflecting others' challenges or launching one's own, along with an understated gracefulness and sophistication . . . And do I have to mention the delivery itself – how the body is controlled, its gestures, facial expressions, vocal inflections and modulations? Or need I emphasise memory, where all of this is filed away? Unless this stands guard over the material collected and elaborated, the material will evaporate, no matter how precious it was in itself.

Aneurin Bevan had, of course, never been tutored in the classics; he was in the same position as, lamentably, with the demise of classics in schools, most of the younger politicians now find themselves. Latin and Greek were part of the cement that helped to hold together the consciousness of nation and provided some continuity across generations; that bonding was part of the speeches of Gladstone and Disraeli. Bevan, nevertheless, although beyond the acquisitive reach of Hellenic articulation, which now seems, after so many centuries, to have found its limits, was, like Lloyd George, within reach of a rich Hebrew articulation, for this determinedly secular man had been cradled in the chapel culture, now dying, of the Welsh mining valleys; and his style and vocabulary so often revealed its source. Tony Blair, for a short while after his mother's death, may have spent his nights in consolatory readings of the Bible and he may make known his church-going, provoke dissent by sending his son to an elitist Roman Catholic school, interpolate, as a sound-bite, a well-worn pacific from the New Testament – never the Old, for that would be too conflictual – but essentially his is the language of the adman's copy; his vocabulary does not suggest that he finds the language of the Bible the main source of inspiration in the expression of his political views.

Increasingly, for many the Bible is becoming a closed book. That is not simply an aesthetic loss for our society; it is a severe deprivation, for the language of our politicians is now that of the sociological and economic textbooks. We find speeches are inflicted upon us that are often well researched, delivered fluently, but are, of course, dreary, unimaginative, passionless addresses; they lack the 'vitality' that Bevan well understood must inform the speeches of leaders if they are to inspire their followers to deeds and selflessness that can create a society more worthy of their humanity.

Many were the times I heard Bevan make vital, unpopular, tactless speeches, but never a populist one; he was an educator not a demagogue. The Labour Party modernisers who would dismiss his philosophy as outmoded and lacking relevance, boast about their capacity to face reality, but their vocabulary betrays them; their mode of expression, unlike his, is abstract rather than concrete, general rather than specific, periphrastic rather than direct. That acute French nineteenth-century political commentator de Tocqueville long since divined how language, when yielding excessively to what he described as the 'democratic dispensation', freed from the need to shape speech not by the standards of a particular class or circle but rather adapted for general acceptance by the overwhelming majority, degenerated in America into populism; and the consensus, conflict-free propositions of the political modernists here in Britain tell us that they are the most extreme of populists. Rabid crowd-rousing is not the only weapon the populist can select to command support.

Contrasting Bevan's pithiness with the linguistic flatulence of the modernisers is, therefore, no mere literary exercise. Words are the tools of thought. If they lose efficiency, that is, meaning, thought itself deteriorates. Thought can only be as precise as language lets it be. If the politicians' words are bloated, continuously euphemistic, then, in power, muddled action will assuredly follow. Euphemism is the effort of the well-meaning to avoid hurting others' feelings; in private discourse it may have justification, but when used by politicians it must be seen as suspect. A Labour Party denying its socialism, and unashamedly stealing Tory clothes in order to appear inoffensive to all, may claim respectability but, in fact, becomes a strumpet of a party, for what are being proffered are fantasies, fairy stories, the delusion that without struggle, without conflict, we can have a society where we can live happily ever after.

Bevan's philosophy infuriated many precisely because he identified and underlined the fundamental conflicts that he believed were endemic to a capitalist society; there was to be no smudging of the issues and the elusive serene society he sought could be reached only by forever increasing the tempo of the struggle. But it would be a misinterpretation to suggest that he was just another wager of class war, albeit an eloquent one. No major politician whom I have known, apart from John Strachey, was more aware of the interior life of man; and he understood that all external changes would be of no avail unless modifications came into our personal vision and conduct; he regarded man as man, and turned away with disgust from those whose political dogmas too often treated man as consumer or productive unit.

Not long before his death, in the 1959 post-election Labour conference, in one of his greatest speeches Bevan reaffirmed his belief that it is the human condition that must be addressed if needed social changes are to be made. Seeking to rouse a dispirited Labour Party, he told the delegates that the principal task now was 'to enlarge and expand the personalities of our young men and women' so that, despite growing material prosperity, they 'again became conscious of the limitations and constrictions that the vulgar, affluent, meretricious society imposed upon them'. And he gave a warning, never more apposite than today, not to adjust policy opportunistically to pollster findings telling us how resistant electors are to criticism of consumerism; with superb arrogance, he denied the proposition that the reasons given by those who voted against Labour in 1959 should necessarily be respected: 'Are we really now to believe that the reasons that people give for their actions are the causes of their actions? Such a naive belief in the rational conduct of human beings would wipe out the whole of modern psychology.' Bevan was insightfully seeking a society more sensitive to the deeper needs of men and women; he believed that an expanding shopping-list was no answer to their personal predicaments or to the ills of society. And he instructed the delegates not to yield to the contemporary mood but to teach, to preach: 'The problem is one of education, not of surrender!' His charisma enveloped the hall and once again I witnessed him galvanising his audience to fight, and not accommodate.

That he could capture the imagination of the delegates and give them renewed hope was in part due to his selection of words; for this stammerer had at his disposal a hard-won vocabulary. Up to his mid-twenties, determined to avoid the pitfalls of his stutter, he had pored almost every night over his *Roget's Thesaurus* searching for synonyms that would not trip his tongue. Moreover, in part, the responses he obtained came from his prophetic stance; he was the preacher of the valleys exhorting and commanding his congregation to fight the good fight, for only by fighting would Jerusalem be theirs. But physical disadvantage and South Wales culture do not in themselves explain Bevan's magic; that sprang from the quality of hermaphroditism, which suffused that last conference speech. His imperiousness induced awe, his mellifluous cradling, solace; from one human being the audience received both paternal instruction and maternal succour.

Thus his audiences could leave his presence with their self-esteem lifted and their hope increased and, for a short while, fitfully, the warm tides flowing between him and his listeners could soothe him too, giving him what his divided nature denied him: 'serenity'. Exteriorising that profound need, the conflict-ridden man, using an adjective unfamiliar to political practitioners, repeatedly insisted that the ultimate goal of the true socialist was 'the serene society'; but, reflecting his own interior battles, he also asserted that that could be reached only by unremitting political struggle.

For Bevan, the private predicament and society's dilemmas were all as one. In singular form, he was acting out, for all our benefits, the biological imperative that some psychoanalysts have suggested governs us: the law of psychic homoeostasis. That decree instructs us that we have, inbuilt, a psychological system that seeks to attain a steady mental state, a condition of dynamic balance.

Such harmony was to be denied to Bevan. His exigent desire to have a united party fighting and winning the General Election of 1959 led him to capitulate to Gaitskell and renounce his allegiance to unilateral nuclear disarmament; his action dismayed his allies, failed in its objective, and killed him. Although he rallied his party in his unforgettable 'meretricious society' conference speech of 1959, he could not sustain himself. When I entered Parliament, I found him in a dangerously depressed mood. No longer able with the old freedom to play monarch in his court, no longer surrounded by his old friends and admirers in his special corner of the House of Commons smoking-room, he prowled around the corridors engulfed in gloom. His participation in debates became perfunctory and revealed too often a lack of preparation. Locked up within himself he could not shift his attention to new controversies. His attacks were no longer reserved for the political enemy; they were upon himself, and it was often hard physically to be near him without sensing his melancholic withdrawal. The end was inevitable. To unleash such massive aggression, as was his endowment, upon himself, meant cancer and death. He was to die as a result of fall-out, as certainly as if the bomb had been dropped.

With his death, whatever curbs might have been placed on the mercenaries of modern capitalism and all hope of a genuinely socialist Britain died too. Only he had the capacity to provide a charismatic leadership capable of fending off the temptations of the affluent slavery proffered by an unthinking technology. He alone in the Labour movement had the magic to persuade a people to choose the holy land, not the fleshpots of Egypt. However Britain is to be reshaped, his untimely death guaranteed it was never to be in the image of the founding fathers of the Labour Party.

Now indeed, if a charismatic leader of Bevan's order was available, he would probably be entrapped by television. It is chasteningly paradoxical that when an orator-leader has for the first time in history the opportunity to speak not to thousands but to tens of millions, no politician can move the nation as their predecessors succeeded in the nineteenth century and earlier part of the twentieth century. With the death of Mitterrand, I doubt whether, in our television age, it will ever be possible to say again of any European politician as *Le Monde* in 1995 said of the French President:

> What he wanted to do, and what he has more or less achieved, was never to lose sight of literature in the smallest details of political life. One felt this profound coquetry in his speeches, where he offered himself the luxury, as did de Gaulle, of rehabilitating an unusual and charming word.

Television quenches such elegance; its debilitating demands can drain even the most distinguished of rhetoricians. Michael Foot, a great wordsmith, and in his day and moment a superbly bellicose parliamentary orator, on becoming leader, was trapped by his integrity. Overburdened with the circumspection leadership imposed and compelled to conform to the orthodox canons of television, with his aggression consequently mortified and his spontaneity suppressed, he lost his freedom and thus, rather than participate in television's mendacious advertising techniques, he became dumb; the public misinterpreted his condition as inadequacy, and Thatcher hugely benefited. Producers made him, as other politicians, a victim of their sly counsel to tread softly, to remember he is speaking to the little old lady in her front room; he must simulate intimacy, speaking as to one or two, although he knows he is talking to millions. Is it any wonder it so often sounds as spurious as it is? On a public stage the inauthentic politician, lacking the marvellous self-created choreography of a Lloyd George or Bevan, could, nevertheless, with some effect, borrow the props of the large gesture and extravagance; but, lacking props and encouraging reverberations from a visible audience, a mimetic exercise in intimacy is so often beyond his histrionic talent, and the resulting dissonances jar upon the listener.

The spin doctors, that odious breed now parasitically clinging to our political process, aware that increasingly the public senses the deception, have, in more recent years, devised for their puppets a new *mise-en-scène*. A more successful confidence trick can be played out if the political leader is televised boldly addressing, with the unseen autocue, a set meeting of adulatory followers; or a meeting so arranged that it is certain there will be a small dissenting minority who, to the applause of the selected majority, the leader will relentlessly crush. The repertoire of imposture is continuously extended as pliant journalists at televised 'press conferences' question the politicians who authoritatively read out the pre-prepared answers. By 1996, the wheel had turned full circle; Major followed Blair to meet people on the streets. Once we in Old Labour went to the street corner and from our soapbox, as agitators, we endeavoured to educate; today, accompanied by television crews, the politician paces a stretch of the high street and rushes through the supermarket. We communicated; they perform.

Meantime, the Commons has been demeaned as genuine debate ceases. Rules now insist that often speeches must be short, and the Speaker, under pressure from MPs insistent that their constituents must see their faces, maintains a rigid roster; prepared speeches for TV and the local paper, often drafted by research workers paid out of the MPs' excessive expense allowance, are hurriedly recited in the intervals between, in the case of many Tory MPs, looking after outside commercial interests. Ministers opt for the *Today* programme rather than the dispatch box, and Prime Minister's Question Time becomes a charade, a mere slot in the week's television programmes.

Within such a degraded political world, the possibilities of the emergence of a charismatic leader, possessed of a sense of reality and a devotion to social aims, diminish. The political failure of Michael Foot, a pure man with selfless commitment, reveals how someone with such a potential becomes a misfit in a society that is so awry, so incorrigibly narcissistic. The man or woman who subliminally may be felt to encapsulate some of the qualities of both the firm, infallible, all-powerful father and a glorified, provident mother is a threat to the Narcissus who at all costs wants to avoid the painful graduation into adulthood that a family unit demands. When hermaphrodite leadership so beckons, the Narcissus retreats.

But in a society tutored by Thatcher to glorify individualism, narcissism is sanctioned, immaturity is tenaciously grasped. Whereas Foot, to his great credit, failed to relate to that wretched society, Blair immediately, and dramatically, succeeded. Foot was a misfit; Blair clicked in. That he did so was not only due to an eagerness on the part of the electorate to be free of the decrepitude of the Tory government, not only because of the attraction of novelty which for some years he was to provide, but because there was a strange and disturbing congruence between the pathology of our society and the configuration of Blair's psyche. The homeopathic 'magic' he proffered to a sick society differed from that prescribed by genuinely charismatic Labour figures of the past; as a remedy for its ails, Blair offered our society its own disease; and, loving its own sores, a credulous electorate, albeit for only a while, revelled in the potions so artfully sold to it in the May 1997 General Election.

Charisma III:
George Thomas:
Order! Order!

George Thomas, secret homosexual, superb Speaker of the Commons, was no saint; nor did he claim to be one. But the nimbus with which he was endowed, and which so strangely crowned him, enchanted all. His very presence illuminated every gathering into which he entered; at dinner-table at Sandringham, or when presiding over Methodist conferences, or sitting in the tea-room of the Commons at the Welsh table commanding the attention of all his ambivalent colleagues, or speaking in the shabby halls where impecunious old-age pensioners assembled – to all alike he brought laughter, a momentary stilling of anxieties, and hope.

And his enemies, of whom there were many, infuriated that they could fall under his spell, found themselves thwarted as, disarmingly pre-empting them, he never ceased to mock his halo. In the Commons, where so often as Speaker he precipitated what the French call a *dérapage* – a blunder, a skid, a temporary loss of control – the House would gratefully forgive him as, to its delight, he laughed at himself and Members would then respond not with censure but, even as he advertised his discomfiture, with non-malicious glee.

Nowhere did he better mask, and simultaneously reveal, his self-depreciation, than in the ultimate title he assumed. Linking his title with Tonypandy may, to a casual observer, be thought of as a homage to his birthplace and to a place to which, in

1920, Churchill had sent troops to quell riots led by impoverished socialist agitators. But the conjunction for George Thomas held other significances and, in Wales, as initiates, we understood and wryly remarked upon his implicit scoffing at the very viscountcy he was assuming, for the ramshackle, down-at-heel township of Tonypandy was always, in snobbish Cardiff, stigmatised as a despairing hole where troglodytes dwelt. Tonypandy attracted in Wales the same undeserved opprobrium as Wigan did in England. It was a barbed raillery directed against himself when Thomas took the incongruous title; he was acquiring his last bauble and felt shame in his desire to add it to his collection. Its absurdity was a joke at his own expense; it was his way of coping with his tragic sense of his own unworthiness.

With no politician in my lifetime did I enjoy a longer friendship than with George Thomas and I believe that occurred because of my insistence over the years, never directly expressed but always understood by him, that far from corroborating his unworthiness, I yielded only to acknowledge his dilemma, never his guilt. And so I lightened his load a little.

Our first encounter was in 1938 when, aged 21, I fought as Labour candidate a council seat in the ward where George Thomas, as an elementary schoolmaster, was teaching. As the years rolled on and he became one of Cardiff's MPs, our political paths were ever crossing; as a city councillor holding within his constituency the largest ward in Wales, as chairman of the Cardiff Labour Party and parliamentary candidate for another Cardiff seat, I was constantly campaigning with him, preaching our political gospels, sometimes on street corners, sometimes in large packed cinemas and halls. When I got married it was George who, in the synagogue, acted as witness, and when I was sworn in in the Commons, he was my sponsor and was by my side as I took the oath of allegiance.

But ours was more than a political alliance; perhaps I alone knew of his personal travail; the help I had been privileged to give him when, as a consequence of barbarous laws and primitive social attitudes, he was endangered, made him feel, quite unnecessarily, that he owed me a debt. But fundamentally it was not the interventions that I had made to ward off the malice that made him feel indebted; this feeling arose from the relief and acquittal that came from my understanding of his torment. In 1959, when he wrote *The Christian Heritage in Politics*, he could not forbear to send me a copy crisply inscribed to record his thanks: 'To Leo, with deep gratitude for understanding friendship through the years'.

He did not deserve to be scorned and stigmatised as a humbug for having written that work, one which eloquently preaches, as he always did, that by our political and social behaviour we must stand witness to God. During his political life, forever emphasising the brotherhood of man, George could benignly sublimate his inclinations, and many, as a consequence, were uplifted by his solicitudes; but not always could those inclinations be contained under the fraternal rubric, and sometimes, overwhelmed, what he regarded as lapses did occur, and then he suffered his agony.

It was in his old age, in the year after he left the Speakership and entered the Lords, that I made my last intervention on his behalf. One morning, at six o'clock, the phone rang; awakened first, my wife picked up the phone. After a few minutes, looking very worried, she handed it to me. 'George here,' came the familiar voice; but now it was strangled. He was sobbing: 'I'm in terrible, terrible trouble. Come quickly.' My heart sank as I feared for him, that after all the years in which he had given so much to the nation, he was about, in the final lap of his career, to be crushed by scandal. I immediately feared he was phoning me from a police station.

I knew I had to dash to him for a man who, with the wit and aplomb to keep himself cool and damp down the passions stirred in turbulent Commons debates, would, I was well aware, dangerously over-act and panic if there was the slightest sign of a crack in the thin ice upon which he skated all his life.

Over the years, given his exposed position, it was inevitable that he would fall victim to blackmail. On one occasion, after a distraught recounting to me of the pressure upon him, I insisted I would meet and deal with the young criminal in his constituency into whose hands he had fallen. My reputation in Cardiff's criminal underworld stood me in good stead in dealing with the wretch for I had so often acted in the courts on behalf of the local prosecution department, and, even more frequently, I had defended the city's gangsters; more, as one-time chairman of the city's watch committee, I had the duty of supervising the local police. The cur, therefore, had no doubt that, unless he desisted, I would carry out my threat to ensure he was put behind bars for ten years; shortly after our encounter he found it was politic to quit the city.

Yet George had always been on the edge of catastrophe. My Sexual Offences Act of 1967, which ended the criminality of private homosexual conduct, was preceded by my being involved for almost a decade in agitation to reform the law; and that brought me into contact with many homosexuals and lobbies seeking to end the grievous discrimination; and they certainly did not lack a talent to operate a rumour mill. There were whispers abroad; and I learned that George was visiting a grubby cinema in Westminster where, under cover of the darkness, groping prevailed unchecked. I warned him against his lack of discretion, and, alarmed that I had been able to know about his haunt, he thereafter kept well away from that pathetic Sodom.

But there had been times when my advice had gone unheeded. While still a backbench MP, he asked me for a loan. George never had any money. As MPs we received in those days a pittance, far removed from the undeserved and swollen salaries and puffed-up expenses now bestowed upon themselves by our legislators; but George was always without a penny because what he had, he gave away. He responded to any hard luck stories and, of course, he was often conned. The specificity and size of the loan, £800, however, put me on enquiry; pressed, he poured out at least part of the story. I urged him to let me deal with this extortioner. But to no avail. That sum – the ticket and resettlement money which were to take the man to Australia – would, George insisted, mark the end of the affair. I had profound misgivings but I could see George was near breaking-point. I gave him the money. What happened to his tormentor subsequently I know not, but years later, and not at my prompting, now receiving a ministerial salary, he one day handed to me in the Commons lobby an envelope, clasped my hand tightly, said 'Thank you,' and moved away, clearly not wishing to reopen what was to him so painful a wound.

He thought he was repaying the loan in full. In fact when I opened the envelope I found he had short-changed me; but with his insouciance about money, for he was generous to a fault and always practised the charity he preached, he could just as well have overpaid me by a few hundred pounds. I preferred to enjoy the incident as my private joke and never told him of his error for I sensed the anguish that still, for him, surrounded the affair.

In his public life he could, unerringly and courageously, ward off the malicious sophistries designed to destroy him; when he was Secretary of State for Wales, not all the calumnies of the Welsh Nationalists and their media fellow-travellers, possessed though they were of tunnel vision and intelligence, could subvert his political initiatives and his high reputation. Yet the slightest tremor of scandal, however faintly reverberating into his private domain, reduced him to jelly.

One such occasion was in 1976 when, summoned to his sitting-room in the Speaker's house, I found him grey-faced and literally trembling. Investigative journalists, some from the BBC, were pursuing enquiries into the adventures of the then Liberal leader, Jeremy Thorpe, and had evidently reached the conclusion that, some sixteen years earlier, under a Conservative government, there had been political intervention that had saved Thorpe from being prosecuted for a homosexual offence against a minor. When, some few years later, in 1964, Thorpe became embroiled in another scandal, he feared that the records in the Home Office of that earlier misbehaviour would, unless suppressed, wreck his efforts to free himself of his own current dilemmas.

The persistent journalist had discovered that Thorpe, using his egregious friend, that smooth-tongued fraudulent Liberal MP Peter Bessell, as an intermediary, had turned to George Thomas, then parliamentary under-secretary at the Home Office, for help and that, yielding to Bessell's importuning, George had set up a private meeting with Sir Frank Soskice the Home Secretary to put to him Thorpe's misgivings.

Now, in 1976, the journalists had indicated they wished to have a probing interview with George Thomas. When I arrived on the scene he felt himself trapped; he feared the interpretation that might be placed upon a denial of their request, yet feared to grant it. He was frightened that his motivation in assisting Bessell was under scrutiny and that the journalists, if denied the interview, would be provoked into becoming interested in his sexual proclivities rather than in Thorpe's.

It was clear to me that if he submitted to an interrogation by the investigative journalists, he was in danger of betraying himself; he could, with unmatched deftness, control the most noisy of Commons debates but, witnessing his anxiety state now, I doubted if, under pressure, he would successfully control the nascent guilt-ridden self-castigations that were just beneath the surface and forever waiting to be released. I had noted at funerals and marriages, as in the marriage of the Prince and Princess of Wales, his penchant for using texts from the Epistle to the Corinthians – by my most unfavourite of Jews – and I wanted not the slightest betraying hint of cleansing repentance to emerge in an encounter with his press tormentors.

On this occasion he gladly took my advice. I told him he must pull rank and in a short reply, which should be sent not by himself but by his brigadier secretary, should indicate the impropriety of the Speaker granting a private interview to discuss any matters which might have taken place during his time as a minister and, in a display of mock helpfulness, suggest that their best plan would be to get in touch with the department concerned – in this case, the Home Office – for they would undoubtedly possess the records of this and other matters of public interest that would be sufficient to satisfy any legitimate enquiries. I knew well from all my experience in dealing over the years with the Home Office that there is no government department that revels more in bureaucratic negativism, and that even the most indefatigable of journalists would, by George sending such a letter, be directed on to a fruitless and a frustrating task. The suggested reply was despatched in those terms and, thus deflected, the investigators turned their attention away from George Thomas and, presumably, pursued their quest to no avail. The heat was off and George, whether he was or was not in reality on the edge on this occasion, within a week or two regained his equanimity and was in splendid form presiding over the Commons.

Thereafter, until I received that poignant early-morning call, George never again turned to me for assistance to overcome any misadventures; presumably he had been exercising more discretion. But that 1984 call fortunately did not come from a police station, but from a hospital. Puzzled and concerned I rushed to him. There was, I well knew, a link between his past flights into illness and dangerous threats of exposure bearing down upon him; once, when he was a backbencher, it drove him into hospital with a bout of shingles; and sometimes, when he had been overwhelmed with praise, his guilt at the encomia being bestowed upon such a 'sinner' momentarily crushed him – as when he collapsed at a party given for him at the Guildhall to celebrate his eightieth birthday. That spasm of shame passed, and a few days later he was in a private nursing-home in Cardiff receiving the Prince and Princess of Wales, and within a week was resuming his public engagements. I wondered, as I approached the hospital that dawn, what ghost had visited the haunted man this time.

Before I reached it, the agitated man had three times phoned my wife who kept on reassuring him that I was on my way. The ward sister was at the reception desk when I arrived; tense, she praised heaven that I had come; she could do nothing with Viscount Tonypandy. I reached George's bed and found him sobbing convulsively; he grabbed my hand and said he was ruined. Soon the whole world would know he was in hospital suffering from VD. Relieved that that was the extent of the problem, I chastened him to get a grip on himself, he had been in worse scrapes than this from which he had been extricated. 'Waterworks,' I explained was the answer; pre-empt enquiries, which would be bound to come on his despatch into hospital the previous night, by allowing one of his journalist friends to know he had been rushed to hospital with prostate difficulties after he had found he could not urinate. That explanation would, I knew, stifle further enquiries. Today, happily, prostate troubles are not spoken of in whispers; increasingly the need of screening for prostate cancer is being advertised; but even fifteen years ago it was one of the unmentionables. I reminded George of a previous Speaker who was temporarily away from the House and how discreetly we were informed that his waterworks were in trouble. No one, I assured him, would follow up his condition if he immediately dropped the hint of a prostate problem. George cooled down and acted on the agreed stratagem. It worked well.

Two days later, obviously fearing that his true condition might, as a result of his importuning phone calls to my wife, be known to her, George entered collusively and enthusiastically into the tale I had created for him and sent me, from the hospital, a card obviously designed to be shown to her. The beflowered 'Thank you' card from the hospital shop read: 'Dear Leo, I shall be for ever grateful. Strangely enough there had been no need for me to worry – it was all in my brain! I am due for the prostate gland operation next Wednesday. Love to you all. George.' My wife laughed indulgently at George's naivety that she would be deceived; but it helped George to think so and very soon he was out of hospital taking, I hoped, the precautions which would avoid him ever again being placed in such a predicament.

Although we never referred to the affair again, I think that for George it was a traumatic experience. My support on that occasion explains in part why he endeavoured so strenuously, even as he lay on his death-bed, to over-praise me to my friends when they assembled in April 1997 at the Savile Club to give me an eightieth birthday party. Fretting that his throat cancer prevented him speaking at the arranged dinner, he twice sent letters to the chairman almost ordering him to read out his laudatory address. With George, psyche and soma were never far apart and if one shares, as I do, the belief of George Groddeck, the father of psychosomatic medicine, that we choose our own dying, I have little doubt that it was guilt that made him opt to be choked, so that his voice, heard so mellifluously on radio calling both the House and the country to order, should be stilled before his death. Had he lived his life through more generous and civilised times, he would not have needed to inflict such grievous punishment upon himself.

In the embarrassing praise he wanted to be heard at my birthday party there was a coded message. He wrote:

Leo is one of my oldest and most steadfast friends. He is undoubtedly to be ranked as one of the most outstanding backbench MPs of this century. His crusading courage, and his first-class intellect, gave him exceptional influence in the House of Commons. He has been the greatest reforming MP since Shaftesbury and Wilberforce and our country is heavily in his debt. His unbridled independence and fearless outspokenness enabled him to make a parliamentary niche for himself, so that he subsequently had greater influence than most of those who contrived to get high ministerial appointments.

And then he gave me his thanks:

Leo has always been his own man. His loyalty in personal friendships is as monumental as his parliamentary achievements. I am proud to know that he is my friend.

Am I now, belatedly, betraying my friend in telling of the shadows in which, away from the pomp and glory of the Palace of Westminster, and, indeed, of Buckingham Palace, he was humiliatingly forced to walk? I do not think he would have thought so. Once, after saving him from the consequences of some escapade, he could not contain his anger against the homophobic hostilities that had so dogged him and, using the only expletives that were part of his vocabulary, with tears in his eyes, he railed: 'Bust them, Leo. I do not care a damn what is said after I'm dead but I couldn't stand them taunting me in my lifetime.' George was a great believer in working for the establishment of the kingdom of God on earth; that was his life's work; but he was no believer in eternity and the kingdom of God in heaven. Pragmatism stood him and the nation in good stead and I take pride that I was able to shield him a little, so that, unbesmirched, when his time came, led by the Prince of Wales, representing the Queen, Westminster Abbey was packed with 1,400 mourners, not only of the great and good but with hundreds of representatives of the charities, chapels and churches to whom he had acted as an inspiration.

And I believe it is proper that George Thomas's homosexuality should be recorded because I believe the gifts he gave to the nation fundamentally arose because of, not despite, his sexual orientation. Too often it is plausibly suggested that inevitably the homosexual in politics tends to be singularly destructive – as has notably been the case with Peter Mandelson; but there are some homosexuals who bring to a legislature a feminine sensibility and empathy, which those outlawing such feelings, out of fear that they could undermine their own fragile heterosexuality, conspicuously lack. These days, fortunately, belatedly, it is possible for Cabinet ministers to come out of the closet, to do their work, without forever dissimulating as was the lot of George Thomas. The charisma that he possessed, and that helped to buoy up our parliamentary democracy, had its source in the extraordinary feminine identification which possessed the man.

That identification was with the one woman in his life – his Mama. The opening words of his autobiography enfold his life's agenda:

> Looking back now I can see how providence has guided my life on a path set by my mother who was the single most important influence in my life.

'Providence' too had ordained that he should be cursed in his first five years of life with a violent, alcoholic and bigamist father who, in drunken bouts, regularly smashed the furniture and beat up his wife and children. It is nowadays almost platitudinous to recite that the Oedipal drama during our earliest years has to be worked through; but the fantasies that accompany a little boy's desire to have and protect the mother, and to dethrone the tyrannous father who, he prefers to believe, forces his mother to bed, were realities, not fanciful imaginings, in the Thomas household; every Saturday night after the pubs closed the father, with his wages spent, returned to make the home a hell, as mother and the young children vainly tried to contain the violence unleashed against them. Relief only came when, never to return, the father left to join the army; but by that time the mother and her favourite child, bound together in an unshakeable defensive alliance, were as one. And so it remained throughout George's adult life.

At every meeting, on every platform, at every social gathering, his mother was beside him; she featured in all his election addresses and all his conversations. His devotion so publicly and ceaselessly displayed would doubtless in other cultures have been regarded as cloying and mawkish. But in Wales the redoubtable bright woman, Emma Jane, was adopted as a symbol of everyone's idealised Mam: caring, concerned and forgiving.

In the Thomas home, to the disgust of the neighbours and the shame of the children, the ruling conventions of the valleys had not been observed but in the general ethos that prevailed, the Mam was the queen. She was not confined to the kitchen although that was certainly part of her territory; she handled the meagre finances, doled out the pocket money to her husband and left politics to him; but the children were shared. She expected, while she was engaged in the chores, that the miner husband would, in no way feeling that his machismo was assailed, take out the baby, wrapped tightly around in shawls in 'Welsh' fashion, to the corner of the street where he would join his similarly attired pals; then, often squatted in a circle, they would all indulge in bantering talk of whippets, rugby and lodge politics even as they tended their little ones. The fathers were extraordinarily mothering. And, in turn, they were always perilously near to being infantilised by their own wives. Even today, absenteeism is unusually high in Wales as wives mollycoddle husbands and urge them to stay at home if they feel the slightest bit unwell.

The encapsulation of the mother into the male psyche played so determinant a part in the South Wales culture that it gave us Nye Bevan's bid, through the health service, to tend the nation; it produced James Griffiths' national insurance and industrial injuries legislation to protect and assist us in adversity. No

Welsh politician, however, had the impress of the mother stamped upon him so deeply as George Thomas and, thus embossed, he was by the overwhelming majority of the Welsh electorate perceived with delight; his very presence brought them the recall of a childhood blessed with Mama and Dada.

In vain did Nationalists rage against him, mocking him as 'Mother's Pride'; and it did them little good to scorn his warm relationship with the Queen Mother by dubbing her as 'Mam with a Tiara'. And when, throwing a few bombs, they sought to sabotage the investiture of the Prince of Wales, George's high-camp *mise-en-scène* emerged successfully to captivate all; the Nationalists were too purblind to appreciate that no one more than the Welsh delights in indiscriminately creating mass myths, whether playing Druids in the Eisteddfod or enthusiastically taking part in the investiture at Caernarvon Castle.

The resonances that George activated, and that brought to him so much affection and admiration throughout Wales, arose because his apotheosis of the Mam was, albeit less extravagantly, the emotional mode of so many of his fellow countrymen. His Welshness came from the heart, not from some cerebral construction; he was adored by so many older voters because he was the good son returning their love; among his male contemporaries his feminine tenderness evoked indulgence, not sibling rivalry and condemnation; and many women, with whom he shared so many lineaments, undisturbed by any threatening sexuality, embraced him as a comforter, half older sister, half brother. When, from the Speaker's chair, in lilting accents, he sent to the world his pacific call for 'Order! Order!', his was indeed the true voice of all that is best and distinctive in Wales.

This subtle interplay between George and his electorate leading him to be the presenter of the quiddity of Welshness to the world eluded the coarse intellectual net of the Nationalists who, in their frustration, unrestrainedly abused him. For them the litmus test to prove a man was Welsh was his capacity and

68   TONY BLAIR

readiness to speak the Welsh language and so, propagating language fascism, they estranged the overwhelming majority of Welshmen. In 1996, in his retirement memoir, the crabbed and bitter Plaid Cymru leader Gwynfor Evans even relegated me to second place behind George in his party's demonology. He whined:

It may be difficult for some leaders to recall how vicious George Thomas could be. He was extremely set in his anti-Welsh sentiments and savage in his readiness – always with a smile – to cudgel a Nationalist about the head and stab him in the chest or from behind. He was the very scourge of Welsh nationalism and the Welsh language. Leo Abse was tender-hearted in comparison . . . At Westminster, with the weight of the British government at his back and his hounds about him baying for blood, he found the lone Nationalist sitting opposite him tasty prey.

Unsurprisingly, given such incitements, when George died, even as Britain mourned his passing, Nationalists and their fellow-travellers danced on his grave just as, undoubtedly, they will dance upon mine. The Nationalist apologists, choked with rage that the obituarists, reflecting public opinion, were recording tributes of so many who felt indebtedness to George, lost their usual articulacy and relapsed into gutter abuse. The obituary in the main Anglo-Welsh literary journal declared him to be 'swinish', 'cynical', '[a] creep', 'possessed of peasant cunning', 'glib', 'tactless', 'pathologically vicious' and 'brutal' – the thesaurus was dredged to find pejoratives to be heaped upon his tombstone.

That they mocked too his 'overheated relationship with his Mam' meant that vaguely they sensed the dynamic behind George's triumphs over them; for, of course, George's mother-tongue was English. Emma Jane, although born in the

Rhondda, spoke no Welsh; her father had emigrated from Hampshire to Tonypandy and, finding only Welsh was spoken in the chapels, defiantly established the first Methodist English-speaking chapel in the area. With such a background, George was certainly not prepared to have himself or his beloved mother defined as second-class citizens disqualified by language from full status. To the applause of the majority of Welshmen he constantly released the full force of his resentment against such Nationalist presumptions; his fellow-countrymen and women had no intention of regarding their ancestry as unhappy miscegenation, nor were they prepared to become aliens in their own land. And so George Thomas's charisma played a significant part in marginalising and, indeed, in taming Plaid Cymru, and thus ensuring Wales was not entrapped in cloacal xenophobia. It was indeed fitting that in the end he should don the robes of the Speaker, acting in Westminster, as he had in Wales, as a custodian of an inclusive British democracy.

Among politicians, a narcissistic breed, many play the part of being their own heroes; with George it was not, however, role-playing; he was his own hero. In sublimated form, unconsciously, he used the Oedipal 'rescue' fantasy of saving the mother from the unwanted attention of a tyrant husband; and he acted out the fantasy that yielded the legend of his namesake, Saint George, the young heroic knight who delivered the distressed and beautiful maiden and saved her even as Andromeda was saved. Because, in the early family life of George Thomas, he suffered a real and cruel corroboration of this unconscious fantasy of every little boy, the zeal and élan he brought to his political campaigning had a special quality; he fought the dragons that he indiscriminately chose with the force of the unconscious.

Rationality was not in his armoury; he relied on his elemental feminine instinct. The banners George unfurled were lettered with words of simplistic, old-fashioned Christian socialism for

he did not read books; he read men. And when he preached, as
he so often did, it was not to save souls but to save human
beings. His was a hermeneutic approach, understanding the
vanities of all of us, including himself. Sometimes he abused
his possession of exquisitely sensitive antennae to manipulate
or disadvantage his opponents but, far more often, his empathy
enabled him to bring balm to the wounded among us.

Always, wherever he moved, he was enjoyed for he brought
gaiety, fun and mischief with him; his charisma lay in its
immediacy. Gaitskell's charisma outlasted his life and disciples
like Roy Hattersley still teach his creed; and, even as I write, I
have become a patron of the Bevan Foundation, a think-tank, to
reinvigorate Welsh politics with the spirit of Aneurin Bevan's
doctrines; but George Thomas leaves no heirs, physically or
spiritually. He was himself, alone, and his charisma died with
him. But it was real and belonged to him, and it lasted his
lifetime. It was not an artificial accoutrement, like that worn by
Tony Blair who, after dazzling his party in 1994 and the nation
in 1997 was, by the year 2001, seen by many as a political
harlot bedecked in tinsel.

Androgynous Politics: Tony Blair

Warning: You Are Entering a Conflict-free Zone

Early in 1984 during the passage of a bill pretentiously entitled 'The Matrimonial and Family Proceedings Bill', I had my first encounter with the newly arrived Member, Tony Blair. This government bill was a very tardy and inadequate response to an agitation I had been conducting since 1979. It was in that year, ten years after I had succeeded, together with my Welsh colleague Alec Jones, in putting on the statute book the Divorce Reform Act which radically altered our medieval divorce laws, that I commenced a campaign to remedy the many blemishes within my own act.

It had been a long struggle throughout the 1960s to persuade the House that root and branch changes were required. When, in 1963, I made a bid to make some tentative changes which could mitigate at least some of the most oppressive features of the divorce laws, Church lobbies were too powerful for me, and my bill reached the statute book in tatters. My renewed efforts in 1969 met with fierce criticism but the wind of change was by then, at last, with me; however, the swinging sixties were certainly not as swinging as popular mythology would have us believe. It was a hard task to move Parliament away from the punitive, guilt-ridden doctrine of proof of matrimonial offence as a prerequisite to the grant of a divorce decree to the doctrine of matrimonial breakdown; and, in order to take the House with me, I had no alternative but to concede provisions relating to finance and to the measurement of guilt in determining financial settlements after divorce, which were either inappropriate or possessed a built-in obsolescence.

The opponents of reform, who wanted no change, had succeeded in arousing alarm and concern among wives who were persuaded that I was sponsoring a bill that could leave them abandoned and destitute. Since, by my bill, for the first time, it would become possible to divorce a wife without her consent if the marriage had broken down many years before, it was only possible to overcome the storm by agreeing to insert in the bill a guiding rule to the courts that in divorce proceedings the parties to a divorce should be returned to the same financial position as they would have been in had there been no divorce. The rule was utterly impracticable and often wholly inappropriate, but it was one of the prices I was forced to pay to obtain the 1969 Divorce Act.

I was, however, fifteen years after my 1969 act, able to achieve a considerable modification of the inequitable financial rule governing post-divorce financial settlements; for by then the rule was causing widespread injustices, particularly to the wives and children of second marriages, who found childless first wives, or those with no dependent children, were receiving a disproportionate amount of their former husbands' incomes and property.

I had anticipated in 1969 that in the end the accumulated grievances would be so weighty that alteration of the rule would become a political imperative. By 1979 I had received hundreds of letters blaming me for the financial injustices which people believed they were enduring. But I was not the only recipient of such letters. MPs were being pressurised by many of their constituents to alter the rules, and, indeed, not a few divorced MPs were themselves suffering from their harshness. By forming an all-party MPs group, which I took repeatedly to the Lord Chancellor, Quintin Hogg – always sulky and irascible when dealing with divorce reform, for the wounds of his own divorce had never been healed – and after an equivocating report from the Law Commissioners, to whom the matter had belatedly been referred, the demand for change, backed by a motion that I persuaded 230 Members to sign, became overwhelming. Hogg, not a man to stay in a dangerously crumbling intellectual dug-out over long, ultimately conceded, and a remedial bill was placed before the House.

When the principle of that bill was debated in the second reading in the Commons, Blair did not participate; but the Whips, doubtless thinking it would be a useful blooding experience for a young Member, particularly one with the advantage of being a barrister, placed him upon the committee that now had the task of considering the bill in detail. Unusually, the bill was to be considered in two committee stages, for, not wishing to create new difficulties while resolving those unnecessarily caused by my 1969 act, I had cajoled the government into using the procedure that enables a special standing committee to come into existence charged with the task of holding inquisitorial hearings on the detailed provisions of a bill in advance of its being debated clause by clause in a conventional committee before returning to the full House for ratification. This special procedure is regrettably now hardly ever used; such a painstaking audit of the human consequences of social and political acts is too onerous a task for our present-day 'professional' MPs, more concerned with gaining attention by sound-bites than, in the shadows, focusing upon the details of legislation.

Today, too often, the false assumption is made that the task of politicians is, by way of exhortation and coercion, to resolve conflicts that have already arisen; rarely, however, do such techniques produce permanent reductions in the tension level in our society. The legislator content to be merely a safety-valve for social protest demeans himself; his role should be anticipatory, ready always to apply social energy to the abolition of the recurrent strains in our society. But these are days of instant politics, and the politics of prevention is unfashionable. Such a mood suits indolent MPs and an executive not wishing its proposals to be subject to unremitting scrutiny. The notorious fiasco that followed the passing of the Child Support Act is certainly not the only recent testament to the well-intentioned but defective legislation now being enacted.

My participation, however, in the prolonged committee stages of the modest 1984 bill gave me not only the opportunity to scrutinise its content in detail, but also, by chance, the opportunity to remark upon the youngster who was so rapidly to become the leader of my party. I have no doubt, however, that Blair's self-absorption made him unaware of my scrutiny. I do not share the view that first impressions are usually misleading; on the contrary, after decades of political experience, I believe increasingly, if not arrogantly, in the assessments I make in the immediacy of a first encounter, particularly with a politician. Freud once remarked: 'He who has eyes to see and ears to hear may convince himself that no mortal can keep a secret. If his lips are silent, he chatters with his fingertips; betrayal oozes out of him at every pore.' The eyes, of course, are not the only windows of the soul. Our frowns, tics and facial contortions are all part of the repertoire of emotions that are revealed and not concealed in our body language. Even as our handwriting is a seismograph, tapping out the secrets of our psyche, so the creases that involuntarily form upon our faces are loquacious messengers, and even masters of histrionics, such as actors and politicians, cannot dissimulate and mask their guilts and conflicts. The initial encounter with another is all-important; love or hate at first sight is not necessarily to be mocked. As time passes, the vision, no longer pristine, becomes blurred and faults are no longer noted; habitude dulls our original keen awareness, and attributes and blemishes fade out of view.

When I first met Blair on the committee and talked to him, I was momentarily puzzled by the ambiguity of his mien. There was a dissonance between the athletic build of this clear-blue-eyed, six-foot-tall, good-looking man with classic broad shoulders tapering down to a narrow waist and the essential sinuosity within his bearing, which became more pronounced as it was accompanied by an over-ready winsome little-boy smile. That night, telling my wife, as was my wont, the day's gossip in the House, I told her (as she reminded me some years later) that an intelligent young rock star had joined our committee. I had evidently believed myself to have picked up Blair's vibes; the androgynous quality that quintessentially belongs to Mick Jagger, a performer whose presentations played a significant part in Blair's life at Oxford, hovered and continues to hover around him. To have made so recklessly such a snap judgement, even if subsequent probings may provide persuasive corroboration, will, I am well aware, be regarded as preposterous by some biographers and political commentators, who, perhaps fearing their emotions, despise empathy and insist, despite the limitations of such assessments, on their over-cerebral evaluations of public figures. Brushing aside what they mistakenly regard as trivial irrelevancies, they bury the real man under an avalanche of easily verifiable facts. They lack the wisdom that lies within the ancient hermeneutical Jewish tradition that contains a disinclination to measure a man with a foot-rule because the corpse is measured in this way for a coffin.

It was the secondary elaborations of Blair's basic psychic configuration that were arresting my attention in my encounter with him in the committee stages of the Matrimonial and Family Proceedings Bill. He had voted against this bill on second reading and I found the coolness of this young newcomer to any implementation of its provisions, to which, with others, I had given so much thought and for which I had long striven, presumptuous. And it vexed me; it prompted me far more than I otherwise would have done to relate Blair's committee contributions to the man himself.

I noted his talent to combine a pronouncement of unexceptional banalities with a distaste to anchor them in the sordid detail of legislation: 'marriage should be viewed as a common endeavour, in a broader sense, as opposed simply to pounds, shillings and pence'. He wanted, he explained, the emphasis in the bill to be changed so that the guiding principle of the bill should be: 'that marriage is a common endeavour between man and woman'. Such a change of emphasis would have meant enacting meaningless mush and a retreat from wrestling, as was the whole purpose of the bill, with the financial inequities my Divorce Act had bequeathed. I was impatient with this attempt to gloss over the realities of the conflictual situations which so often, unhappily, arise when a marriage breaks down and financial disputes abound. But Blair, by his approach, was giving to me my first intimation of his need to place himself and his politics in a conflict-free zone; he was clearly unhappy that we should be acknowledging the realities of the fierce marital struggles, expressed in pounds and pence, that wretchedly accompany many family breakdowns. I noted too the emotional overtones in his condemnation of my view that support should be given to a clause permitting the divorce court, when the funds within a marriage were available and when there were no children or when they were grown up, to order a complete and final distribution of the matrimonial assets. Blair eschewed the clean break which I advocated, a break that could encourage parties to build up new lives untrammelled by past or renewed financial obligations. Such an approach was blunt, unblurred, and did not commend itself to Blair's mindset; he abhorred the principle of the clean break. 'That principle,' the moralist told the House, 'shuffles off the lifelong responsibilities of marriage and brings a change in the nature of the marriage contract by permitting an easier clean break even where the parties may not consent.'

It was unpalatable for Blair to acknowledge that there are dead marriages, that conflict can be mortal, an acknowledgement that he was still reluctant to make in 1996, when the Conservative government presented the bill which, whatever its blemishes, was a genuine attempt to remedy the more substantive defects of my Divorce Act. Then, he again muddied the waters rather than assisting forward a valuable bill. In debates explicitly agreed to be governed by a free vote, Blair sought to taunt the government and accuse them of disarray when one of the Lord Chancellor's clauses was defeated. A justifiably angry John Major accused Blair, as did *The Times* and many others less partisan, of being unprincipled. The charge was inappropriate; Blair was acting according to the prejudices of his principles, which he had already displayed in 1984, when he wished to have in statutory form an idealised mutuality and an avoidance of acknowledgement of strife, a wish that reflected his essential mode of thought: all differences of views should be minimised.

Unsurprisingly, given Blair's prejudices, the 1996 act was still not being implemented in 2003 under the then Lord Chancellor. Lord Irvine, himself a divorced man and a former head of Blair's chambers, accommodatingly found that implementing the act would be too expensive, and so it is to be binned; but the painful sequelae of broken marriages cannot be hidden. Nor can they be overcome through a public relations exercise, by way of a white paper, as Blair wished in 2000, to 'promote' marriage. The brutal fact is that unhappily four out of ten marriages end prematurely, and the woe that that often brings, not least upon children, cannot be wished away.

I had repeatedly found in my divorce reform efforts that an upbringing within a tension-ridden, stricken family unit, such as Tony Blair had, and those who had suffered the fate of being born into a dysfunctional family, as was Cherie Blair's sad lot, can be most resistant to any changes in the divorce law that frankly and honestly acknowledge the existence of the conflictual situation that brings about marriage breakdown; for such, it is better to idealise marriage and affirm its immutability than to contemplate the debris of the broken relationship, even although that may lead to picking up at least some of the pieces. For some there can be terror in the evocation of early childhood and, denying that unhappy past, they are more comfortable with a divorce law that hypocritically insists that a spurious consensus should be maintained between the estranged, and societal obstacles be placed in their way to rebuild separate lives. And in a Roman Catholic environment such as prevails in the Blair establishment, theology doubtless provides support to such a sacramental view of marriage and a belief that sacrifice of personal happiness is the price to be willingly paid for redemption; at all costs, even at that of happiness, consensus must be maintained.

Far from avoiding a dialogue in which objections, considerations and counter-examples may be introduced, what is essential is to encourage them, whether one ends up altering one's position or whether one chooses to maintain it. Only thus can a decision or view be less blind and one-sided, and can it acquire a greater warrant. The goal should be an authentic, uncompelled consensus, not the pap of false agreement; and to reach such a consensus, healthy engagement in confrontation is necessary.

I saw at close quarters the man who, on reaching the premiership, became, with fatal consequences, the outstanding practitioner of false consensus. For Harold Wilson it was an art form and, one apparatchik praising another, caused Jim Callaghan at Wilson's memorial service to call on us to admire, above all, Wilson's skill as the party manager. It was indeed remarkable how Wilson, to avoid at all costs even acknowledging that he was facing antagonism, would, to disarm and placate an internal party opponent, deploy all his considerable intellectual powers to prove that even the most mutually exclusive objectives were not incompatible and would indeed often attempt to pursue all of them; and, as a consequence, usually did not properly achieve any of them. Elsewhere, in my 1973 book *Private Member*, I have written about Wilson's notorious Walter Mitty fantasies, his misplaced optimism, his dream that the outside environment was ever benevolent and never hostile, that no enemies need exist, that all could join in consensus, a stance he often endeavoured to maintain intact by having no one around him who disturbed his worry-free dream; no voice in his circle was to be heard murmuring that the emperor had no clothes. Although the aetiology of Blair's spurious consensus-seeking is to be distinguished from Wilson's, I became aware during the committee stages of the Matrimonial and Family Proceedings Bill of the parallels between Wilson's approach and that of this arriviste. An awareness of these parallels alerted me; this was no sweet, asexual, gentle Bambi, as the media was initially to depict Blair. Reconciling the irreconcilable, practising all the Wilsonian artifices of denying the existence of contradiction, insisting there was no difficulty in the lion lying down together with the lamb, may bemuse and comfort the credulous; but peddling such soothing political opiates can become a sinister occupation. In Blair's case it has led him to repudiate any hint of partisanship in Labour's policies, to affect that the tatty fabric of our society can be splendidly restored without raising taxes, without extending the powers of the state, without compulsorily taking back the nation's natural resources and public utilities into civic hands, and without any imposition upon what the presently privileged describe as their individual freedom.

Blair, in short, is the populist who, at a time when the incompetence and sleaze of governance had left many disenchanted with politics, pandered to this widespread mood by seeking to de-politicise the Labour Party. He went even further than Wilson, who proffered a magic solvent, a new technology, whose white heat would dissipate yesterday's struggles and conflicts, and precipitate an electoral coalescence, a Labour Party that would be the natural party of government. That goal does not satisfy Blair. Propelled by profound inner needs that are more significant even than his wish to take up heroic stands against those he knows are in retreat, he ceaselessly continues expanding the boundaries. His wish is to become the leader of a party above party, representing society as a whole; Labour, he told the 1995 Labour Party conference, was the one-nation party, a claim that comes perilously near to acclaiming the ideal of a one-party nation. It follows that those who demur, and would dare to mock this impossible and, within a democracy, sinister dream, must be treated as cranks or outlaws; by the autumn of 1995 he was declaring in an *Observer* interview that 'those who fail to fall in' with his modernising project 'need their heads examined' and added an ominous comment, reminiscent of Soviet incarcerations of political opponents in mental hospitals, that in his view, although he was a politician not a psychiatrist, such opponents 'require not leadership but therapy'.

The Ashdown diaries published in 2000 reveal how unflagging Blair's efforts have been to thwart his fractious activists and to come together with a Liberal Democratic leadership, and so, together, to hold power through the 21st century; but Blair here is not simply engaged in a practical manoeuvre to gain the support of more and more voters however diverse in reality their interests may be. It is an irrational and compulsive project that becomes Blair's temperament, and because our democracy is pinned together by adversarial party politics, it can develop into a dangerous assault upon parliamentary democracy; opposition denied expression at Westminster is an incitement to democrats to turn to extra-parliamentary action.

An assumption that one party, binding together all strands of opinion, can be representative of a society is a credo suitable only for an authoritarian state and is alien to British democracy.

This is a lesson that I relearned in the first few minutes of my entry as an MP into the Palace of Westminster. On my arrival the attendant in the men's cloakroom pointed out to me the coat-hook assigned for my personal use. A loop of pink ribbon was tied around it, as around everyone else's hook. Intrigued, I questioned the flunkey, who told me, unsmilingly and with hauteur, that the loops were to hold the swords that must be deposited by MPs before they entered the Chamber. Evidently combativeness was traditionally expected, indeed demanded, from those entering the Chamber. But adversaries must confine themselves to verbal violence; and inside the Chamber each Member must know his defined territory, for it is not permitted, while speaking, to cross the thin red line woven into the carpet of the aisle that divides the two front benches, an aisle which itself is the length of two swords. Any Member whose foot does cross the line, if only by an inch, is immediately called to order by angry colleagues from all corners of the House. Such rituals and procedures should not be mocked; they are outward expressions of the belief that party divisions are essential to the working of our parliamentary democracy. We want no truck with round chambers – the plan of the building ensures that government and opposition face each other squarely; and there are no cross-benches in the Commons. Although in the present Parliament there are too many oafs who, colluding with the cameras, would reduce party politics to institutional paranoia, Disraeli's belief that 'without party parliamentary government is impossible' should be regarded by those who value parliamentary democracy as unchallengeable; the unpalatable corollary to Disraeli's finding is that without partisan party politics, democracy must needs find expression in extra-parliamentary modes.

Those like Wilson and Blair who seek to define their leadership not by their beliefs, which they prefer to remain suspended, but by proclaiming how representative they are of the whole nation, inevitably find the parameters set by our healthy tradition of party conflict intolerably constrictive; all of them attempt to escape from their dilemma in ways which can be strikingly similar. Matthew Parris, writing as *The Times*'s unerring and perspicacious parliamentary observer with the advantage of experience as a former Conservative MP, as participant as well as observer, noted the parallels between Wilson and Blair that had prompted my own early misgivings.

Parris was struck that Blair, at Wilson's memorial service, chose to praise him by repeating the dead prime minister's words:

> The Labour Party is a moral crusade or it is nothing. 'Let', said Blair, 'that be his epitaph . . .' But, of course, Wilson's Labour Party was not a moral crusade. It was anything but. His career was many things, but never that. It was marked by his failure to become any sort of moral crusader. His enemies came to execrate (and his admirers to celebrate) the skill with which, time and again, issues of principle were sidelined, skirted or postponed.

Acquitting Blair, unlike Wilson, of any open attempt to celebrate his own rectitude, Parris, however, continued:

> But the language tells another story. Scan his abstract nouns and you will sniff a curious blend of pulpit and school assembly. The vocabulary is of trust and honour; of compassion, conviction, vocation; of humanity, integrity, community, morality, honesty and probity; of values, standards, faiths and beliefs. In the Commons he slips into the habit of implied superior virtue. With indignation just a shade too righteous and eyes just a mite too wide, he appeals to the heavens to be his judge.

The large, intangible claims and aspirations to which Parris finds Blair is wedded were already nascent when I found Blair sitting next to me in those early committee proceedings. Although the cautious, high-minded young man clearly found my approach too combative when I sought to amend or defend a clause in the bill, he nevertheless was unpleasantly careful to avoid any direct confrontation with me. The most he did was, with a sweet smile on one occasion, to suggest 'with respect, that the Honourable Member for Torfaen had gone slightly over the top in some of his rhetoric'.

At the time, as now, I find such studied circumspection in the young unbecoming, not necessarily deferential or courteous. I concluded then that there was no danger of this man going 'over the top' to fight a domestic enemy genuinely capable of retaliation. Appeasement has proved to be part of his mindset; the enemies he conjures up in Britain are often non-existent ones whom he can bravely overcome. His well-publicised 'battles' have been bloodless charades, sometimes fought against non-existent enemies against whom he can strike an heroic 'posture'; even his 'modernising' abolition of Clause Four involved, as all political initiates know, a fake struggle since he was pushing against open doors. And when, at Prime Minister's Question Time, he was faced with a confrontational stance by even so meagre a politician as William Hague, all parliamentary correspondents agreed that Blair almost invariably fumbled and was disadvantaged.

In retrospect, having become alerted to Blair's relationship with his father, Leo, I now have no doubt that the particular circumspection he showed towards me in those 1984 committee proceedings – and, indeed, when chatting with him in the intervals before they would begin or after they ended – came from an inhibition to challenge someone bearing the commanding father's name. Blair's evasion of confrontation and his accompanying manipulative placatory style arise, I believe, from his failure to cope with the unconscious guilt that burdens him for daring to surpass his father, the man who, but for the appalling stroke he suffered, would probably have become the Conservative MP for Hexham. Leo, the aspiring parliamentarian, did not even reach the back benches; Blair, in my view, continues to be torn between the pleasure of triumph of accomplishment and the displeasure and fear of punishment for having vanquished the ailing father and so gaining the office to which the father had aspired.

All of us who, as little ones, rival the father for the affection of the mother, unconsciously have death wishes against the man we see as an interloper; if such wishes appear to be fulfilled, leaving the father dead or cruelly disabled, the resulting guilt can be crushing; and certainly, it can find expression in fearing, in confrontation, to provoke in adult life another 'murder' lest this time the punishment be capital. When, after so much extravagant heralding, the time came for Blair to give a name to his son, it was not fortuitous that he called him Leo; bestowing the grandfather's name upon the babe was no ingratiating gesture to Leo Blair. It was, I believe, at one level, an attempt, by way of reparative guilt, to bring to life the father he had 'slain' and so to feel cleansed of his own guilt.

Much indeed has occurred since my first meeting in 1984 with the young Blair, but the pattern of elusiveness and non-confrontation, which I then remarked, remains in place; in such bespoke suiting, as I then anticipated, he has travelled a long way in the Commons – but not in the right direction.

Exhibitionism: Do I Exist?

The theatricality, the overacting in speech and demeanour, from which Parris recoils had from the beginning already jarred on me. Grey politics, ill-designed, without drama or colour, is, of course, a poor thing; an emphatic declaration in dress and gesture can capture the attention of the unheeding. There was a time, indeed, when my waistcoats and garb, created by my designer wife, would, as I entered the House each Budget day, capture the attention of television viewers and the readers of the national press. My gesture was not mere self-indulgent exhibitionism. It made a statement founded on the socialist principles of the artist-craftsman William Morris, which as a boy I had learned from those wise elders who had permitted me to attend the proceedings of the Cardiff society bearing his name; a well-designed society should have well-designed accoutrements, buildings, furniture, fabrics and dress to be enjoyed by all. My act was in fact a defiance of the covert sumptuary laws maintained by those Tories who patronisingly believed that finery was for them and socialists should wear cloth caps. Of course my gesture shocked some, not least the puritanical petit bourgeois Jim Callaghan, who, after my first Budget day entry, priggishly told me my political career was ruined and that I had no future as an MP. My constituents thought otherwise; and so did a substantial section of the public, who, having focused upon my attire, were now much more ready to focus on my words, on my campaigns for social reforms. I do not therefore despise the controlled introduction of drama into politics; but form must match content. Theatre is one thing, theatricality, lacking wit, another.

Samuel Johnson, when told by the great Shakespearean actor David Garrick that every time he played Richard III he felt like a murderer, made the rejoinder: 'Then, Sir, you should be hanged.' Evidently in Garrick's performance there was no gap between the portrayal and the hunchback king. A great actor belongs totally to his part; but only too often one sees an actor observing and appreciating his own performance and, by his preening, by his estrangement from the assigned role, he leaves his audience no less estranged and unconvinced.

A politician faces a greater hazard, for his artificiality, if such is his condition, would be betrayed not only by his demeanour but, as Parris underlines, by his vocabulary. The politician uses – or, in these days of speechwriters, chooses – his own words; and these may subvert rather than corroborate his affirmation of genuineness. Even a good actor can be perceived as second-rate when provided with a shoddy script; and with the politician, the individual nouns, verbs, adjectives and adverbs he has chosen, even as much as the content of his speeches, can nullify his persuasions and leave his audience to categorise him as a phoney. Such an accusation may be attracted not only by an obvious B-feature ham actor like Reagan; the discerning may find more sophisticated appeals suspect.

Abstract nouns for which, as Parris has pointed out, Blair has a penchant, can act as a shield, keeping complexities and painful realities at a distance. He ensures that nouns that possess an excessive resonance, likely to offend the politically timorous, are gutted. His wordplay is dextrous; by the use of a hyphen he sought to bury socialism, telling his supporters: 'Once socialism is defined in this way – as social-ism – we can be liberated from our history and not chained by it.' And then, in turn, to placate suspicious traditionalists impatient with such decorous redefinitions, he introduced in May 1996 at the Welsh Labour Party conference a fresh phrase into New Labour's lexicon, one that could mask the incompatibility of consensus politics with fundamental change; the Labour Party, he told bemused delegates, was now 'the party of one-nation radicals'. By 2001 in his opening salvo of the General Election campaign, he was still pushing this absurd quest to reconcile the irreconcilable: his government would be 'radical but firmly in the centre'. Yet in all these various presentations one notes that he is like an actor who does not belong to his part; despite his attempts by over-emphases to surmount the difficulty, he often repetitively uses an adjective or adverb to claim a condition that does not truly belong to him. He is forever claiming he 'passionately' believes, that he has 'passionate' convictions. Such declarations of passion are reminiscent of a wooing hero in a Victorian melodrama. In our public lives, as in our private lives, genuine commitment is not expressed, hand on heart, in adolescent protestation. Still, not babbling, waters run deep.

Blair so often flounders in the shallow but defined channel that divides the actor from the authentic politician. Nye Bevan, the exponent of Old Labour, well understood that distinction and had the strength to resist any tide tugging him towards an histrionic shore. He warned:

Over-prepared speeches rarely succeed. The audience in the theatre is radically different from that of a deliberative assembly or a political meeting. People go to the theatre in a mood to give themselves to the magic of illusion. They expect time and space and the constrictions of reality to be set aside in the service of theatrical conventions. They expect . . . that the actors and actresses should speak their lines with clarity of diction because they are fundamentally mimes subordinated to their parts in the performance . . . the political speaker is in an entirely different category.

But Blair does not fall into an entirely different category; it can certainly be pleaded in mitigation that he is living in the world of the autocue, and the spontaneity which Bevan demanded of the politician is no longer possible, but I do not think the content, manner and delivery of his set speeches can be explained solely in terms of modern technology. His personal history tells us otherwise. He has always been attracted to the stage, even as were his music-hall dancer and occasional actress grandmother, and his Pierrot-performing and straight actor grandfather. Singing in the choir of his prep school, standing as the Conservative candidate at thirteen in the school's mock election, playing at his public school at fifteen the part of Mark Antony in *Julius Caesar*, and then the lead in R C Sherriff's World War I drama *Journey's End* while singing tenor in Mozart pieces at school concerts; he was soon at Oxford to become a prominent member of the troupe in St John's College revues and lead singer in one rock band while playing in another. He left Oxford untutored in politics but not in stagecraft; in his present performance there are far more than vestigial traces of the extracurricular qualifications he acquired as an undergraduate.

In a quest to identify the particular and distinctive qualities that have led to Blair's present dominance, it would not necessarily be of assistance simply to remark that he has been stage-struck for, among politicians, exhibitionism is a generic condition; indeed, it is a qualification required in the CV of any budding politician. No MP is a shrinking violet; but Blair's persistent display of his mimetic talents, whether playing Shakespeare, in St John's revues, or in public impersonations of Mick Jagger, reveals, even for a politician, exhibitionism in an unusually undisguised and exotic form.

When exhibitionism becomes overt, when it shows itself in the behaviour of the pathetic 'flashers' for whom I used to plead in magistrates' courts, or when it becomes obtrusive in unpleasantly histrionic behaviour, it tells of a failure to transmute the narcissism that is the endowment of all of us in our earliest years. The ultimate test is to be found in our capacity, as we grow into adulthood, to transmute our original feelings of grandiosity, of omnipotence, of narcissism unlimited, into a self-esteem and self-confidence which can show themselves as a genuine concern for others as well as ourselves. For that transmutation to take place successfully, the psychoanalysts tell us, our first carers must not regard our earliest narcissistic traits as arrogant and self-serving; as demands to be fiercely denied. Instead, they should acknowledge them joyfully and with empathy until the soothed baby – no longer compelled to test his power to command – weans himself away from the need for total narcissistic gratification, gains self-confidence and, in the end, obtains his self-gratification and esteem from his own activity and creativity. But when the child's self-assertive presence is not adequately responded to by the mother, then the narcissistic injury thus inflicted never heals; in adulthood the prohibited exhibitionism, raw and untreated, exudes, at its worst, criminal perversion and, at its best, less antisocial responses.

But the failure of a babe to receive the corroboration of his healthy narcissism always leaves him bereft, and can lead to him being uncertain of his very existence. Indeed, latter-day psychoanalysts define exhibitionism as a manic defence against loss of identity: 'I must be real because I'm being looked at.' I have seen this syndrome dramatically presented when meeting famed actors and actresses and finding them empty, vapid and colourless, yet they become miraculously alive when on stage and given an identity they themselves lack.

And, of course, although usually in milder form, the same signs of early deprivation of corroboration abound among politicians; forever they clamour for attention. There are some optimistic psychiatrists who would seek to persuade us that the psychopathology of the politician, thus expressed, is not important; what is important is the creative use they make of

their psychopathology. And it has to be conceded that sometimes their flow of provocations, ideas and manifestos, giving
them the attention and thus the comforting confirmation of their
own reality, results in net gains for the nation. Too often,
however, the consequences are less than benign; and certainly
that is how I would categorise the consequences that come from
Blair's existentialist waverings. As actor or performer
doubtless he brought pleasure. His small step from stage to
political platform in search of identity may have assisted him in
his personal resolution, but it has left my Labour Party shorn;
he has taken away the identity of Labour and reshaped it to suit
his own psychological measurements. This operation is
described by his supporters as 'reform'; I call it theft.

We can note the exhibitionist symptoms of unassuaged
infantile narcissism when a politician is forever belatedly
seeking an identity corroboration denied to him as a babe.
Although in the generality we can rest upon the clinical
findings of the paediatricians and psychoanalysts who affirm
that the source of such restlessness lies in the absence of 'good-
enough mothering', perforce, evidentially, there are grave
difficulties in establishing the fact in the particular; but
although these obstacles necessitate caution, we should not be
deterred when the exhibitionism of the individual politician is
so florid and various that it is undeniable that it has stamped
upon it all the hallmarks delineated by the clinicians.

And we should be quizzical when such politicians, finding it
too painful to accept that they received anything but unstinting,
exclusive love and care from their mothers, indulge in
idealisations of their mothers.

Predictably, Blair's overpliant biographer tells us how Blair
'adored' his mother, the 'down to earth' daughter of a Glasgow
butcher, and how, in turn, we are informed: 'It was absolutely
clear she doted on Tony.' She may have provided him with an
audience but when she died, tragically early, Blair's declared
handling of his grief does not present a picture of a satiated man

who felt he had received adequate recognition from his mother. No stillness appears in his mourning. All of us pass through a kaleidoscope of emotions on the death of a parent, but with Blair, his odd dominant response was to use the occasion in an extraordinary self-directive manner. He has said that the death 'strangely galvanised him'. He converted the death into a spur to drive himself on, frenetically, to achieve rapidly his narcissistic satisfactions:

> I think the death of someone very close to you does act as a spur to you, because as well as your grief for the person your own mortality comes home to you. And you suddenly realise – which often you don't as a young person – that life is finite, so if you want to get things done you had better get a move on.

Getting 'a move on' immediately manifested itself, despite his previous lack of interest in politics, in his joining the Labour Party; to Blair 'moving on' and 'moving up' carried the same meaning.

One of Blair's aides has quipped that when travelling in a car with Blair the item that gets most used is the passenger's vanity mirror; but the mirror-gazing is not to be dismissed as mere vanity. Psychoanalysts, particularly those who are followers of Heinz Kohut, who made many emendations to classic Freudian theory, stress that for a healthy self to develop, to gain cohesion and balance, the babe requires adequate satisfaction of what they call 'mirroring' needs. These are the babe's needs to feel affirmed, confirmed, recognised, to feel accepted and appreciated especially when he displays himself. If those needs are unsatisfied, mirror-gazing in adulthood is a belated attempt to obtain the reassurance that he is there, whole and in one piece. These days, this fear of dissolution, which was formerly overcome by many a politician in the confirmatory audience response at public meetings, is warded off by television.

Thanks to the recording video, a politician can now indulge his exhibitionism on television and then, subsequently, see himself on the screen. The MP guards his videotapes of himself jealously; they have freed him from having to find someone else to look at him and confirm that his identity has not gone missing.

The technology is new but not the phenomenon. I can recall, long before I came into the Commons, a meeting that I chaired in a Cardiff cinema addressed by the then Foreign Secretary, Herbert Morrison, grandfather of Peter Mandelson. Despite the attraction of being outdoors on a hot Sunday afternoon, the meeting was packed and, in that pre-air-conditioning era, the hall became uncomfortably warm. As I opened the proceedings I was aware of the understandable listlessness of the audience, and I hoped the inquisitiveness which had brought them to see and hear the Foreign Secretary would overcome their somnolence. It was not to be. For an hour Morrison pompously read his prepared Foreign Office brief, cautiously never departing from the text; the audience wilted, and the applause when Morrison eventually concluded was so muted that even Morrison's conceit could not sustain him. He grumpily accompanied me to the small dinner party that had been arranged at the home of a supporter. After the first course, as our proud hostess was carrying in her *pièce de résistance*, Morrison abruptly commanded the service and eating to cease; he was aware, as we were not, that lengthy recorded excerpts of his speech were to be given on the wireless, and on his order one of his officials placed a radio on the dinner table and once again we were subjected to his verbal torture. As the broadcast speech droned on, we drooped in despair and embarrassment but Morrison's moroseness left him and he became the famed chirpy Cockney. Even more than most politicians, he was in love with his own voice; and thus supported, while we disconsolately ate our now cold fare, he pronounced the evening a great success. Indeed, so pleased was he with himself, and thus with me, that the following day he told regional officers of the party that they should endeavour to find a South Wales seat for me. His good opinion of me was not to last long; when I did reach the Commons, in a xenophobic tirade he endeavoured to smear left-wing MPs by pointing out we were a bunch who, from A to Z, from Abse to Zilliacus, with Mikardo in the middle, had doubtful origins. Given his prejudices, or perhaps because of them, it was ironic that his daughter married the well-liked advertising manager of the *Jewish Chronicle*; for her offence, Morrison cut her off and was to see almost nothing of her children, and Peter Mandelson's pretence that his politics come from the influence of his grandfather is faction, not fact.

On the occasion, when Morrison used his recorded voice to gain the approbation denied to him by his audience, his behaviour was but a caricature of the technique we all use when we are, literally, uncertain of ourselves. In the dark, feeling alone, we ward off the threats we fear from without and within by humming or whistling to ourselves; total silence can depersonalise us. Whistling in the dark is not a practice confined to politicians; but one of the sources of their notorious loquacity, like their gregariousness, is their particular incapacity to be alone. The jibe that they like their own voices too much is justified, but there is a plaintive plea lurking behind all their prolix outpourings. Respond to us, applaud us, tell us we are here; we fear our dissolution; give us not only your vote but cheer us, and so, by your voices, give us the corroboration that we did not receive as babes in our mothers' arms.

Donald Winnicott, the paediatrician whose work has so influenced contemporary English psychoanalysis, has spelled out the origins of this incapacity to relish solitude, this extraordinary need always to have the presence of others with whom one can communicate. Incapacity to be alone originates, Winnicott tells us, with the infant's experience of being alone in the presence of his mother. If the child's immediate needs

have been satisfied, if he has received warmth, physical contact
and food, and if the babe sees the approving mirroring gleam in
the mother's eye, when there is no further need for the mother
to be concerned with immediately providing anything more,
nor any need for the babe to be looking immediately to the
mother for everything, then, at such moments, there is a blissful
silence. The relatedness between mother and child, Winnicott
tells us, is the basis of the capacity to be alone:

> The paradox of the capacity to be alone is based on the
> experience of being alone in the presence of someone and
> without a sufficiency of this experience the capacity to be
> alone cannot be developed.

So many of our compulsively gregarious politicians suffer
from, and make us suffer for, their insufficiency of that experience; and, since a prerequisite to enjoying that experience is to
have the blessing of a succouring empathic mother who, with
love, tends and feeds the child, it unsurprisingly follows we
find so many politicians who fall into the category described,
75 years ago, as 'oral character types' by Karl Abraham, the
man regarded by British Kleinian analysts as their founding
father. Abraham traced the link between the babe who had
received inadequate gratification by way of sucking and the
incessant adult talker. In infancy all of us have an intense
pleasure in the act of sucking, but Abraham insisted that this
pleasure was not to be ascribed entirely to the process of taking
food but that it is conditioned in a high degree by the
significance of the mother as an erotogenic zone; some of that
early enjoyed erotic activity finds a place in the kissing of
adult lovers, but such is our oral erotic endowment that this
outlet is insufficient to deplete its supply. The primitive form
of obtaining pleasure through sucking has to persist in all sorts
of disguises during the whole of our lives, and Abraham
thought that certain traits of character can be traced back to

singular displacements, particularly by those feeling orally deprived:

> Their longing to seek gratification by way of sucking has changed to a need to give by way of the mouth, so that we find in them, besides a permanent longing to obtain everything, a constant need to communicate themselves orally to other people. This results in an obstinate urge to talk, connected in most cases with a feeling of over-flowing. Persons of this kind have the impression that their fund of thought is inexhaustible, and they ascribe a special power of some unusual value to what they say.

For thirty years, daily, in the great talking-shop of Westminster, I found clinical material that all too chasteningly illustrated Abraham's theory. The most insufferable confirmation came from Harold Wilson. In public he had no reputation for brevity and many of his speeches were ruined by their longevity; his book rendering his account of his governments stands witness to his disregard for economical presentation. But he was no less unendurable in private. On not a few occasions, arriving late in the Members' dining-room and finding all the smaller tables occupied, I fled the House to an outside restaurant rather than sit at one of the vacant places at the large table over which Wilson presided; there, his role as leader of the party meant he commanded the deference which enabled him to talk without interruption – and he would take advantage of his position.

When Wilson spoke to you, it was not a rapport that was being established; rather, you felt he was relating to you in the only way open to him, by way of oral discharge. And not content to leave his words to be spoken once, a disproportionate amount of his conversation would be spent on what he had recently said to the women of Bootle or the Trades Council at Llanelli, and how large were his audiences, and how well they responded. And he would recall unimportant meetings of long ago with an astonishing wealth of detail, savouring them yet again as would an aged man recalling the *affaires* of his youth. If he stopped his compulsive talking, you wondered if he would disappear into thin air. Wilson revealed all the inner apprehensions of the incessant talker which Logan Pearsall Smith, the famed literary critic, once sensitively described: 'It is the dread of something happening, something unknown and dreadful, that makes us do anything to keep the flicker of talk from dying out.'

But garrulousness is a vulgar stratagem to ward off fears of dissolution; I have observed, when sharing platforms with some sophisticated politicians, auditory ruses that are much more inventive. James Griffiths, the architect of our National Insurance scheme, as his speeches advanced and his decidedly chapel oratory held his audience, while speaking would close his eyes as if in a trance, and Roy Jenkins sometimes, if not so emphatically, could similarly shut his eyes. These gestures are not to be dismissed as mere mannerisms. By having the audience look at you while simultaneously listening to yourself, you have the double assurance of your own presence, of your own reality. You can obtain the applause of the audience while at the same time lulling yourself into security by listening to your own lullabies, the ones you did not receive but wanted when clasped in your mother's arms. The gesture, of course, can be interpreted as an attempt to blind yourself to painful truths, past and present, internal and external; but the quiddity of the eye movement is the protection it affords against disintegration. It has not been part of the protective armoury of Blair; he has used another technique to reach the same ends. He opens his eyes wide, too wide, sees his admiring audience and then, in song, Mozart or rock, has obtained his listeners' approval while having the solace of hearing himself. He is thus more shameless in his exhibitionism, but doubtless his need is greater.

The Outsiders: Leo and Tony

The very desperation of Blair's need for corroboration leaves one unconvinced, despite all the inferential evidence that can be marshalled, that the sole source of this hunger for external approbation is to be found in his unassuaged infantile narcissism. Moving at an extraordinary pace, unencumbered by any serious political baggage, en route from earliest infancy to Downing Street, what else, one wonders, has spurred on this man? One incitement is his place within the family constellation, which ensured he would not lack for sibling rivalry. Second sons, forever attempting to elbow their way to the front, striving to obtain the priority their birthday has denied them, have often been remarked upon in the Labour movement, where second sons with able elder brothers have, from Stafford Cripps and Harold Laski to Tony Benn, frequently provided significant leadership. The dynamism behind sibling rivalry can be benign or destructive, and sometimes both, and its force should not be underestimated politically in a family where the resources of the mother-provider are meagre and the brothers begin their lives fighting over small morsels of love and recognition. The wish to blaze high in the family firmament is effortlessly displaced in adult life to the political party whose members, as part of its trades union inheritance, so recently, until sanitised by Blair and his kind, addressed each other as 'Brother'.

And does yet another incitement to be way out front come from the particular circumstances of his Scottish origins? Or is he, as some of his Scottish colleagues would have us believe, *déraciné*, the grandson of the English land-owning class, educated at Fettes, 'Scotland's Eton', and at Oxford, suitably representing an English seat? Those questions are certainly politically relevant but to obtain answers we should focus not upon his formal schooling, but upon his upbringing within a family dominated by a politically ambitious father. It is true that, by chance, Tony's father, Leo, was brought up in Scotland, but it is an exploration of the geography of Leo Blair's mind, not the venue of his first home, that provides us with some of the answers we are seeking.

Glib, too glib, in his oft-repeated affirmations of family values, Blair has told of his good fortune in coming from a 'very closely knit family', and certainly he remains tied to a father who is a case study of the outsider striving to become the insider. Blair's sympathetic biographer has described Leo as 'a walking advertisement for social mobility'; he was the illegitimate son of the daughter of a wealthy land-owning family in West Sussex and was dumped upon a Clydeside shipyard rigger and his wife, to be brought up in a tenement in near-poverty, and forced to leave school at fourteen in order to find work. His predicament and the resentment of the class from which his mother sprang made Blair's father an active communist but the war gave the outsider the opportunity to get on to the inside track. He left behind his secretaryship of the Scottish Young Communist League and in the army took another route; he rejoined the class from which he had been expelled. He rose from being a private to become a major and in the postwar world became one of the leading Tories in the Northeast and, but for the cruel misfortune of his suffering a severe stroke, it is likely he would have entered the Commons. He had moved a long way from Govan in Clydeside. Forever determined to belong to the establishment, which now, thanks to his son, is New Labour, he has effortlessly glided from the Conservative Party to join New Labour. With him as an exemplar, his son continues to thrive on political lability.

If he had entered the House as a Conservative MP, Leo Blair would have been one of those who come from the 'outer margins' and whom Isaiah Berlin has contrasted with those born within the solid security of the dominant settled society and who look upon it as their natural home. Berlin notes the fiery vision, noble or degraded, of the outsiders: Napoleon from Corsica; Gambetta from the southern borderlands; the Austrian Hitler; and Theodor Herzl and Trotsky from the outer rim of the assimilated edges of the Jewish world. Berlin could certainly have added to his list the Welsh Lloyd George, the most notable outsider since Disraeli to attain the premiership. Berlin too could have underlined his contentions by pointing out that Napoleon, born in Corsica of Italian origin, had an imperfect knowledge of French; that Garibaldi, born in Nice, a French citizen, spoke clumsy Italian; and that Herzl, a secular Western European Jew, found the majority of his followers among East European Jews whose language, Yiddish, he hardly knew. Given the dreams, some misshapen, some idealistic, of these outsider leaders, Berlin concludes that, in contrast, the insider leaders 'tend to have a stronger sense of social reality, to see public life in reasonably just perspective, without the need to escape into political fantasy or romantic inventions'.

Tony Blair, unconvincingly, seeks to explain and justify his father's trajectory in quite different terms; he presents him, speciously, as a 'gut Conservative' chafing against the restrictions imposed upon him by the collective society and does him the serious injustice of comparing him with Norman Tebbit, a man regarded by many as an exponent of gutter politics. But if we leave fiction for fact, then the strivings of the outsider and ersatz Scot, Leo Blair, no Essex man, are seen to be of the type explicated by Isaiah Berlin when writing of outsiders' craving for recognition:

It is an effort to escape from the weakness and humiliation of a depressed or wounded social group by identifying oneself with some other group or movement that is free from the defects of one's original condition; consisting in an attempt to acquire a new personality, and that which goes with it, a new set of clothing, a new set of values, habits, new armour which does not press upon the old wounds, on the old scars left by the chains one wore as a slave.

When we note the swing of Leo Blair from Young Communist to High Tory, we wonder how apposite to him are Berlin's comments on those, suffering discrimination, who start their lives feeling they are excluded from participation in the governance of the community:

They are liable to develop either exaggerated resentment of, or contempt for, the dominant majority, or else over-intense admiration or indeed worship for it, or, at times, a combination of the two which leads both to unusual insights and – born of overwrought sensibilities – a neurotic distortion of the facts.

But for the terrible fate of suffering a stroke at forty, Leo Blair would undoubtedly have become an insider, feeling confident that he had become part of the 'dominant majority', a Tory MP with the drive and intelligence to become a minister. As it was, his son was to be brought up in a home where the stricken father, intensely buttoned up about his origins, had nearly, but not quite, rid himself of his past and nearly, but not quite, obtained the recognition that would have meant that he had achieved what he most wanted: to belong, to cancel out his rejection and his illegitimacy. How did that enforced limbo, physical and psychological, endured by Leo, impinge upon his young son – and with what ultimate political consequence?

The influence of Leo Blair upon his son is, in some respects, blatant, most obviously in the young Tony's fledgling politics. The boy in his earliest years was immersed in Tory politics, with his father as chairman of the Durham Conservative Association receiving into his home many of the leading Conservatives passing through the Northeast; and, after his father's enforced retirement, his son remained loyally and firmly attached to the doctrines in which he had been reared. His role as a would-be Tory candidate at thirteen in his school's mock elections shows not only his political precocity but, more significantly, the continuing strength of his father's influence. I know how family influences had shaped my politics when, at the same age as young Tony, I stood as a Labour candidate in a mock election held at my valiant run-down secondary school, and I wryly recall my presumptuousness in writing to the then leader of the Labour Party, George Lansbury, asking him for a letter of support – which brought back a sensitive and warm commendation which, well passed round the school, ensured my victory. And even as the Welsh socialist pacifist tradition within my family shaped my boyhood politics, so did the influence of his family bear down upon the young Tony as he strove to emulate his father. The impress of my early family conditioning remains deeply embossed upon my political thought; and, similarly, if less unequivocally, does the impress of Leo Blair upon the political stances of his son.

But more subtle, yet no less pervasive, paternal influences appear to have been at work. All feelings of rejection, of not belonging, which Leo Blair had so courageously attempted, with partial success, to overcome, would surely have been reactivated as once again he found himself within a hostile environment, one in which a cruel and debilitating stroke had left him as a baby, for years speechless and utterly dependent. The man who had so courageously battled to break out from an outer wilderness found himself expelled from the centrality of his political life and reduced to a peripheral role even within the family he had commanded. Tony Blair was thus brought up in a home overcast by the estrangement of his father, a man who by his own efforts had become in the postwar years a successful academic lawyer, and then, at forty, was tragically fated to be reduced, by his physical condition, to being once again an outcast even as he had been as an illegitimate child. Those feelings of Leo Blair, of not belonging, of alienation, have been picked up, as the record shows, by his son. Repeatedly, surveying Blair's passage through his public school, university and party, one's attention is arrested by the incapacity of this good-looking, intelligent and seemingly socially fluent individual to feel, despite his advantages, at home within the institutions which house him; sometimes, indeed, so acute is his discomfort that he cannot forbear not to make it public.

When I have spoken to some of his contemporaries at the Durham Cathedral Choristers' Preparatory School, their recall always emphasises his non-participation, outside the organised school games, in the play of the kids in nearby open spaces; he was often ferried in from the nearby village of executive houses, where he lived, by his father – remembered as a stern, forbidding figure – and then, after school, Blair returned home direct. He was a 'good boy', average in his studies, but doing well in scripture and thus conforming to the religiosity that pervaded the all-male establishment and was felt, at least by some of the choirboy pupils, as sickly and tinged by a vague eroticism. He is also remembered at the school by his ever-present smile directed towards the teachers, a smile which then was successfully used to deflect any potential hostility and which now he still so notoriously deploys, and which indeed has become his political trade-mark. That compulsive smile, in my judgement, falls into the category that the insightful research psychotherapist Valerie Sinason has identified among patients suffering from severe emotional traumas and severe physical disabilities. She has termed it 'the handicapped smile', an anxious, studied grin, used as a defence against unhappiness;

and other psychotherapists, like Brett Kahr, working with profoundly handicapped children have remarked on their strained smiles, which are used as a protective mechanism against their extreme fear of being unloved or even hated. Certainly at his school, Blair used his smile to considerable effect; it enabled him to ingratiate himself with his canon headmaster so that, side by side, they would fervently pray together.

Blair's biographer, Jon Sopel, was evidently over-persuaded that he was very much at home at the prep school. A closer scrutiny of the facts and the recall of some of Blair's contemporaries more strongly suggest a façade, a priggish adaptation by a stress-loaded boy, which accommodated to the environment but which failed to be sustained when he left the prep school for the rigours of Fettes public school.

At Fettes, often called 'Eton in a kilt', Blair would have encountered the highly disciplined and structured environment of an old-fashioned and rigid public school. Doubtless many boys found it tough, but few would so fail to adapt to its group ethos. Blair packed his bags and, literally, ran away; it needed all his father's persuasions for him to be taken back. Only in fantasy, in the school drama productions, could he find himself, and the only extant commendation of Blair at Fettes appears to be the comment in the school magazine, after he had appeared in a school play, that the college had been 'very fortunate in having so experienced an actor as Blair for the central figure'. Whether his continuing histrionic ability is fortunate for the Labour Party is another matter.

As for Oxford, his alienation there is, on the surface, quite extraordinary. He has told his biographer that, 'looking back', he felt he 'never really belonged to Oxford'. Absurdly patronisingly and, given his second-class degree, defensively, he says: 'Oxford, far from being intellectually invigorating, is actually rather stifling. There was very little room for fresh or original thought . . . all the time I was at Oxford I felt an outsider.' When in the past I visited Oxford to speak to student societies, I found youngsters from comprehensive schools in my constituency, sons of miners or steel-workers, who understandably felt lost in the ancient university. But why should the public school boy, coming from an upper-middle-class family, good-looking, with a string of undergraduate girlfriends, 'enjoying himself', he says, performing in revues, in sketches and playing music, be so wretchedly afflicted with estrangement? The cause is not to be found in Oxford or in any other external circumstances of his undergraduate days; it was older and more deep-seated. Tony Blair carried within him the depression and grief in which, as a member of Leo Blair's family, he had, as a boy, been engulfed.

Feeling the outsider in Oxford was part of Blair's personal travail; but carrying that estrangement into the Labour Party has made the personal problem a public one, for he could no more 'belong', in the full sense that Nye Bevan stressed, to the Labour Party than he could to his schools and Oxford. In July 1995, after the special conference called to gut Clause Four of Labour's constitution, he made a comment which, even as he made it, astonished him as much as his *Guardian* interviewer; he announced that the whole process of effecting the change had been an education for him, belatedly introducing him to the Labour Party: 'I know my Labour Party very well now. It may be a strange thing to say but before I became leader I did not.'

It may be 'strange' to him but, given his particular psychic disablement, and the consequent repetitive pattern of his tenuous relationship with the institutions he has joined, it is not strange to me; but it is offensive, as it is to others within my dwindling generation of Old Labour. Our entry into, and our understanding of, our party did not come by way of some blinding Damascus revelation; nor did we qualify for our membership by filling in an application form in a glossy magazine. My experience is not atypical even if, as has been reported, in standing as a candidate seventeen times in local and national elections, I have been the standard-bearer for Labour more times than anyone now alive, and even although, as becomes a Labour veteran, I have been arrested and for a very short while imprisoned because of my political activities; some such experiences, victimisation in the workshop, appalling exploitation in mine or factory, prolonged periods of unemployment and poverty, shaped most of the political activists of Old Labour. Displaying the same hubris towards them as he has towards his old university, in the same interview in which he revelled in his efforts to create Labour in his own blemished image, the young politician patronisingly added: 'The Labour Party is much nicer than it looks. Labour often looks as if it is about to engage in class war but in fact it is full of basically rather decent and honest people.' Unsurprisingly, vexed by his presumptuousness, some traditional supporters accused him, in 1995, of 'betrayal'. Now, six years into Labour government, those accusations mount. It is a government which began with relinquishment of the Bank of England which, after years of struggle, Labour had nationalised in 1945; and it ended its 2000 parliamentary session striving to privatise the air itself, to take air traffic control out of public ownership. In 2003 we find the government insisting on top-up fees at universities and proposing the creation of 'foundation hospitals', which are to be given the right to raise their own financing. Labour activists see such pusillanimity as treachery, and dub Blair a traitor to the party. They are in error. When the notorious alienated spy Kim Philby was stigmatised as a betrayer, he protested: 'To betray you must first belong.' Tony Blair could indeed be granted the same defence.

Disavowals

All of us, to a greater or lesser extent, seek to blot out our painful experiences, to disavow past fearsome or humiliating events in our lives. But the defence mechanism of denial is defective; it is liable to backfire. Our refusal to acknowledge the existence of our past agonies guarantees that, slyly, they will return in disguised forms, and often will demand a ransom from us for daring to ignore them. Our past pains and fears will never be tempered unless we face them.

Any overview of Blair's personal and political life reveals a man who depends upon denial as a principal weapon in his psychic armoury; predictably, this leaves him, as man and politician, vulnerable. Freud uses the term 'disavowal', *Verleugnung*, in the specific sense of a mode of thinking that consists of a refusal to recognise the reality of a traumatic perception. With Blair, disavowals of that quality abound. They are to be seen in his descriptions of his relationships with his mother, his father, his school and university, and in his account of his early life within the Blair family.

By idealisation of his mother, he denies any emotional deprivation he may have felt in her arms. That judgement, thus baldly stated, has, it is immediately conceded, been reached only inferentially, by linking his marked exhibitionism to unassuaged narcissism, to a failure to have received, initially, sufficient loving corroboration; no other explanation seems to be available. And certainly such little as has been made known of his mother does not subvert that judgement.

Hazel Blair came out of a harsh, austere climate, that of the conservative Protestant farming community of the borderlands of Ulster. Blair's over-generous biographer Jon Sopel, who received much aid and time from him and from his office staff, has recited a list of her virtues. He tells us that she was a 'practical', 'down to earth', 'shy' woman who reared her family with 'stoicism' and instilled into her children a 'sense of duty'. One is left feeling admiration for a woman who clearly met family adversity with resource and courage, but the choice of words in the eulogy is discouraging; it bears an uncomfortably close resemblance to the encoded masking vocabulary found in many an obituary notice. 'Shy' could mean uncommunicative, withdrawn; 'practical' could mean non-academic and perhaps rather dull; 'down to earth' suggests unimaginativeness – all the qualities one would associate with a dutiful but unempathic mother. Blair himself, when recounting her main attribute, uses a noun which conveys a hard adamantine quality: she was the 'cement' that kept the family together.

Blair's use of the mechanism of denial is more explicitly revealed in the turmoil of his schooldays. Sopel has concluded that Blair 'at Fettes College found himself in a completely alien world' but does not offer any explanation why Blair, the son of a professional man, should be at odds with a school that was not peopled by lairds but by the sons of Edinburgh's merchant classes. Nevertheless, despite this alienation, and despite the rigours of the highly disciplined and oppressively structured environment imposed upon him, and despite the humiliations of the fag system, of which 'aspect of his school life he displays a marked reluctance to speak', Blair tells Sopel that 'for all the pettiness of Fettes' he came 'eventually to enjoy his time there'. The travails of his schooldays are distanced, almost totally denied, as his recollections dwell upon the comforting escape to fantasy in the school theatricals.

And in Oxford his flight from the predicaments of his inner loneliness as an 'outsider' took on a manic quality. Psycho-analysts define denial of psychical reality as a manifestation of a manic defence; it consists of denying the inner significance of experience, and in particular of depressive feelings. His biographer is forced to acknowledge that 'for all the fun of wine, women and song', Blair was 'restless' at Oxford. The biographer overstates the fun and underrates the significance of the so-called restlessness. Blair was attempting to cope not with unease but with dis-ease.

Almost frenetically he flung himself into the social whirl of undergraduate societies like the Archery Club, which had nothing to do with archery and everything to do with the affectation that its members were latter-day characters out of *Brideshead Revisited* having a 'good time' drinking at dinner-parties, which would be concluded by throwing champagne glasses out of the window. And thus Blair 'enjoyed' himself, dressing up on and off the stage in bizarre styles, sporting what he believed were trendy clothes, a vile synthetic skin coat or a curious black coat with well-displayed red lining. With his hair halfway down his back accompanied by a severe fringe, his father going to collect him from Oxford literally did not recognise his own son; and he would have been more taken aback if he had seen him wearing in his revue or rock-band appearances a hoop-necked, trumpet-sleeved T-shirt 'which stopped just beneath the ribcage, leaving a large acreage of rippling bare torso and beyond that there were the obligatory purple loons, topped off by Cuban-heeled cowboy boots'.

But for one factor, it would be priggish and irrelevant to comment on Blair's undergraduate behaviour. Many of the undergraduates, particularly those from public schools, burst out of their earlier shelterings and containments in similar fashion, and when I would speak at the Oxford Union at the time Blair was an undergraduate, I noted how prolonged and delayed was the adolescence of the public schoolboys compared with working-class young men, often married with a child, employed in the factories in my constituency. Given, however, the unconvincing explanations by Blair, telling us why he never in any way participated in the Union or the political societies of the university, his immaturity at Oxford is a legitimate subject for comment. He found, he says, the activities of the Labour Club: 'a complete turn-off . . . I could not be bothered with that. I've always had a fairly practical turn of mind and student politics at Oxford never seemed very practical. Instead I generally enjoyed myself performing in revues, sketches . . .' He 'loathed the falseness and pretentiousness and wanted no part in the affectations of would-be prime ministers'. These muddled rationalisations, with all their non sequiturs, telling how the 'practical' man preferred the falseness of the footlights to politics, would be bewildering unless we understand that here the adult Blair is masking the predicaments of young Blair at Oxford. There, as described by a much older fellow-student, an ordained priest who influenced Blair, he was a 'lost soul'. 'I think his life kind of lacked purpose and direction. Beyond getting a degree I don't think he knew what he was doing at Oxford, and I think he felt unsatisfied.'

If indeed his extraordinary claim that he was too practical to join in student politics had any substance, then he could have followed the example of not a few Oxbridge students who escaped the confines of the student societies and endeavoured to enter the real world by joining the local branch of the Labour Party. I often encountered such students during the short time that Robert Davies was the Labour MP for Cambridge – a man with whom, after he came into the Commons from a distinguished service on the local authority, I formed a friendship. Rigid, ideological but scrupulous, his rectitude was a personal disaster. Accustomed to need and to obtain, as can often occur in local government, speedy and useful results, he found himself on the back benches lacking function and, in an ineffectual limbo, despising the compromises of the 1966 government and those indigenous to Harold Wilson's temperament, he bravely, but desperately and fatally, hurled himself at the institution. In vain I counselled him to cultivate more detachment; but his fury and impatience with the political charades, the half-truths and evasions of Westminster, dangerously blew back upon him. Still in his forties, after fifteen months as an MP, this gifted man died of his honesty and the House of Commons. But during the time that he was in the Commons I sometimes accompanied him, at his request, to speak to his constituency party and there I found Cambridge students receiving tutorship from him and guidance from adult working-class fellow-party members, unavailable to them in the student societies.

If, similarly, Blair, too fastidious to participate in the politics of his fellow-students, had joined the Labour Party, he would undoubtedly have been exposed to some of the realities of the outside world. It would have introduced him to those in the local party from the Oxford working-class of Cowley and to those in the car plant there which, at the time of Blair's sojourn in Oxford, was a hotbed of political activism; and he might then have understood, through his contact with the trade union delegates on the management committee of the Oxford party, the intimacy existing between the Labour Party and the trade union movement and how the federal nature of the party, which in 1995 it was discovered he clandestinely was seeking to dismember, was its very lifeblood.

And if it was not that he was engaged in a flight from, and not a fight against, his alienation, the 'lost soul' could have found the 'communality' about which he forever prattles in the trade union branches where, tacitly, it is practised. I had found it there before the war when, as a teenager employed in a factory doing work, like Blair's father and so many of his and my generation, which denied our potential, I joined the Transport and General Workers' Union. When, with the opportunities made available to ex-servicemen in the postwar world, I became a solicitor, one of my greatest professional satisfactions was my capacity to repay my indebtedness to my union by giving its members legal aid and advice. The 'brothers' should not be mocked. Inside branches of the unions and the lodges of the miners there can come into existence loyalties and support of a rare quality; but their bonding has been formed not according to some fanciful theories but in struggle, and their allegiance of one to another has sprung out of conflict and confrontation.

Blair's notions of communality, however, come from a totally different source. In the latter days of his undergraduate life, he came under the influence of his friend Peter Thomson, the 36-year-old ordained priest who, as a mature student, was studying theology and whom Blair found 'spellbinding'; the spell never seems to have broken, for in 1995 Blair took his family across the world to spend his Christmas at Thomson's Merrijig home in the backwoods of Australia and there enticed him to return to Britain. Uninterested in heaven since leaving behind his cathedral prep-school prayers, under Thomson's influence the bewildered young man once again got into religion and became confirmed. He pursued it with all the enthusiasm of a novice and soon the priest had led him to the works of John Macmurray, which totally 'fascinated' him and which he now says are central to his political thinking; that is a claim which requires scrutiny.

Blair's biographer says Macmurray was 'an obscure Scottish philosopher'. He was certainly not obscure to me. Thirty-five years before the young Blair trekked to Scotland from Oxford in the hope of sitting at the feet of his elderly guru, I had, when I was the same age as Blair, listened to him lecture; but the professor of moral philosophy did not make the same overwhelming impression on me as he did on Blair. I recall him, a man as short as I was and no less loquacious, lecturing on dialectical materialism and, in conciliatory tones, seeking to accommodate Christianity to Marxism; even as a twenty-year-old socialist, I found his ecumenical expositions strained but, of course, politically welcome. The Macmurray that Blair encountered, however, was a man who had long since ceased to make his gentle, political forays. Indeed, in his later book, the one specifically named by Blair as his guidebook, the earlier neo-Marxist essays are not listed among his previous publications; this erasure evidently did not convince the old Etonian sneak George Orwell who in 1949 stupidly placed Macmurray on the notorious secret list of so-called potential traitors that he so shamelessly supplied to the credulous clandestine section of the Foreign Office.

Blair most certainly would not have obtained from Macmurray any encouragement to seek any political answers to the woes of the human predicament. On the contrary, the late works of Macmurray that Blair was reading mocked politics and politicians; community, Macmurray insisted, was to be found in religion, and politics were to be eschewed:

> If we track the state to its lair, what shall we find? Merely a collection of overworked and worried gentlemen, not at all unlike ourselves, doing their best to keep the machinery of government working as well as may be, and hard put to it to keep up appearances. They are, like ourselves, subject to the illusion of power. If we expect them to work miracles, we flatter them, and tempt them to think they are supermen . . . Those of them who are wise enough to know their limitations, and to be immune to the gross adulation of their fellows, will resign; and government will be carried on only by megalomaniacs.

Blair's claim in 1994 that at Oxford Macmurray had led him to see the 'coincidence between the philosophical theory of Christianity and left-of-centre politics' is demonstrably fiction. Not for the first or last time, Blair rewrites his political biography. In submitting himself to Macmurray, Blair was not in any way being baptised into mere politics; he was being 'saved', preparing to enter the Kingdom.

For Macmurray had become a great one on despair, a word he would place in his books in italics; and, of course, he was therefore addressing himself to the very condition suffered by young Tony. My gurus, when I was young, taught me the wise adage: 'Beware when you find what you are looking for.' Tony Blair could have done with that advice, although it is improbable that he would have found it acceptable, for the lure of a philosopher who claimed that he not only knew the source of despair but also an unfailing antidote was, for Blair, irresistible. Needless to say, such extravagant claims could not be made in the context of politics but only in religious terms; and the ultimate resolution that Macmurray taught was that proposed by hundreds of vicars throughout Britain every Sunday morning: celebration of the fellowship of all things in God.

Macmurray's reputation as a philosopher deservedly did not survive the war and before his death he had been relegated to a minor figure in academic theology; but with the future prime minister of Britain persisting in telling us in 1994: 'If you really want to understand what I'm all about, you have to take a look at a guy called John Macmurray. It's all there', some scrutiny of Macmurray's dated mixture of homespun psychology and on the hoof sociology has to be endured. Not all is there, but it does become clear why of all the masks Blair wears to deny and conceal his wounds, Macmurray is the one he finds most comfortable.

What Blair has plundered from Macmurray comes from the moralist's distinction between society and community. For Macmurray, the term society refers to 'those forms of human association in which the bond of unity is negative or impersonal'. He illustrates this assessment of society by proposing that 'Hobbesian society is based on force, Rousseau's on consent, but both are aimed only at the protection of the individual associates in the pursuit of their private interests'.

In contrast, community associations have 'positive personal

relations as their bond . . . it is a personal not impersonal unity of persons'. This philosopher, ever the preacher, tells us the path to be taken is away from the negative societal values – they are based on a:

> categorical misconception, a misconception of one's own nature which must affect all our actions for we shall misconceive our own reality by appearing to ourselves to be what we are not, or not to be what we are . . . It is a misconception that is 'categorical', making action inherently self-frustrating, for in the end such a misconception leads us only to the discovery that all objectives have the same illusory character; this is the experience of despair.

And then, lest his student listeners – who were the bewildered Blairs twenty years before Blair himself read the published lectures – should find the professor taking them out of their depth, he repeats himself in a simple homily:

> When two friends quarrel and are estranged each blames the other for the bad relations between them. Or, to put it otherwise, if my motivation is negative then I appear to myself as an isolated individual who must act for himself and achieve whatever he can by his individual efforts, in a world which cares nothing for success or failure. Yet in reality, my isolation is self-isolation, a withdrawal from relationships through fear of the other. This attitude which expresses the experience of frustration and despair is nothing but the sophisticated adult version of the attitude of the child whose mother refuses to give him what he wants. Its unsophisticated formula is 'nobody loves me'.

It is not surprising that the isolated Blair resonated to such a diagnosis; and no less unsurprising that he responded to the balm Macmurray proceeded to apply to his wounds:

If we isolate one pair as the unit of personal community we can discover the basic structure of community as such. The relation between them is positively motivated in each. Each then is heterocentric; the centre of interest is in the other not himself. The other is the centre of value. For himself he has no value in himself, but only for the other; consequently he cares for himself only for the sake of the other.

However:

If their relationship to the other is negative . . . this will destroy the realisation of the exclusive relationship itself. To be fully positive, therefore, the relation . . . must be inclusive and without limits. Only so can it be a community of persons. The self-realisation of any individual person is only fully achieved if he is positively motivated towards every other person with whom he is in relation.

We can therefore formulate the inherent ideal of the personal. It is a universal community of persons in which each cares for all the others and no one for himself . . . if the negative motive could finally and completely be subordinated to the positive, in all personal activity, the redemptive function of religion would be complete; and only its central activity would remain. Religion would then be simply the celebration of community – of the fellowship of all things in God.

Macmurray's instruction brought Blair to the Lord, but not to the Labour Party. No one could have been more anti-political than Macmurray, and if he had the stamina to hack through the thicket of Macmurray's often dense prose, the only serious politics he would have discovered was Macmurray's tirade against Marx's irreligious doctrines. Macmurray, as a young man, had translated some of the early Marx but his early flirtations with Marx are vigorously repudiated in the late works to which Blair had access and which so moved him. In seeking to persuade his biographers that he found his brand of socialism via Macmurray in Oxford, he is proffering credentials which he does not possess. I have no taste for politicians offering false political prospectuses, or for those who, to gain credibility, would adapt their own CVs according to the circumstances of the time.

If it were not for Blair's repeated and misleading assertions that Macmurray is the source from which his membership of the Labour Party sprang, one would pay scant attention to his undergraduate infatuation with philosophy and religion. A young man going through a delayed adolescence, assailed by new and, to him, frightening awakenings, turning to religion, is a commonplace phenomenon, oft remarked upon, not least by Byron:

> In thoughts like these true wisdom may discern
> Longings sublime, and aspirations high,
> Which some are born with, but for the most part learn
> To plague themselves withal, they know not why:
>
> 'Twas strange that one so young should thus concern
> His brain about the action of the sky;
> If you think 'twas philosophy that this did,
> I can't help thinking puberty assisted.

Young Blair, in his philosophical meanderings, was provided by Macmurray with a religious base that could support him in his personal travail; but the self-abnegation that Macmurray urged upon his acolytes was clearly unacceptable to Blair's exhibitionism, so he took Macmurray *à la carte* and later, after Oxford, chose another vehicle, the Labour Party, which he hoped could carry him away, would distance himself from his own Furies. But meantime in Oxford, buoyed up by

Macmurray, he faced the world with that now well-known toothy smile, the butt of so many caricatures, with a countenance that persuaded the president of St John's, Sir Richard Southern, to remark in his end-of-term report in 1974: 'Seems extraordinarily happy'. Extraordinarily is the apposite word; maniacal evangelical persuaders rarely totally convince the sophisticated. The president seems sceptical, and evidently was on enquiry, asserting in his final 1975 report: 'Needs to be tougher in thinking through his ideas', a criticism which, 28 years later, causes us to admire the president's perspicacity.

When Blair eventually arrived in the Labour Party he came garbed in vestments stolen from Macmurray's wardrobe; he had selected his plunder with care, rejecting the ill-fitting, those that mortified his address, and choosing only those that he found were custom-made for his figure. Repeatedly, during his political life, these are the clothes he wears.

The moral philosopher taught friendship, pure unadulterated friendship, free from 'negative' motivation, as the basic structure of the ideal community. He spelled out to the priest who had taken Blair to Macmurray 'that the noblest form of human existence is friendship'; that in friendship, as in community, antagonism and estrangement lead only to 'despair'. This immature, Boy Scout ethos pervades Blair's political thinking; never a speech goes by without him calling for 'partnership'. The model of the altruistic 'friendship', the 'pair', that is the starting-point of Macmurray's discovery of his 'universal community', is a fable that may beguile those moved by tales of chivalry, even as Blair's tales of partnership between government and industry, between the Labour Party and the City, between capital and labour, although leached away from reality, attract all those seeking an illusory safe political option.

The essential congruence between the mode of thought of Macmurray and his disciple is their neurotic denial of the simultaneous existence of contradictory feelings or attitudes that envelop every human relationship and are endemic to all born of woman. Both these men seek to disavow ambivalence; they cannot tolerate, and hence cannot acknowledge, the coexistence of love and hate.

When Macmurray selected as his model for the 'community' the 'pair', the pair he chose was 'friendship', not flesh and blood lovers, for passion, with all the tumult that must bring, overtly shows what Macmurray seeks to mask: the opposite to love is apathy, not hate, and throughout our lives the ambivalence we have towards our first carer, wanting full, absolute and unconditional love and simultaneously resenting our dependence, is a concomitant, as every school of depth psychology affirms, of all our later relationships. Afraid of his own resentment, fearful that aggressiveness against the 'other' may lead to the destruction of the carer upon whom he depends, Macmurray stumbles upon basic Freudian insights as he warns against what he describes as 'negative' feelings; and significantly, to explicate his philosophy, he admonishes us to repudiate those feelings, for they bring us despair, the frustration 'of the child whose mother refuses to give him what he wants'.

Macmurray correctly diagnoses the source of our discontent but his proposed remedy, the banishment of all aggression, may be an option open to saints on their way to heaven but it is unavailable on this earth. Meantime, for some afflicted with 'negative' feelings so murderous that they are ever fearful of the consequences of releasing any aggression, religion may be of assistance; in Macmurray's case, predictably, his renunciation of aggression led him to the supreme practitioners of absolute pacifism, and before his death he had joined the Quakers. The same syndrome embedded in Blair's consensus politics prompts him to attempt to de-politicise the Labour Party and proffer policies expressing his love to all and his hostility to none, excepting only those who would dare to disturb his conflict-free dreams; any voice heard to say the emperor has no clothes is, in Blair's infelicitous phrase, 'in need of therapy'. By the autumn of 1995, while he basked in the warm approbation of the tabloid *Sun*, his displeasure that his consensus politics should even be queried led him to accuse the *New Statesman*, *Guardian* and *Tribune* of producing 'claptrap written as fact'.

To unravel this curious convoluted but fanatical insistence of Blair's upon consensus by diktat, we need to take the unguarded hint of his mentor, and his warning that 'negative' feelings, breaking up consensual relations, would bring about the despair 'of the child whose mother refuses to give him what he wants'. Unwittingly, Macmurray points us to seek elucidation of his and Blair's shared idiom of thought not from philosophers or politicians but from the paediatrician; and we are encouraged in such an exercise by a no less unguarded hint of Blair's when, replying to an interviewer wanting to know what had brought him into politics, he gave the distinctly odd and evasive reply: 'Well, I suppose you could go into all the slightly twee motives.' 'Twee', sweet, dainty, are certainly not words one associates with adult male motivation; it is a colloquialism that belongs to the description of the world of childhood and it is in that world we can find the sources of Blair's fantasy of a politics without discordance or schism.

No one in Britain in the twentieth century more elegantly addressed himself to those sources than the fortunately influential paediatrician Donald Winnicott, and his teachings have resulted in many children receiving the sensitive care that lays the foundation of a confident sense of identity. Those denied such care may, by impersonation, on stage, in politics, or in their daily lives, be forever borrowing someone else's persona; but those blessed with a mother tuned into her baby's emotional needs have the greater opportunity as adults to possess a secure ego. The empathising mother, letting the child feed at his own time, willingly allowing him, within her own embrace, to sleep peacefully and restfully, gives him the most complete experience of security possible in human life; this is where the foundation of identity rests. I am because I *feel* secure and, therefore, real; and since the feeling 'I am' leads to the question 'What am I?' it brings the experience of 'being' and leads on to the growth of self-consciousness, self-knowledge and self-realisation.

But Winnicott, like the psychoanalysts W R D Fairbairn and Harry Guntrip in their seminal works, gives warning of the consequences of those unblest as children with such empathising carers. No one can regain the paradise lost linking us to the cosmos within the womb. As the ancient Jewish saying recounts: 'In the mother's body man knows the universe; in birth he forgets it.' But as far as the initial pre-natal condition can be recaptured, it comes from the mother knowing her babe by feeling and identification. Winnicott has taught us that the motility that exists in the intra-uterine life as the babe kicks in the womb, and that exists when a babe of a few weeks thrashes away with his limbs, is the precursor to the aggression that has to be positively organised by the child if he is to become a person. And for that to successfully come about, the babe, without overwhelming fear, must constantly discover and rediscover the environment by using his motility as he snuggles and struggles within his mother's arms; and thus, and only thus, he can enjoy the primal erotic experience within which he can fuse his love and aggression.

But what of those who, by environmental chance or by less than good-enough mothering, have been denied the circumstance that permits such a fusion to take place, those who are not provided with the series of individual experiences that enable them to learn that, despite the aggression they felt against their first provider, despite their hatred of their dependency and their anger that, to adapt Macmurray's phrase, the mother 'refused to give them what they wanted', despite all their 'negative' murderous wishes, they were still secure in their mother's love? One of the variants in adult behaviour that tells of such an early determining pattern, marked by empathetic disharmony, is, I believe, seen in Macmurray's pacifism and Blair's consensus politics. Those unconsciously terrified that their aggression, unglued to love, is so dangerously at large that it would bring dire punishment upon them, make the vain attempt to outlaw it entirely; but aggression, like sex, will out, and if repressed, not faced, governed or constructively sublimated, can bring about similar distortions of the human spirit. It may be that such attempts to banish aggression can, within a religious context, have some benign consequences for the worshipper and society; and it could be urged that in the politics of Gandhi's India they had an honourable place. But in the politics of contemporary Britain, it has one certain consequence: it ends in tears.

Already at the TUC conference of 1995, unlike the Labour Party conference a month later, there were overt intimations of the turbulence lying ahead. Never have I observed Blair so uncomfortable, so uncertain, as he faced the suspicious delegations wary of the man who wished to distance them from government, and who would deny them the right to pursue aggressively their demand for wage-earners to have a greater share in national income, a share then running at its lowest level since records began in 1955.

The delegates did not need the confirmation of the Central Statistical Office telling us that had wages maintained the same share of GDP as in the mid-1970s, employment income would now have been more than £60 billion higher; this translated into a loss, compared with what might have been, of £2,750 a year for every worker. One of the oldest economic debates in which the trade unions have played so prominent a part is about how the national scale is, or should be, divided. That is the battleground on which the struggles between labour and capital have taken and will take place; and, presently, capital is winning hands down. No wonder that the delegates were sullen; and no wonder that some of the leaders immediately after the conference expressed to me in private their contempt for what they regarded as Blair's naivety, his belief that in the social market capitalism would be wooed into voluntarily accepting the need for social justice. Less eloquently, but certainly no less robustly, they put the view expressed by Hugo Young: 'Labour, the tyro party of capitalism, has yet to understand the full brutality of the capitalistic logic.'

It is not only the fat cats of the privatised utilities who make the inherent antagonism between capital and labour glaringly obvious; management throughout a capitalist society will look after themselves and, as they conceive it to be their duty, look after their shareholders. On many occasions during my stewardship of my constituency I was called in by unions and, not infrequently, by employers to help prevent or resolve industrial disputes. I learned to distinguish between what was intractable, the antagonism of capital and labour, and what was tractable. What was important was the creation of a balanced truce in which each side knows its clearly defined boundaries, presses them to the limits, but knows that overstepping them leads to disaster for all. The trade unionist who had, in my youth, a considerable political influence upon me was that lovable communist Arthur Horner. During his presidency of the South Wales miners, the coal fields were almost strike-free; his controlled aggression was feared by the owners and he knew how to take his miners to the very edge but not, like the paranoid Scargill, over the edge.

The delegates at the TUC 1995 conference, with the television cameras focused upon them, out of loyalty to the Labour movement, not to Blair, dutifully gave the required standing ovation to the Labour leader; but the delegates had sat on their hands as sceptically and sullenly they listened to his call to have 'a revolution in our attitudes at work, in management, in unions, in government. All of us need to address a new agenda. Instead of conflict, partnership'.

Blair felt a cold wind blowing into his cosy kitchen cabinet. It was a wind from a real outside world 'swept with confused alarms of struggle and flight', where ignorant and not so ignorant armies clashed by night and, indeed, by day; it is a world that cannot be wished away.

The alarm bells were ringing, awakening Blair's personal aides; if the 1995 Labour Party conference was to be all consensus, sweetness and light, ground had to be yielded. Privately, Blair or his authorised aides held talks with union leaders and accepted that the reduction of the union vote at Labour conferences to 50 per cent was to be the final settlement, and other specific commitments were given. It was to be announced at the conference that a Labour government would put money in union coffers by abolishing the restrictions on check-off; by introducing legislation giving unions the statutory right to recognition if 50 per cent of a workforce balloted for it; the principle of the national minimum wage would be affirmed; compulsory competitive tendering, uncompromisingly opposed by local government unions, would, under Labour, be abolished; railways would be brought back into public ownership; and the commitment to full employment as a policy goal both domestically and in Europe would be unequivocal.

Old Labour, through the unions, thus obtained a respite; but it was to be a short pause. Blair well knew that a government genuinely implementing the commitment to the 1995 conference could not bring about a national consensus; rather, there would be fierce resistances from many vested interests. So in 1996, to avoid precipitating such confrontations, and true to the weaknesses of his temperament, Blair came up with his Big Idea: the Stakeholder Society, where the lion would lie down with the lamb, and all would be peace; each man and woman possessing the sense of belonging in workplace and boardroom; trust restored between stakeholder-worker and business; unemployment tackled at its source; abdication of power by corporation and unions and interest groups – all combining to empower the individual, all holding hands in one great happy John Lewis Partnership. Apple pie and motherhood and Amen.

Only a few spoilsports doubted such a vision; most enthusiastically rummaged through the runes of the brave
declarations, and there found their salvation. But a few asked
the needed foreboding questions. Anatole Kaletsky, then
economics editor of *The Times*, doubted whether Blair would
ever move from the:

> hideous business school jargon of the stakeholding
> society to the language of social revolution; to tackle
> unemployment at source would require a transformation
> in the conduct of economic policy in Britain. The
> minimum would be root and branch reform of the
> Treasury and the Bank of England, including the removal
> of most of their senior officials, and a total repudiation of
> the monetarist orthodoxy that government must never
> take risks with inflation sternly endorsed by Blair.

Now Kaletsky's scepticism is seen to be well-founded. The
stakeholder society has vanished into thin air while accommodation to the City and big business has proceeded and a
respectability has been gained in international financial circles;
and, with prudence and caution as the watchwords, Britain's
infrastructure and its health services have been left to
deteriorate further. The contrast between the aggressive Labour
government of 1945, ill-prepared though it may have been,
immediately on taking office, tackling head-on vested interests
and taking into public ownership so many industries and
services while simultaneously establishing the welfare state,
illuminates the essential pusillanimity which, despite its huge
majority in the Commons, has informed New Labour government; it is a timidity that fully reflects the temperament of
its leader.

Meanwhile, to accommodate pressures from employers,
every EU directive is watered down; now the government is
trying to wriggle out of the ending of Britain's shameful

exemption from the 48-hour Working Time Directive, which is due to expire towards the end of 2003. No wonder the trade unions are dismayed when Britain's long-hours culture, that of the hardest working yet least productive EU country, is described by Tony Blair, boasting instead of blushing, as the 'least regulated market in Europe'. The unions' dismay increases as Blair, in his second term, favours the CBI on every major issue. The TUC request in 2002 for European-style works councils was peremptorily refused. This is no marginal issue; the development of works councils and workers' involvement in managerial decision-making goes to the heart of contemporary trade-union thinking and European legislation provides a legal framework that entitles workers to such rights and limits the authoritative power of employers.

That, of course, is contrary to what members of the CBI desire; they strongly oppose any legislative measures at all on the matter and Blair, in thraldom to them, has instructed his acolyte, Alan Johnson, the employment affairs minister, to reject any such legislation. The government, Johnson has said, is prepared to acknowledge the need for 'better consultation' between employers and unions – but only on a voluntary basis. The TUC have ridiculed that argument but are aware that they have been sidelined and, smarting at this and similar rejections of their legitimate demands, are too often responding by electing jejune left-wing leaders whose clumsy clamour estranges the general public, thus leading Blair to believe that he has nothing to fear from any confrontation they may mount. That may prove to be a serious miscalculation. In May 2003 John Monks, the departing general secretary of the Trades Union Congress, so often a key ally of Blair, warned that even the diminishing number of left-wing union leaders still advocating keeping the historic links of unions with the Labour Party were insistent that this be dependent on Blair quitting the leadership. In June 2003 the rejection of Blair's favoured candidate and the election of Tony Woodley, a fierce opponent of Blair, as head of the TGW, a traditionally moderate union with 900,000 members, will ensure that attacks on government will come from the mainstream and not just militant elements in the union movement.

Before the summer of 2003 was over, Woodley hosted a 'summit' of union chiefs to review the level of union funding to New Labour and to co-ordinate a strategy to ensure Blair responded to their demands; the storm clouds are gathering. The forbearance and goodwill that Blair could count on in the nineties from so many, including trade unionists, are no longer in place. Blair's initial magic, which once persuaded so many that all could be achieved harmoniously and that a New Labour-One Nation party would see us through without strife, is now perceived as legerdemain.

Since June 2000 the spell has been broken; that was the time when, with molars flashing a boyish smile, and with a deeply sincere timbre to his voice, exuding charm, he so unsuccessfully wooed the gathering of 10,000 members of the Women's Institute. Encouraged by his coterie who concoct, and with whom he rehearses his speeches, and believing in the omnipotence of his own dream-thoughts, presiding over a paradisical society where warm consensus prevails, he had given a speech replete with all his usual pious platitudes. The prepared speech was being given to a predominantly rural audience and was utterly devoid of practical relevance to country folk; nothing about the paucity of rural transport, of sustainable land use, food production costs, petrol prices, rural post office closures. Only a prime minister and his advisers who are not just deeply urban but metropolitan to boot could have been so crass. Silver threads might have predominated among his listeners, but age does not increase credulity; Blair's soaring oratory left these down-to-earth women unimpressed and, refusing to stomach his condescending claptrap, they gave Blair the bird.

Only someone who, together with his early personal biography, was burying the political past could have been so entrapped. The bruising I received, when standing several times as a candidate in local elections during the early 1950s, was inflicted by the British Housewives' League; it was the women of the League who enabled the Tories to recover their popular support, especially among women voters, by exploiting resentment over food and controls on consumption generally. Food rationing, necessary to ensure fair shares for all, was derided; its continued existence was used by the Conservatives, with the powerful support of the League, as a means of demonstrating the distinction between socialist bureaucracy on the one hand and individualism and enterprise on the other. No one who lived in that period, or who was genuinely aware of the political history of post-war Britain, could doubt that the Housewives' League enabled the Conservatives to create a distinctive image for themselves as the champions of the hard-pressed housewife; with women as the more volatile part of the electorate, the Tories thus forged a key weapon in their electoral recovery; and, thanks to the League, the gender gap kept them faithfully in power throughout the 1950s.

The lessons that 'Old' Labour learned from that searing experience were unknown to Blair; for him, the history of the Labour Party began with his entry into Parliament. He was, consequently, taken by surprise at the Wembley Arena. What occurred inside was the echo of the tumult in the outside world, a restlessness that spread throughout Britain in 2000. By many the years of New Labour's government were seen to have been squandered. Blair's folly, the Dome which he had insisted upon, stood as a symbol of his vacuousness. His fear of attacking, his insistence on avoiding confrontation even when essential, left the agro-chemical industry and greedy farming interests free to spread BSE, the privatised railways to look after their shareholders and kill their passengers, the petrol companies to collude with hauliers to wrest undeserved tax reductions, the biotechnology companies to sow their threatening genetically modified products; government decision-making has lacked bite for the master does not wish to offend the strong – whether they be press lords or tycoons.

When action becomes unavoidable, Blair behaves like a child with a kaleidoscope, shaking focus group reports and opinion polls, and rearranging his mental furniture in a bid to create the impossible matching response of pleasing everybody. Offending may lead to retaliation, his ever-present fear. And so his major speeches have continued invariably to include lists but lack verbs – for verbs are the 'doing' parts of speech, and action, with its concomitant risks, must be postponed or avoided; and none can help him more to procrastinate than the 318 advisory bodies, involving some 2,500 people, funded by millions of taxpayers' money which, within three years, he has caused to be created. In the past, during my lifetime, I suffered too often as a member of government advisory committees not to be aware of their negative aspects; prolonged study of the condition addressed can result in a proliferation of diagnoses – and, meantime, the patient dies.

Before 2000 ended, faced with the reality of the resistances and protests that had come into existence, so removed from his fantasised conflict-free society, Blair did what cowards fearing punishment for their acts always do – proffer apologies as profuse as they are insincere. In September Blair sang a plaintive *mea culpa* air admitting 'mistakes'; too late, Mandelson, in November 2000, added to the mournful threnody by expressing the government's collective contrition and asking for pardon for its over-enthusiasm which, by over-selling the enhancements to ordinary life which its policies could bring, had led to disappointment. That disappointment was to be shown in the June 2001 General Election when just over 40 per cent of the voters refused to go to the polls. This was by far the worst turnout since the advent of universal adult suffrage in 1928, and 12 per cent lower than in 1997. Blair was back in government with the wholehearted consent of only 21.4

per cent of the British voting public. It was not over-enthusiasm that led to this shattering result; it was lack of conviction in government; too little conviction can cause no less havoc than excess.

Lacking the courage of the conviction that drove Attlee's Cabinet to mock consensus and release its aggression against vested interest abusing power, Blair has few resources to overcome the inhibition that pulls him back from any assault on the undeserving privileged. There is consequently no sobriety in Blair's promises; he cannot handle his own aggression; he gains release, in excess, of his aggression only against distant enemies where there is no serious danger of retaliation – as in Kosovo, Sierra Leone or Iraq – but on the domestic scene, he cowers. He, as an adult, is the selfsame boy who suppressed in his home his rage against the accusing eye of the authoritarian, speechless, stricken father, lest release bring about his own destruction. The roots of the immunity that the vested interests of Britain have gained under consensus New Labour are to be found many years ago amidst the tragic circumstance at the home of Leo Blair Senior.

Traumatic Families

Sociologists have paid much attention to what they describe as 'homogamy'. In this context, homogamy means that people are attracted to one another because they are similar in character, family and social background, and experiences. This unexceptional and prosaic observation has, however, been considerably sophisticated as the sociologists, confirmed by the clinical findings of psychotherapists and reinforced by the clinical findings of the paediatrician John Bowlby and his followers, have directed greater attention to the phenomenon. Now they stress that the catalyst precipitating attractions may often be hidden, that the less obvious similarities may be more determined and decisive, and that, in particular, those who have undergone separate but similar early traumatic family experiences, resulting in parallel later emotional problems, can be compellingly attracted to one another. The sociologists illuminating the condition claim their research reveals that bonding between those who have endured traumatic childhoods can be so intense that it can come into existence without the protagonists being in any way consciously aware of the dynamic behind their motivation, and indeed sometimes even in the absence of any verbal communication.

The bold sociologist David Aberbach has insightfully put forward the hypothesis that this silent bonding operates beyond the area of personal relations; that there are circumstances when it comes into play between a political leader and the society in which he dwells:

> Much as individuals silently bond with each other on the basis of shared trauma, so also a society and leader may bond together when external crisis intersects with private trauma.

The lives of Tony and Cherie Blair, and the relationship between Tony Blair and the electorate, provide a surfeit of clinical material validating the sociologist's conclusion.

Blair hesitates to recall the full agonies that, during his childhood, enveloped his family. Justifiably he dismisses a suggestion of his critics that because he went through the private educational system, finishing at Oxford, 'it must have been a bed of roses'. 'Don't get me wrong. It was a happy childhood,' he protests and disavows, 'but it did seem as though I was spending every spare minute in Durham hospital visiting . . . and there was a lot of worry and uncertainty attached to that.' He concedes that the disabling stroke suffered by his father was 'one of the formative events' in his life. But he draws back from commenting on the anguish the 'event' brought him; rather, he emphasises the beneficial instruction it brought: 'My father's illness impressed on me from an early age that life was going to be a struggle, that there were a lot of losers.' That seems as far as he is able to acknowledge the effect on him of the family turmoil.

More usually he attempts to distance himself entirely from the pains he suffered as a child; he strives, as at the 1995 Labour conference, to displace them from the private to the public area, eloquently but over-determinedly emphasising the overriding importance of the stable family, and denouncing the iniquities that result from its instability:

> Look at the wreckage of our broken society. See Britain through the eyes of our children. Are we really proud of

it? Drugs, violence, youngsters hanging round street
corners with nothing to do.

Families can be destabilised not only by separation; other early
traumas endured by children and adolescents also result in the
catalogue of vices enumerated by Blair. His catalogue is,
however, not exhaustive and if it were more comprehensive, it
would also note that whatever the lifelong burden personally
carried by the traumatised children and adolescents, society
very occasionally can be the beneficiary as well as the victim;
and, indeed, sometimes in the person of a political leader with
a history of traumatised childhood or adolescence, society can
be both beneficiary and victim.

My generation has felt the full force of political leaders who,
after being traumatised by severe loss, neglect or upheaval in
their early years, established for a while an astonishing rapport
with their nation; a homogamous relationship bound them
together, a relationship founded on the affection one had for the
other because of common strength but, more usually, common
frailties. Such leadership is hazardous, sometimes bringing
benefits but too often bringing disasters. Hitler's brutalised
childhood was within a family that suffered early multiple
losses culminating, when he was fourteen, in the deaths of his
father and, a short time later, of his mother. Stalin lost three
siblings in early childhood and his father at eleven. And
Churchill had an appalling childhood; his son, Randolph,
conceded: 'The neglect and lack of interest in him shown by his
parents were remarkable even by the standards of late-
Victorian and Edwardian days.' Leaders emerging traumatised
from the epicentre of domestic upheaval and loss need to be
especially scrutinised; and Blair is such a leader.

For the doleful consequences of the blows that concussed the
Blair family in Tony's childhood are far-reaching; they are not
limited to his attempt within a public life to overcome the
personal feelings of estrangement that acutely dog him. His was

not, as he claims, 'a happy childhood'; it was a terrorised childhood, and the mésalliance, substantially involuntary and irrational, between Blair and large sections of the electorate is a bonding between an alienated man and an alienated society, each attempting within a homogamous relationship to find a magic analgesic to relieve them of their pains, to heal their wounds and erase their scars.

It is true that there can emerge leadership of inspirational character when, at a particular time, a member's agonising private experiences correspond with, and become virtually symbolic of, the group. Weber long ago illustrated unforgettable correspondences of this type. Hosea's marriage to a prostitute symbolises the 'prostitution' of ancient Israel; Jeremiah's childlessness represents national loss and barrenness and brings home the fact that procreation on the eve of mass slaughter and exile by the Babylonians is futile; the death of Ezekiel's wife is a symbol of the destruction of the Temple in Jerusalem, to which the Judaeans were 'wedded' in faith.

These ancient Jewish prophets did not speak in mellifluous tones to their people; they did not collude with them, gloss over their frailties. They identified the evils in their society and raged in memorable language against those who perpetrated them. There was no compromise with iniquities. The New Jerusalem was not to be reached by temporising; they certainly did not believe the route was via the middle ground. Such men, however, are not the exemplars chosen by our contemporary puny politicians. The prophets suffered grievous losses, infertility, infidelity, death of near ones, but they were the exceptional men whose traumas were transmuted into creative leadership; they mastered grief by transforming it into a creative motivation.

For most ordinary mortals, being traumatised by loss or upheaval in their early days results in inescapable chronic handicap. For a few individuals, however, the grief, the residual anger and depression that can spring from their earlier setbacks, the idealisation and alienation that have resulted, contribute to their becoming political leaders. Unfortunately, whatever leadership early trauma yielded in biblical times, the experience of the Western world in the twentieth century tells us that our prophets have all been false prophets. In certain limited circumstances they can be of considerable social and political use, as is witnessed by Churchill in the war years. But the general rule is that when a traumatised leader suddenly emerges as a microcosmic correlative and symbol of a specific and usually transient societal condition, then trouble lies ahead.

In Blair's case, all his dissimulations cannot mask the severity of his early trauma. In an instant all the hapless boy's security was shattered as a massive stroke reduced his towering father to a speechless babe. Financial constraints immediately imposed themselves upon the patriarchal family. Like many men of Leo Blair's background and generation, a working wife would have been regarded as subversive of the husband's authority. This was a widespread view, one I found deeply embedded in the culture of the mining villages of my constituency, where, up to the late 1960s, a miner who let or encouraged his wife to work was despised. So Hazel could not seek outside employment to supplement the now diminished family income. New school uniforms became hand-me-downs, treats became rare, planned foreign holidays abandoned.

There had already been little anchorage in the family as Leo climbed out of his class, living in rented, sometimes austere, accommodation, moving from one town to another, from Edinburgh to Glasgow, even as far as Adelaide in Australia, and then on to Durham, forever seeking to improve on his lowly positions. Geography and the desperate uncertainties of upward mobility had continuously destabilised the family during Tony's short life. A family so utterly dependent upon the father as it moved peripatetically between different environments could, with such a history, have been ill-prepared to receive the shock when the pilot who had literally steered them round the world utterly lost his direction.

In a curious attempt to deny his essential rootlessness Blair, in 1994, was claiming that in Durham he had been influenced as a child by the traditional socialism of the Durham miners, 'a feeling which has stayed with me ever since'. By what process of osmosis this took place is not explained; his childhood was in the shadow of the cathedral at Durham, a city which has a very different feel from the surrounding area, and in any event, by the time Blair came to live in Durham most of the pits in the county had been closed. Blair's romantic recall has little credibility; his creation of an imaginary evocation does tell us of his sense of loss of lineage.

His wandering father had bequeathed him only a Romany inheritance and had deprived him of any tradition of strong religious conviction, of commitment to socialism or firm attachment to class or locality. A few months after his fanciful nostalgic excursion to his Durham childhood, in another interview he truthfully acknowledged: 'We moved around a lot when we were young . . . I never felt myself very anchored in a particular setting or class.' And thus, inadequately anchored, young Blair was, by a cruel fateful wind, blown from his frail moorings.

In later life this nomadic childhood has contributed to his facility to move with ease from one piece of political territory to another; not all of us have a taste for the gypsy political life, but he is a man untutored in reverence for the fixed place of abode, the new holds promise, the old is discarded. Converting his original handicap into personal political advantage and persuasively claiming it was to national advantage, he has on the political plain succeeded in making lability a virtue and fealty a sclerotic disease.

But the trauma inflicted on the singularly vulnerable ten-year-old, unlike his family vagabondage, does not lend itself to being so artfully used in the public arena. However cunning the handler, it remains too explosive to be displaced from private psyche to public argument, for it is charged with the retaliatory threat of what Ernest Jones, one of the greatest Welshmen of the twentieth century, the carrier of psychoanalysis from Vienna to the Anglo-Saxon world, described as 'aphanisis' – the terrible condition of a living death where all sexual desire in any form, however attenuated, is utterly and irrevocably extinguished. It brings a fear even more profound than the fear of castration, and Jones, following Freud, asserts it can arise from the death wish which, in our ambivalences, we unconsciously direct against our loved ones – as Wilde put it: 'each man kills the thing he loves, By each let this be heard . . .'

And when the death actually occurs, when our buried death wishes are seemingly fulfilled, attributing omnipotence to our evil thoughts, burdened with guilt, irrationally taking responsibility for the death, we fear awesome retaliation will result, that we will, as murderers, suffer the deserved punishment. Freud tells us:

> A hostile current of feeling . . . against a person's nearest and dearest relatives may remain latent during their lifetime, that is, its existence may not be betrayed to consciousness either directly or through some substitute. But when they die this is no longer possible and the conflict becomes acute.

And then, comfortingly, Freud adds that the taboo against acknowledging the retaliatory fears can, through a mourning process, fade away: 'When in the course of time the mourning runs its course, the conflict grows less acute, so that the taboo upon the dead is able to diminish in severity or sink into oblivion.'

But what if, as occurred to Blair's father, death strikes but does not slay, leaving the victim dumb but with accusatory eyes staring for years, day in and day out, at his wretched little son, denied the relief of mourning, denied 'the course of time' when 'the mourning runs its course' and 'the conflict grows less acute . . . is able to diminish in severity or sink into oblivion'.

With the stricken father lying in the house, young Blair was compelled to live for years with the threatening consequences of his unconscious ambivalences to his father; and the usual Oedipal rivalries that are part of all our growing up would inevitably have been continuously stoked up as his mother was compelled to give her whole attention to her helpless husband. When one remarks upon Blair's constant and repeated retreat from acknowledgement of ambivalence in his public discourse, a mode of thought which frequently invalidates his political judgement, here is one of the sources: each resentment felt against the appurtenances of the illness enveloping the household would have brought new guilts, renewed fears of retaliatory action. No wonder that, like his mentor Macmurray, any sign of ambivalence is interpreted by him as a red light warning him of dangers ahead.

Young Blair's burdens could not be shared with his siblings. His older brother was away at public school and, to add to his woes, even as his mother's attention was still directed to the slowly recovering father, yet another catastrophe suddenly engulfed the family. Still's disease, a form of infantile rheumatoid arthritis that erodes the cartilage and eventually burns out the joints, hit his youngest sister, who was to spend two years in hospital as doctors battled to save her life using toxic immuno-suppressant drugs which had distressing side effects.

The boy therefore entered his teens fearful that he was being pursued, frightened that he would be the next victim of a hostile invisible disabler intent on mowing down his family; for Blair lived in a house of secrets, in a haunted household where ghosts stalked – the ghosts of the wild promiscuous mother of Leo, the mother of whom no one dared speak or enquire, and the spectre of Leo's irresponsible musical father whose names, genuine and assumed, can never be erased from Anthony Charles Lynton Blair's birth certificate.

Adolescence was to bring no respite to the teenager; his boyhood fears of a ruthless stalker were soon to be inflamed, not stilled. The Terminator struck yet again. Cancer attacked the thyroid of his mother; for five years she bravely struggled, in and out of hospital, before dying when Tony was 22 years old. 'It was,' his elder brother recalls, 'traumatic for all of us.' Tony crumpled completely. His friend Peter Thomson heard that it had 'knocked the socks off him.' Clearly he was on the edge of a nervous breakdown; he withdrew into himself and, as is his wont, for solace took to intensive Bible-reading.

How inadequately Blair has come to terms with the anguish of the traumas of these early years, and how he has sought to bury rather than confront them, is well illustrated by his incredible claim that until 1994 he had no idea of the origins of his Christian names. He told his biographer, Jon Sopel, that it came as a bombshell when, midway through his leadership campaign, the *Daily Mail*, in revealing the truth about his grandparents, pointed out that Blair's middle names, Charles Lynton, came from the music-hall grandfather, Charles Parsons, whose stage name was Jimmy Lynton. Blair said he had never questioned why he was given these names; he simply assumed it was a family tradition. And when his older brother was contacted by the prurient press, he corroborated Tony's response. He was nonplussed: 'The names Charles Parsons and Jimmy Lynton don't mean a thing to me.'

That Tony Blair should have raised no questions about having three Christian names is just possible; that he should have not queried his conventional second name is credible; but that he and his brother never queried why he had the curious third Christian name, is surely because they knew that was a question they must never ask. Tony Blair has told his biographer that he 'had known his father had been adopted but it was something Leo did not speak about and equally something the children didn't ask about'. That was secret, forbidden territory.

Even although we may wish to conceal it from ourselves, those of us who are parents know how within a household children will divine the existence of our secrets; and when they know a secret exists, but one to which they have no access, then left in ignorance of its details the secret can become more not less menacing and the emotional content of the parents' secret, one they feel is too agonising to expose, is passed on. There is, unhappily, these days a grim plenitude of clinical material illustrating how far-reaching the deleterious effects can be of the unarticulated traumas of parents upon their children; the children of the silent scarred survivors of the Holocaust, like the children of the guilty murderous Nazis, can both become victims of the parents who cannot bring themselves to talk of the horrors of their past.

Freud, in his *Totem and Taboo*, long ago spelled out how vain was the attempt by one generation to conceal their traumas from their successors:

> We may safely assume that no generation is able to conceal any of its more important mental processes from its successor. For psychoanalysis has shown that everyone possesses in his unconscious mental activity an apparatus which enables him to interpret other people's reactions, that is, to undo the distortions which other people have imposed on the expression of their feelings. An unconscious understanding such as this of all the . . . dogmas left behind by the original relation to the father . . . make it possible for later generations to take over their heritage of emotion.

It is such a 'heritage of emotion', a trans-generational pathology, with which Tony Blair wrestles. At a time when the shame, and the legal disabilities, of illegitimacy were real, his father, after initially as a baby being dragged from lodging-house to lodging-house while his parents were on tour, was soon to be treated as an encumbrance, and was dumped as a little boy on the family of the Glasgow ship-rigger James Blair. Neither of the two biographers of Blair tells us at what age his father was wrenched away from his natural parents, or whether he entered a house where there were other children. Indeed, both biographers display surprisingly little curiosity about Tony Blair's grandparents. Even in John Rentoul's more detached biography, the biographer naively and dogmatically asserts 'the story of Tony Blair's real grandparents is a colourful one, although perhaps of limited relevance to all but genetic determinists'. But I believe that traumas endured by Tony Blair's father continue to reverberate.

The actor-politician able to play, in politics as he did on stage, many parts, possessing a political agility which enables him with excessive fluidity to discard the old for the new, reflects the identity confusions that can so often afflict the adopted child unable to model himself upon a certain fixed father figure, ever asking himself what was his sin that caused him to be rejected, uncertain as to who he is, and from whence he came. The essential political rootlessness of Tony Blair, the man who came from nowhere, tells us of the 'heritage of emotion' bequeathed to him by his father.

The burden of such a heritage is not to be minimised. Leo Blair was one of the thousands of children who, at the time he was placed into what was to be long-term fostering, were treated as the property of parents with children lacking any individual rights and who were able to be disposed of at the caprice of the natural parents. It was the battle that I commenced shortly after I came into the House to erode the discriminatory laws against the illegitimate that brought me to a fuller understanding of the malignant consequences that came from Britain's lack of a comprehensive adoption service giving support and guidance to the unmarried mother as well as to would-be adopters. The unavailability of such a service to all those needing it throughout the country meant that the choosing of new parents by natural parents or by society was little more than a sinister game of roulette with thousands of children often being the losers.

Adoption is an ambitious technical method of resolving sterility, illegitimacy and the nature of the rejected or unattached child; it is also an imaginative and sensitive human enterprise where biology jostles passion, and where irresponsibility, inadequacy or wickedness is met by pity, concern and love. To presume to intervene by laws in this subtle and complex process is to invite condemnation as an intruder; reason and insight embedded within such laws, however mildly corrective, can be speedily resented. Perhaps, in retrospect, it is not surprising that, given the delicacy of the issues, it took me more than a decade to bring about by legislation the needed sweeping changes.

As a solicitor dealing with adoption applications, I had already found, before becoming an MP, that the scores of voluntary adoption societies then in existence were of a strikingly uneven quality. They were unevenly distributed throughout the country, some purportedly serving a locality and others claiming to operate nationally. Many of them had standards of service that were abysmal, lacking professional skills, and dealt only on the basis of bizarre criteria with a selection of adoptive homes and the placement of children with parents who were often considered primarily simply on the basis of their declared religious belief. This dilettante characteristic of so many of the adoption societies was encouraged by the perfunctory surveillance to which, by law, their standards were subject. Indeed, approval of their registration had been reduced to little more than a formality so far as the local authorities were concerned, as they far too often feared to exercise their powers to make their own social work departments act as adoption agencies. Outside the purview of the adoption societies of such varying quality came those adoptions arranged privately by matrons, gynaecologists, solicitors, busybodies or someone a hard-pressed unmarried mother met in the local launderette or fish and chip shop. Choosing parents for someone else's child was in my view certainly too awesome a responsibility to be left to any one person, but the muddlers and the meddlers, who for morbid or mercenary motives were able to intervene to play God, under the laws then in existence were being given a dangerously free hand.

After I had formed an all-party group of MPs committed to pressurising the Home Office to review those adoption and fostering laws, the wind which, following devaluation, blew Jim Callaghan in 1967 out of the Treasury into the Home Office, brought me good fortune in my quest; for both my personal relationship with Callaghan and his own personal biography, which left him with good reason to be concerned with the fate of children unendowed with two ever-present and certain parents, acted in my favour and, despite the department's resistance, he set up, at my request, an advisory committee on which I was to sit. Apart from, for politically correct reasons, one Tory MP being appointed, the other members all already had, as directors of social service departments or adoption societies, as paediatricians, child psychiatrists or jurists, considerable fieldwork experience in adoption. For almost three years we sat taking evidence from all the regions in Britain in our wide-ranging enquiries, and finally produced a unanimous report.

Not waiting for the dust to gather on our recommendations, I persuaded David Owen, then a back-bencher who had drawn in the Private Members' ballot the right to have time to introduce a bill, to sponsor an Adoption bill. Together we were well advanced in putting through the legislation, when the government, and thus our bill, fell; the incoming Labour government took over the bill, which reached the statute book as the Children Act of 1975. Of all the acts with which I have been associated, it is the one with which I continue to enjoy an unalloyed satisfaction, for if political life is ever worth the candle, it is when you have persuaded society that it is to be judged by the concern of one generation for the next.

But during the long trawl of evidence-seeking which preceded the Children Act I learned many lessons – not least among them the imperative need to avoid the maladroit placements and concealments of the type that seem to be illustrated by the experience of Leo Blair. He apparently was never formally adopted and his status was left in limbo, enabling his feckless parents, when he was twelve, to try to reclaim him. His foster-mother evidently attempted to conceal his origins, blotting out his real birthplace in Filey, Yorkshire, and affirming he was born in Glasgow. He was old enough, when his natural parents finally decided to formalise their relationship and his mother married for the third time, to have been likely to have received bewildering intimations that something was afoot; it is clearly possible that at a young age he was aware that he was the child of an adulterous mother, an illegitimacy that would have brought him, in those unenlightened days, a particular shame. That the tensions and ambivalences of his early upbringing pursued him into adulthood is poignantly displayed in his later juggling of his own names and those of his children. When he married, Leo gave his name as 'Blair, formerly Parsons', and took Charles and Lynton, a combination of his natural father's original and stage names, as his middle names. To his first son, William, he gave his foster father's name, James, and Lynton as middle names, and his own middle names, of course, he gave to his second son, although it is evident that he never told them where they came from. The sinister silences that Leo Blair, as a consequence of his early casual and unfeeling placement, imposed upon himself and his family left Tony without the endowment of an authentic father possessing a certain and confident identity. Despite the anchorage provided by the dutiful and stoical mother, the family unit would inevitably have had a fragility ill-equipped to withstand the traumas that fell upon it. The severity of the emotional disturbances resulting from the ambience within which Tony was matured in my view invades both his political and his personal choices; and those who would scoff at such a belief should note the corroboration provided by his significant personal choice.

Wives of politicians, detached from the politics of their husbands, most certainly have as unequivocal a right to privacy as any private citizen. It would indeed be presumptuous to delve into the private life of the diffident Mary Wilson or the politically non-intrusive, kind and eminently sensible Audrey Callaghan, whose warm realism and lack of pretension always left me gratified when I dined with her family at No. 10, as insulated from politics as from the flunkeys and officials below. But that right to privacy can legitimately be denied to wives who actively and enthusiastically join in the political fray. Such a wife is Cherie Blair, who not only shares her husband's abilities but, more relevantly in our quest to uncover the singular relationship between Blair and the electorate, like him emerges deeply scarred from a traumatised family, one from which tawdry stagecraft and narcissism continue to wreak havoc. Once a woman ready to use legal injunctions and press complaints procedures to protect her family privacy, by contrast in a limitless and compulsive display of exhibitionism, in 2003, she invited journalists and photographers to witness a soft-porn scene with sapphic overtones. She was viewed with her body adviser on the king-sized marital bed, being taught how to apply phallic lipstick; as part of the sick *mise-en-scène*, she allowed the press to gaze upon her kinky ankle boots and a dressing table overflowing with knickers, tights and cosmetics.

Much of the responsibility for such weird behaviour must fall upon her actor father, the notorious Tony Booth, the 'Scouse git' of the television series *Till Death Us Do Part*. When Cherie was young he abandoned her, her sister, Lyndsey, and her small-time actress mother, Gale. His autobiography, *Stroll On*, makes no reference to his children by Gale except to ask for their forgiveness in the dedication; that request is presumably also directed to the four or five other children he had by other women. He does not even specifically mention Gale in his book. At the time he was supposed to be married to her he presents us with a lewd account of his boisterous 'crumpeteering'. Gale, a tough and brave cookie, meantime gave up the stage and, fortified by a no-nonsense Roman Catholic Labour working-class family background, was prepared for the sake of the children to take on any job including one in a fish and chip shop. It says much for that woman, as it does for the resource of her daughter, that Cherie is now a highly competent QC.

Given the early adversities endured by Cherie Booth, and the political commitment of her mother's family, it is unsurprising that, unlike her husband, she was already a member of the Labour Party by the time she was sixteen. She took too from her actress mother an obvious desire to be on stage, and soon put herself forward as the potential Labour candidate to fight Shirley Williams in the Crosby by-election in 1981, the high point of the SDP's march out of the Labour Party; the eyes of the nation were on that by-election and Cherie clearly had an appetite for the publicity such a candidature would attract. Two years later, identifying with the left-wing pressure group the Labour Co-ordinating Committee, she was, as candidate for Thanet, speaking on the same platform as Tony Benn, declaring that he had 'inspired' her in her 'quest for socialism' – hardly a claim she would presently make. Opportunism and narcissism would be charges she would require all her considerable forensic skills to ward off today. Indeed some may conclude that, provided she has the opportunity to display those skills publicly, she shows an unseemly readiness to take up causes unbecoming to the wife of a Labour leader; although she may have acted in accordance with the best traditions of the Bar, her championship before an industrial tribunal in October 1995 of a Conservative council against allegations made by some fifty dismissed black and Asian employees alleging racial and sexual discrimination was received with distaste by many in the Labour Party.

But it is in other respects that the corroboration which she provides in her partnership with Tony Blair should cause greater public unease. More intelligent than her husband – she gained a top first in law at the London School of Economics and came top in the Bar exams, while her husband obtained a second-class degree at Oxford and an undistinguished third-class at the Bar – she nevertheless displays disconcerting negative traits, giving every indication that they flow from her early abandonment and traumas. Her tenseness and humourlessness, her curious atactic mien, her much remarked upon public holding of hands with Blair, her rapturous gazing at, and kissing of, her husband at conferences, are outward symptoms of much painful insecurity. At best her early bruising can lead her to champion causes like Refuge, the charity that provides accommodation for battered women; and she speaks out in favour of the Labour document 'Peace at Home', advocating a national helpline for women victims of irresponsible violent partners. But less benign public consequences can stem from her early bitter experiences.

Little girls require the admiration of reassuring fathers if they are to grow up confident in their own bodies. A daughter's relationship with her father is critical to the opening up of wider horizons of difference in order that she, later, at ease with her own body, can manage her intimate relationships with men. As family therapists Pincus and Dare have written:

> The little girl needs to know that her father is a bit in love with her (just as the adolescent girl whose father feels absolutely no erotic interest in her cannot believe that anyone else could love her); a little girl needs also to

believe that her mother takes her seriously, as a rival to her father's affections . . .

Bereft of a father's presence in her earliest days, Cherie Blair shows her deprivation in her body language, which is asyntactical, ungrammatical. Her desperate endeavours to correct the faulty grammar led, in 2002, to her undoing when Carole Caplin, the body grammarian she employed (who was a former topless model turned lifestyle guru whose mother claims to be a psychic), involved her in the imbroglio that has permanently damaged her reputation. The stress management techniques that Caplin used to give Cherie Blair's body the repose and poise she lacked enabled the tabloids to present the toxin-scrubbing routines followed by the trainer as the most gruesome shower scene since *Psycho*. Certainly the relationship that appears to have been established between the two women has had dire consequences. The whole miserable story of Cherie Blair in 2002 using Caplin's criminal lover as an intermediary and to engage on her behalf in property speculation has been unsparingly spelled out in the media; her first failed attempt to cover up the squalid tale by evasions forced her on to the television screens to apologise, unconvincingly, and to acknowledge her 'mistakes'.

And the same concatenation that links her early deprivations with that mêlée was in place when, in Australia in 2003, Cherie Blair found irresistible the temptation offered in a freebie of wildly enhancing the body which, if she does not despise, she finds so uncomfortable. She interpreted a suggestion by a Melbourne fashion store that she choose a few pieces for her family as an open invitation to help herself and her children, and cleared the shelves of 68 items of designer clothes. She was then to compound her silliness by attending the solemn Anzac Day ceremony in provincial Perth, where staidness rules, dressed in a jacket with a disrespectfully plunging neckline, drop pearl earrings and hatless. The poor woman's ambivalence towards her own body leaves her never knowing when to dress down and when to dress up, when to cover and when to reveal. The little girl who never received the corroboration of a father's admiring gaze has been left with no certainty or confidence in her own bodily existence. The detrimental effects of her sad childhood are deeply embedded; no masseuse can scrub them away; and still the scars of those detriments will show, despite all the camouflage of all the PRs she has now hired.

For these detriments lie in the symmetry that exists in the family backgrounds of Tony and Cherie Blair, a symmetry that is a paradigm of the sociologist's developed theory of homogamy. Both were abandoned by their fathers, the one literally, the other's powerful father dissolved into dependency; both act out their lives against theatrical backdrops, the one bearing the names of the errant actor grandparent illustrating the Roman adage *nomen omen* – destiny can lie in one's name – the other burdened by the irresponsible actor father giving her nothing but a surname; both have responded to dutiful but insufficiently tender mothering with an obtrusive narcissistic assertion in their careers; both have used politics and the law to triumph over a parent by fulfilling the parents' thwarted ambitions: Tony went to his father's desired destination, to Westminster; and Cherie, as a successful barrister, has made the High Court her stage.

The danger of a binding between those who have similarly disturbed family backgrounds, and undergone similar early traumas, resulting in comparable emotional problems, is that the handicaps each partner possesses are compounded, rather than contained or cancelled out; a *folie à deux* can result. It is true that there may be many differences between such partners and the attraction may involve a complex matrix of aims and motives; but the homogamic principle is, in the case of the Blairs, too insistently illustrated to permit the symmetry in their personal biographies to be dismissed as coincidence. We were treated to one such illustration of the Blairs' narcissistic bonding, in this case one more bizarre than inimical, in the spring of 2003. Blair, wishing to totally merge with his Catholic wife, and putting aside the sternly Protestant teachings of Macmurray, the mentor of his youth, had illicitly taken to joining her as one in communion. Given his ambivalence about his father, the Eucharist has singular attractions for him; Freud has claimed its origins lie in the totem meal of the tribal primitives who had murdered their father and believed that by incorporating parts of his body into the act of eating, they acquired the qualities he had possessed:

> One day the brothers . . . came together, killed and devoured their father and so made an end of the patriarchial horde . . . In the act of devouring him they accomplished their identification with him, and each one of them acquired a portion of his strength.

The Pope invests the Eucharist with no less importance than Freud gave to the totem meal; taking communion is no act of symbolism, the worshipper literally eats the flesh of Christ and drinks his blood. The sanctity of the occasion is in no way to be treated as a shibboleth, to be belittled by an interloper lacking the faith of the true Catholic. Following the Pope's directive, which was to be reaffirmed in 2003, Britain's Cardinal wrote to Blair telling him to desist. In bad temper Blair, denied the narcissistic wish of fusion in prayer with Cherie, reluctantly submitted. In a characteristic show of egocentricity, making the assumption that the Lord would be personally interested in his disqualification, Blair ended his reply to the Cardinal: 'I wonder what Jesus would have made of it?'

Blair's petulance over this affair is not to be treated as an understandable response to a minor personal frustration; such is the interdependence between him and his wife that he clearly finds it intolerable that she can soar to the heavens and partake of the divine, while he is left standing alone in the church aisle. The pair appear to have little capacity to disengage from each other and have a real separate existence.

At a time when increasingly we have an executive-driven democracy, it is disturbing that we have in control in Downing Street a pair who are unlikely, as between themselves, to contain the fall-out from their severe early traumas; on the contrary, with Blair as Prime Minister and she playing the 'first lady', the excitations have continued, and indeed increased, as, to mutual satisfaction, each acts as a mirror to the other. It is a private affair if individuals silently bond with each other on the basis of shared trauma; but a bonding between markedly intelligent and histrionic partners can find a pathological expression in the public domain if their leadership is proffered to a bewildered, insecure society shocked by unmetabolised technological change and frightened by the collapse of traditional and conventional religious values.

An affiliation can arise between such leadership and the estranged afflicted with the fears abounding within a society ridden with anomie. A prosthetic relationship can be established, leader and a fractured electorate each yearning to find in the other a wholeness they lack; but only rarely can such a resolution be accomplished, for this is a bonding infected by pathogenic elements.

Exceptionally, a traumatised leader may for a short period effectively and realistically meet the societal needs. Winston Churchill, forever suffering severe depressions as a result of his traumatised childhood, was such a leader and the historian A J P Taylor emphasised:

In 1940, any political leader might have tried to rally Britain with brave words, although his heart was full of despair. But only a man who had known and faced despair within himself could carry conviction at such a moment.

But far more usually, as the impossible yearnings of the leader and his followers are increasingly felt to be unfulfilled, disenchantment, often accompanied by disaster, follows. Leaders like Robespierre, who lost his mother at six and then, together with his siblings, was shortly afterwards totally abandoned by his father; or Ayatollah Khomeini, whose father, when Khomeini was an infant, was murdered by bandits, are far more typical, if somewhat dramatic, examples of traumatised leaders, and tell us of the dire consequences such leadership can bring to a nation.

Within the milder political climate of Britain, with its unwritten constitution of checks and balances, even traumatised dyadic political leadership has not had the capacity to inflict such catastrophic damage, but the difficulties it has brought should not be underestimated. It is clear that the Blairs, unlike Churchill, have most certainly not been able to transform their handicap to public advantage, to confront crises and overcome them; for their bonding is hermetically sealed with narcissism.

To bask in widespread public approbation needs an avoidance of expounding discomforting but necessary solutions to public dilemmas. In theory the pain of their traumas could have been used to understand, empathise with, confront and resolve the pain within our society, but such a salutary transmutation is not to be achieved by the Blairs. The armour-plating of their narcissism acts as a shield against insight. Only if they had thrown away this defence and had been prepared to endure the stress of uncovering the sources of their traumatically conditioned public stances would the electorate have been likely to gain advantage from the early sad personal experiences of the Blairs.

The quality of the Blairs' bonding leads one to a pessimistic prognostication, to scepticism that they have the capacity to master the grief of their early years and transform it for the public good into a creative motivation. If one departs from the sociologist's homogamous theory and turns to the schematic distinctions made by classical psychoanalysis when reviewing the motivations operating in one's choice of partners, our pessimism unhappily finds increased justification.

Freud, anticipating in 1914 in so many respects the current sociological view, put forward his belief that there are two basic types of choice of a love-object, the anaclitic and the narcissistic. One choice, the anaclitic or attachment option, is governed to a greater or lesser degree by a dependence on images of parental figures. The love-object is selected on the model of parent figures who had guaranteed them, as children, nourishment, care and protection. But the narcissistic choice of partner operates on the model of his relationship to his own self, with the love-object representing some aspect of himself. Freud makes clear that the two types of object choice are to be looked upon as purely an ideal or image, and as liable to alternate or to be combined in any particular case. His exploratory elaborations, however, of the notion of narcissistic choice indicate, in some circumstances, how dominant an element narcissism can become.

Freud set forward a schema for such narcissistic expressions under four headings: a person may love what he himself is, what he himself was, what he himself would like to be and someone who was once part of himself. When Freud writes of the search for a partner who was once part of himself, he has in mind a mother's narcissistic love of her child who was 'once part of herself'. The yearning for someone who was once part of yourself is for someone not necessarily resembling yourself as a unified individual but rather someone in whom you can recover and restore your lost unity.

In many cases, of course, some or all of these fourfold elements play a part in our choice of partner that may cumulatively amount to little more than a sharing of a few common traits; but the relationship of the Blairs is not of that order. Their personal biographies, their early traumatic experiences and mothering, have conspired to create an intensely narcissistic bonding. When Cherie avidly publicly gazes at Blair, we recall Narcissus seated by the limpid spring, so fascinated by the sight of his own image that not for a second could he avert his eyes; and so he died of languor.

The myth contains warnings. When a dyadic narcissistic leadership emerges, there can arise a conjunction that is not limited to the immediate protagonists; the psychological traits of the leadership in some circumstances and at some particular times can mirror the general characteristics of society. The private correspondence of the pair extends wider. The 'Me' society, where individualism has been sanctified by Thatcher and her ilk, is singularly vulnerable to the fatal attraction of a leadership that reassuringly confirms, not seriously challenges, its own narcissism; and when, simultaneously, such a leadership proffers a vague communitarianism that, without pain, will relieve the man and woman living in our atomised society, deadened by all the insecurities of menacing and threatening technological changes, then the temptation for electorate and leader, each in a self-induced trance, to consummate the relationship becomes irresistible. And that was the nature of the consummation that took place between Blair and the electorate in the 1997 General Election.

Since, however, there are no never-never lands except in fairy stories, this is the romance that has not ended with all living happily ever after. With floods swamping homes that public investment could have warded off, with commuting on the privatised railways a daily exhausting misery, with the mounting anxiousness – particularly in mothers – over a tainted food supply brought about by government dalliance, greedy animal feed manufacturers and avaricious farmers, with government protection given to the biotechnological industries' feared GM food production, and with evaporating confidence that the National Health Service has the capacity to succour them in adversity, the electorate has entered a new millennium feeling unloved. Narcissus loves himself, not others; and Blair, wrapped up in himself, lacks the ability to extend love, to reach out beyond his dyadic relationship to empathise with an electorate wishing for comfort in their predicaments; and so the voters feel abandoned by Blair and, by extension, by all politicians. Thus politics has become a dirty word and all politicians are condemned as self-seeking.

We cannot contain the threat to the democratic process which such cynicism brings by affecting that the public face of politics is designed only for the pursuit and resolution of public issues; that since they cannot handle the intrusions of incendiary private matters, politicians must be accorded a right to present only a public face and to be so judged. The narcissistic politician in particular must not be given such exemption; for him the private is public, the one totally enmeshed in the other; for him no private matters, however intimate, are insulated from the policies he publicly invites us to pursue.

There were times when Blair publicly unloaded even his immediate family irresolutions; a public man cannot claim a right to privacy when, lacking insight and endeavouring to exorcise hurts felt within his private domain, he externalises and rages against them on the public stage. Speaking at the Global Ethics Foundation in June 2000 to an audience many of whom were soaked in the sickly religiosity that Blair finds so appealing, he suddenly vented his rage against the anti-social behaviour of the young and claimed that a suitable way to combat such conduct was to give the police permission to pick up drunks and disturbers of the peace, take them to a cash-point and levy on-the-spot fines of £100. The applause in the hall was loud and long. There were rather fewer panegyrics in Britain; police and penal reformers alike joined in mocking the extravagance and impracticability of such a policy. But there was one poignant resonance to Blair's call for punishment. A few days later his sixteen-year-old son was found by the police lying drunk and alone in the gutter.

Few parents escape the acted-out rebelliousness of their adolescent children; but, nevertheless, public sympathy for Blair in his embarrassment was certainly measured; and his sanctimonious religiosity, his cloying affirmations on family values, and the absurd repressive remedy he had just advocated to deal with ill-behaved youngsters, no doubt all played a part in an unpleasant gloating over Blair's discomfiture. Yet, at least subliminally, there were too other sensibilities operating that caused the sympathy of many to be engaged with the hapless lad, not with the parents; his behaviour was perceived as that of the victim not the perpetrator; the same sympathy arose for the youngster as had been extended in 1997 to William, Jack Straw's teenage son, who, when set up by a tabloid newspaper, was found to be dabbling in marijuana, a practice so denounced by his Home Secretary father who rages against those who advocate the end of the existing impracticable laws against its use.

Psychiatrists have pointed out that at the time when a man's children become adolescents, he can experience what is described as 'decompensation in retrospect'. The adolescent boy prompts the reactivation of the father's own adolescent struggles with auto-erotic, homosexual and Oedipal conflicts. Few fathers are likely, when faced with their adolescent young, to be unmoved by the reverberations which echo their own struggle to cope with the threat once felt to their own authority as a clamorous sexuality assailed them; that recall, in an empathic father, may move him to understanding and support of a turbulent son. Then the father can absorb and tolerate the deployment by his son as, using the classic defence of projection, the youngster works out and exteriorises the internal revolution his awakened sexuality has precipitated by rebelling against his father and the institutions of his father's generation. But, from a less understanding and more narcissistic father, there can be other responses to the provocations he is enduring. Adolescence is the period of rebellion and it befits the adolescent; but it is not fitting for influential middle-aged men, on becoming fathers of adolescents, to overreact against their own reawakened adolescent passions by imprisoning themselves, and by condemning adolescent rowdiness and permissiveness.

Blair's irrational outburst at Tübigen University in June 2000 was surely such an overreaction; the rowdy destructive youths he condemned were the excluded ones, cut off by our society's narcissism from any feeling of belonging; and that boy in the gutter, without any mates, tells too of exclusion. While affecting coyness and spurious pleading for privacy, the Blairs colluded in promoting the arrival of baby Blair as if it were the second coming. When, on the birth of the child, the tabloids asked me what were my thoughts at the boy bearing my name, they correctly recorded my reply, that having stolen my party, it was unsurprising that Blair should have stolen my name, but that I was relieved to learn that the baby had not been born in a manger. When the Blairs' 2000 card came along from Downing Street *The Times* tartly commented: 'The last time the babe appeared on a Downing Street Christmas card, it was Jesus. This year it is Leo Blair.' In other years Euan had been seen on the card; this year he was absent but Cherie, boasting of her product, was protectively shown with Tony and the baby. Mrs Blair may have considerable intelligence; but simpler mothers-to-be, not wrapped in themselves, not preening themselves on their own creativity, know how much attention during pregnancy and following the birth of the new baby must be focused on an existing child, lest he otherwise feel displaced and betrayed.

And that sense of betrayal would be felt even more keenly by an adolescent finding that, once again, he was to yield his priority as the eldest child. It is clinically well recorded that the Oedipal rivalry of the earliest few years of our lives, after a period of quiescence, are reawakened as puberty arrives and, unless sensitively handled by the parents, the arrival of a new babe totally takes away from an adolescent sibling the protection that an unconscious denial of his parents' continued sexuality may hitherto have afforded him; and, feeling abandoned, he can, in a public act of revenge, protest against his parents' seeming indifference. It was impossible not to remark upon Cherie Blair's taking the baby abroad with her husband in a well-publicised visit, leaving Euan behind. Euan certainly has had his provocations.

A half-century ago the famed American sociologist, Talcott Parsons, emphasised the hazards of an excessive withdrawal of binding libidinal urges away from the larger collectivity and loading them upon the dyadic couple; those whose chronic narcissism is sealed within the dyad, leaving little libidinal overspill even for the children in their immediate family, are disqualified from emerging as genuine, benevolent leaders. A true leader acts as an exemplar, inciting the led to societal allegiance, wooing them to yield up some of their excessive investment in the personal. Man's libido is essentially finite; the libidinal diffusion, the social cement binding the wider community together, needs constant replenishment. If it is drained, if it is starved of sustenance, it suffers energic impoverishment and then those larger co-ordinate aggregates, the maintenance of which gives us the possibility of a civilised society, can collapse.

These are selfish, Thatcherite-cum-Blairite days, a time when the balance between intimate family and supra-family collectivities has become seriously disturbed; the glue that binds us together – patriotism, religion, political ideology and comradeship – has become unstuck. Now, led by a dyad that excludes all but themselves, there is no encouragement for an electorate to feel engaged, to feel committed to a larger collective. In 2001 as in the subsequent local and European Assembly elections, polling booths lost their allure; many preferred to abstain, and others voted reluctantly, fearing abstention would bring worse. But the 2001 General Election was not, as in May 1997, an election day of rejoicing. We voted in the 'dilemma of twilight, Never glad confident morning again!'

I have lived through times when political leadership had the courage to call for adult not indulgent infantile responses, when Churchill offered blood, sweat and tears, and when Stafford Cripps, Labour's Chancellor of the Exchequer in the immediate postwar years, successfully called upon the nation to continue its sacrifices, to practise austerity and sharing, so that the foundations could be laid for a fairer society. We cannot hope for leadership of this calibre from the Blairs; more likely, those early traumatic experiences that have so shaped them will continue to become, through a symbolic resonance, catastrophically enmeshed in the public domain.

Rock

At Oxford two passions governed Blair: indifferent to politics and scholarship, his enthusiasms were reserved for religion and rock. Both he pursued with extraordinary zeal. And even as Blair's heavy flirtation with Macmurray's religiosity illuminates his present-day political stances, so does his undergraduate infatuation with Mick Jagger's rock.

His commitment to rock music has proved to be no mere phase-appropriate scream; his was not the transitory allegiance of so many public school boys at Oxford who, released from the artificial constraints of their schooling, in their delayed adolescence, found risk-free liberation in the exuberance of the beat. With Blair his fidelity continues into his fifties. 'Rock music is the absolute love of my life,' he declared in 1995, although characteristically, while declaring for rock in general he refused to specify to his *News of the World* interrogator which were his favourite groups. All for pleasing everyone, when pressed, his response was electorally impeccable: 'All the bands that everybody loves.'

An interview he gave for his fiftieth birthday displays his continuing enthusiasm. His interviewer records:

> He has played his guitar more in the past few years than for a long time, having taken it up again when some friends invited him to join their band. Like his Oxford

rock group, Ugly Rumours? 'Ah yes, Ugly Rumours,' he says, beaming, 'those days were great. Every so often I feel I should graduate to classical music, properly. But the truth is, I'm more likely to listen to rock music. I listen to what the kids play.

At Oxford his favourite icon was Mick Jagger, upon whom he subsequently bestowed a knighthood. Blair, as the lead singer in his public school rebel band, The Ugly Rumours, was famed there for his Jagger impersonations. His long hair down his back, his purple loons and his cut-off shirt undone to his navel, finger-wagging and punching the air, the man to be prime minister of the United Kingdom snarled out his and Jagger's favourite 'Live With Me'. The ambivalences within the well-known words, calculated more to repel than to capture an adult lover, and enveloped in the imagery of the archetypical pre-pubescent nasty little boy, were accompanied by a display of sensuous gyrations, all designed to emphasise the essential androgyny of the singer.

We have seen Blair posing in the tabloids with his Fender Stratocaster guitar, throwing a few tentative shapes on the fret board, demonstrating that he has not forsaken what he has intimated were those 'lazy crazy days' when he 'modestly fronted a college rock group'. His attachment to rock is his present, as well as his past. He recalls his fascination for the Rolling Stones and the Kinks when he so readily presents current magazine music awards, but his presence on such occasions is to him no mere photo-opportunity.

In no sense too is it an exercise in nostalgia, the memories of his early twenties. If it were, it would be readily understood by those of my generation, for when Vera Lynn presided over the 1995 commemorations of VE-Day, for most of us veterans it was her songs above all else that evoked for us our wartime youth, the partings, pains, tragedies and hopes of so formative a period in our lives.

Following upon publication of my book *Wotan, My Enemy*, which addressed the question of whether it was now possible within the European Union to live with the Germans, I was invited to lecture upon a D-Day cruise of American and British veterans, which ended by accompanying the Queen's yacht as it came up the English Channel. Vera Lynn came aboard our ship; my meeting with her gave me, as it would most ex-servicemen, an extravagant pleasure; and when she sang for us the songs that I had first heard again and again over the tannoy of troopships sailing in hazardous convoy, the bittersweet emotions they stirred were totally disproportionate to the slightness of the lyrics, simple and banal as they may appear to the more detached.

But the quiddity of those songs, in striking contrast to those coming from the rock icons, is their unequivocal commitment. As wartime youngsters in our twenties we joined with Vera Lynn in a celebration of fidelity; we responded in 'Yours' to a pledge to be joined to our absent lovers until the end of life's story. When, upon our return from distant lands, there would be bluebirds again above the White Cliffs of Dover, when the lights would go on again, it was to be a homecoming to a romantic, tranquil domesticity. There would be the sound of wedding-bells; we wanted to be, or return to be, husbands. We were being hurled across continents from one theatre of war to another, but we were involuntary rolling stones; we wanted to gather moss. We did not believe like Jagger, still revelling in his fifties in his inability to find 'satisfaction', that, as he told us in his interviews in 1995, the trick in life is to keep on the move.

And there was no misogyny or ambivalence, as in rock music, in our singing; we did not fear entrapment. We wanted to run to our woman, not away from her. 'The archetypical rocker/rapper,' the perceptive Suzanne Moore observed in the *Guardian*, 'who regards woman as the "architect of conventional life" is still in revolt, still on the run from mother.' For youngsters rock may be an imaginative space in which they strive to gain their own individuation, to cut the umbilical cord, to find a sexual identity or stretch and indeed escape its limits altogether; the androgynous dimension of their rock idols helps them unthreateningly to engage in what Moore has called 'gender tourism'. Rock can no doubt be such a rite of passage on the way to adulthood and, within its ambit, the bewildered adolescent may temporarily find his bearings; but it is not a place to tarry.

It is because there is a widespread understanding that rock is essentially age-appropriate only that there was so much raillery against the forty- and fifty-year-olds who attended the Rolling Stones' 1995 European tour concerts. The comments made at the time by Mark Simpson in the *Independent* were singularly apposite:

> pop music must bear a great deal of the responsibility for spreading Peter Pan-it-is. Beginning by worshipping youth and turning it into the commodity of the late twentieth century, it has ended up by populating the charts with ghastly mummified spectres like Mick Jagger and Cliff Richard, performers who became stars when they were young but now employ all the technology that royalties can buy to slow the maturation process.

The *Financial Times*'s contributor similarly jeered: 'The 50-something Rolling Stones and their gaga middle-aged fans should accept that youth is gone'; and he approved of the kids' mockery of the wrinklies, 'because they know that those pumped-up songs and sad pelvic thrusts hide the fact that youth, whether gilded or wasted, is ultimately lost'. These 'grown men should have been doing a bit of gardening, polishing their Volvos or topping up their pension plans instead of checking in their adult years at the Wembley box office'. Resentment of this order against the would-be Peter Pans reveals more than vexation with unbecoming juvenilia. It tells us of the subliminal fears that rock encapsulates: the threat that this gender-free music could be emasculating; that this music lures the listener away from his achieved heterosexuality back to the hesitations and diffidences of an androgynous condition with no commitment to another, no responsibilities to flesh-and-blood women, for in rock's perception women represent everything that the rocker is not: domesticity and social norms. Ambivalence, therefore, towards the adult feminine domain is the defining mark of classic instances of rock rebellion from The Stones to The Doors, Led Zeppelin, The Stooges, The Sex Pistols, Guns N' Roses and Nirvana.

And the BritPop groups like Oasis and Blur have continued to express the same fears of the commitments of adulthood. 'Peter Pan-itis,' Simpson writes:

> seems to have had a peculiar effect on British pop and a new batch of young(ish) acts. The only way to get attention in British pop these days, apparently, is to be derivative and deferential to your ancestors. Bands like Blur and Oasis sound like 'Q' readers singing karaoke. Paradoxically, in a world where boyishness is now preferred to manliness everywhere, BritPop seems to have decided that the best way to avoid becoming your dad these days is to impersonate his heroes.

These rock rebels certainly have no wish to become real, caring dads; they are always in retreat from adult mature life. Their defiances should not mislead us into believing that they are brave revolutionaries breaking new ground. Their stance is that of insubordination not that of radicalism. And, in political terms, they are highly suspect for they are secretly complicit with the order against which they affect to revolt. As the music critics Simon Reynolds and Joy Press in their extraordinary, illuminating 1995 work *The Sex Revolt* stress, Jean-Paul Sartre's distinction between the rebel and the revolutionary is apposite when applied to the rocker. For Sartre the rebel's goal is not to create a new and better system; he wants only to break the rules. In contrast, the revolutionary is constructive, aims to replace an unfair system with a new, better system, and is therefore self-disciplined and self-sacrificing. Because of his irresponsibility, the rebel has access to the ecstasy of dissipation and living in the now; the revolutionary, however, enjoys the satisfaction of merging his identity with the collective and long-term projection of improvement whose fulfilment lies in the future. 'We take it as read,' write Reynolds and Press, 'that rock is not a revolutionary art, that its insubordination and ego tantrums are complicit with or bound within the terms of capitalism and patriarchy.'

No comfort, therefore, can be obtained from Blair's enthusiasm for rock, no intimations can be obtained there of someone genuinely prepared to challenge and transform the body politic. What can perhaps be deduced from his addiction is his fear of the ebb-tide within rock, dragging back the stricken to androgynous irresponsibility. His over-determined efforts to resist that dangerous tug lead him, strenuously and tactlessly, and to the offence of many one-parent families, to sing paeans of praise for the traditional family, even as he revels in the music which subverts all its best values. One such extraordinarily over-determined effort took place in the spring of 2003. With his spin doctors warning him of waning female support, he made an attempt to ward off women's unease and suspicions of an androgynous quality; astonishingly, given that he was preoccupied with the Iraq turmoil, he gave a series of carefully crafted interviews to popular women's magazines all designed, by advertising his procreative capacity, to prove his unequivocal maleness. And, to compound this onslaught of ostentatious displays of his fatherhood, he caused a government subsidy to be given to a new magazine called *Dad* in which he undoubtedly will be represented as a role model, a man taking most responsibly his duties as a father, a man far removed from a rebel rocker in retreat from the supreme commitment of caring fatherhood.

Undoubtedly, reassuring presentations of domesticity of this kind did, way back in 1997, have an electoral appeal to not a few middle-aged men of middle England who shared with Blair an enthusiasm for the rock of their adolescence. Blair, then the wide-eyed, fresh-faced, goody-goody leader, the man who had played rock at Oxford and who, when all around him in his rock circle were taking drugs, listened to his father and eschewed them, gave an air of respectability to their nostalgia. They did not dare to overtly reveal their immaturity by attending Rolling Stones concerts, but in the secrecy of the ballot-box or in the anonymity of the opinion polls, resonating to the 'freedom' androgyny so spuriously offers, they imagined themselves liberated from their burdens of mortgage and family.

Not all thus respond. The more emotionally adult, sensing the androgyny, find the quality turns them off, not on. Michael Heseltine, in the Commons in 1995, quoted the poem 'A Political Kiss' by Fleur Adcock, who had in fantasy dreamt of kissing John Prescott. That was a rhyme from a woman to a man; but Heseltine would have been more effectively politically mischievous if he had been able to draw attention to another discerning rhyme of Fleur Adcock's:

> Can it be that I was unfair
> to Tony Blair?
> His teeth, after all, are beyond compare;
> but does he take too much care
> over his hair?
>
> If he were to ask me out for a meal,
> how would I feel?
> Would I grovel and kneel,
> aflame with atavistic socialist zeal?

No, I'm sorry, he doesn't appeal:
he's not quite real.

In the House he sounds sincere,
but over a candlelit table, I fear,
his accents wouldn't ring sweetly in my ear.
Oh dear.

I'd love to see him in No. 10,
but he doesn't match my taste in men.

Although rock icons may masquerade as political leaders,
grown-up women are wary of their attractions; and, of course,
that wariness is reciprocated by the icon. What he wants is not
a woman but a sheltering womb. For him, having a real woman
brings the threat of parenthood, the quenching of his restless
desires and the resolution of his emotional tumult. Rock is
enveloped in such fears; and the rock icon's apotheosis by the
young and immature comes from such shared apprehensions,
anxieties often declared explicitly as, for example, by the group
Nirvana.

Nirvana's 1992 multi-million-selling *Nevermind* contains
songs like 'Breed' and 'In Bloom' that are riddled with this fear
of reproduction and what is perceived as emotional stagnation.
Nirvana's work, like so much rock, tells us of what Reynolds
and Press have described as 'the regressive impulse to
repudiate manhood and seek refuge in the womb'. These music
critics draw our attention to the cover of *Nevermind*, which
features a baby swimming under water: in front of him dangles
a dollar bill on a fish-hook luring him to abandon his amniotic
paradise for a corrupt world. Indeed, Nirvana's 1993 follow-up
was unequivocally and simply entitled *In Utero*. In its first
single, 'Heart-shaped Box', Kurt Cobain, the group's lead
singer, begs to be hoisted back to safety with his head in an
'umbilical noose' and declares his longing to be sucked into

'your magnet tar-pit'. He is expressing what so often can be heard amidst rock's clamour: the call to refuse manhood in a world where, the rocker screams, most manifestations of manhood are loathsome. In Cobain's case, his desire to retreat from the world into numbed-out sensuality passed through heroin addiction, then blossomed into a full-blown death-wish, and so he reached his Nirvana; in April 1994 he shot himself. Rock is not always fun; it can be very, very sick. Only the naive can regard a political leader's infatuation with rock as simply an engaging caprice; it can be as sinister as Hitler's love of Wagner.

For almost invariably the music is in retreat, back to the womb and back to the imagined bliss of the pre-natal condition, back to Mamma, away from reality. Not only Nirvana proclaims its fantasy goal. Dozens of rock music groups assume names telling of their yearnings. Genesis, The New Birth, Babes in Toyland and so many others produce songs or albums confirming the group's longings. Like *In Utero*, *Mothership Connection*, *Mother's Milk*, *Sowing the Seeds of Love*, they are all replete with womb and birth imagery. Indeed, in an arresting 1994 paper, the American Professor of English Alvin Lawson, spelling out the conclusions he draws from his study of rock videos, proposes that the worldwide appeal of much of rock's thumping beat originates in unconscious pre-natal memories of the maternal heartbeat.

Lawson can certainly turn to the musicologist for aid to justify his contention, for rock's music rhythm is less simple than it seems:

> The tempo of much rock at first appears to be a rapid 100–160 beats per minute or more . . . but these false tempos are deceptive because rock drummers usually emphasise alternate beats (often counts 2 and 4 or what in effect are the upbeats), so that the perceived thumping pulse is slower by half. Thus most rock tempos effectively

fall into the 60–80 bpm range, about the same as the human heart at rest.

Expressing the view that the rhythmic model of so much rock music is a heart-pulse, Alvin Lawson affirms:

> Many bands devise (consciously or otherwise) ingenious rhythmic echoes of the heartbeat sound – for example, three or four quick beats followed by a pause (often played on higher pitch drums, but also by unison guitars or keyboards). The effect simulates an actual pulsing heart. These various heart-pulse rhythmic patterns not only support . . . birth/rock music co-relations . . . but they also imply that the sonic honorary presence of the maternal heartbeat is more significant than its bpms. Remember that foetal ears are a mere four-six inches from the booming maternal rock beat for most of their first nine months of life – all but a few hours of which pulse along 60–80 times a minute.

It is, however, not only the titles of rock albums or the insistence of the rock beat that are so richly suggestive of the pre-natal and birth events. Rock's central instrumental symbol is Blair's favourite – the guitar; and the guitar's neck which he and fellow-guitarists hold is not only a hesitant phallic intimation, it is also essentially umbilical and, because of its abdominal position and the typically frenzied musician's alternately loving and destructive interactions with it, the guitar's soundbox or body can be seen, and has been so described by Lawson and others, as a placenta.

Such a perception certainly accords with the challenging conclusions of the psycho-historian Lloyd Demause, who, in order to advance his view of the importance of the psychological imprinting that he contends takes place in foetal life, has assembled an intimidating collection of obstetrical and clinical evidence relating to the role of the placenta. It would seem that, during the second trimester, while the amniotic sac is rather roomy, the foetus is able to float peacefully, kick rigorously, turn somersaults, urinate, suck its fingers and toes, grab its umbilicus, become excited by sudden noise, calm down when the mother talks quietly and rock back to sleep as she walks about; but a change of scene in the foetal drama comes about during the third trimester when, as its length and weight increase, the foetus becomes distressed. The crucial problem of the foetus in this newly cramped womb lies in its outgrowing the ability of its placenta to feed it, provide it with oxygen and clean its blood of carbon dioxide and waste. Demause postulates that when the blood coming to the foetus from the placenta is bright red and full of nutrients and oxygen, the foetus feels good, but when the blood becomes dark and polluted with carbon dioxide and waste, the foetus feels bad; the foetus contends, therefore, with a placenta both nutritious and poisonous, alternately or simultaneously.

On such an interpretation the love-hate relationship between rock artists and the placenta-guitar has its precursor in the ambivalence of the foetus to its own placenta; and when the 1960s rock star Jimi Hendrix used to smash and burn his guitar on stage, his violence can be seen as an acting out of the anger of the foetus against the overworked placenta which during birth deprives it of fresh, oxygenated, waste-free blood. Such a display of rage is not peculiar to Hendrix. Many rockers, as in Toad the Wet Sprocket's 'Walk on the Ocean' and in Pearl Jam's 1993 show, continued to destroy their guitars. The phenomenon may be an outcrop of mnemonic accumulations originally stored pre-natally as Lawson and Demause appear to suggest; or it may be the product of an extraordinary regressive imaginative fantasy of the rocker. What is unequivocally clear is that it is yet another illustration of the pre-natal and birth imagery which envelops rock – illustrations that are sometimes embarrassingly obvious.

Rock artists clinging desperately, and, in these days of modern sensitive microphones, so unnecessarily, to their microphones and cords, move around like the foetuses that have been photographed clinging to the umbilicus where they find comfort and, it seems, emotional security; and some rock artists, as in Peter Gabriel's video album *P.O.V.*, are not content with the subliminal message they are transmitting but have a wrestling match with the mike cord-umbilicus, after which they collapse on stage in a foetal position. And often in many rock concerts there is a 'mosh pit', a standing-room-only area at the front of the stage, where in a symbolic birthing ceremony some of the young head-bangers lose consciousness in the crush and are lifted up and 'delivered' to safety on the hands of the crowd. The performing stars often participate in this midwifery rock and at climactic moments in their performances leap, often from risky heights, into the pit, where they are caught and 'delivered'.

Such antics reveal that what the rock star offers is not simply a route to a paradisical womb insulated from travail – although sometimes this fantasy is on offer – but, rather, he is holding out the opportunity to be reborn. This offer of rebirth is often remarkably explicit. The language of an authoritative musical review of the 1993 performance of the song 'Cherub Rock' by the group Smashing Pumpkins is redolent of birth experience, and the nature of audience participation which marked the rendering of the song, enabled Lawson to comment confidently:

Actually, the audience is in deep group perinatal fantasy; entranced by the (remembered maternal heartbeat) rhythm, it identifies (ie, bonds) with the foetus singers/(birth) passion, repeating hypnotically its cry for freedom (ie, delivery), let me out, let me out! Stimulated by the music, the beat, and the rocker's voice and body movements, the fans relive in fantasy their unconsciously remembered emotional peaks and nadirs from the ambivalently benign/oppressive late-stage womb and birth.

The fans are engaged in struggle as they respond to the rocker's call, as they would to a preacher's call, to be born again.

Much rock music tells of that struggle, for it is replete with analogous material relating to the pre-natal drama, to the struggle of the foetus to gain liberation from the asphyxiating womb. The yearning to flee from the threats of external reality to a fantasised comfortable womb is powerful, and some music can pander to the wish, but most rock contains the reminder that the womb's attraction may lure the listener into a trap; the sought-after peace will be reached only in Nirvana. The gynaecological fact is that the foetus lives in a world of pain as well as pleasure and the ultimate price for the foetus is to die or to get out. Rock is an incitement: 'Let me out and be born anew!'

For the young, therefore, rock can act as a liberation, affording the gain of a second chance, providing an opportunity to start again and, in androgynous state, hold sexual and gender identity in suspense before the final decisions are taken, adolescence left behind, and adulthood reached; it is a case of *reculer pour sauter*. Even if a grown-up man may playfully indulge himself in an occasional dalliance with rock, to be seriously 'into' rock in your fifties is surely an arrest, not a hobby.

We are entitled to be on enquiry when we find such a man in the role of a political leader; it is disturbing to find a prime minister who so persistently immersed himself in this born-again world of rock, the world without commitment, of gender disorientation, of sexual nomads, of the Rolling Stones, who, in their restless name, enshrine rock's stance. This man has never freed himself from a need to enter into the trance-inducing rock where, as in the Stones' 'Prodigal Son', the hero whose prototype is the footloose rebel of the biblical legend, rejects, as rock music critic Simon Frith has explicated, 'the constant behavioural calculus and moral accounting of settled existence, makes up his life as he goes along' and lives for the now and the new. Why is Blair so gripped by a medium which above all else is a manifestation of the fantasy of rebirth, the myth of regeneration?

Most importantly and relevantly, Blair's politics reveal themselves as only one more displacement of the symptoms so exotically displayed in his love affair with rock. His much-publicised involvement with rock in the run-up to the General Election of 1997 was a meretricious advertisement, a trailer, inviting the Labour Party and the nation to join him in an unbecoming adolescent dream of new regenerative politics. Only the deaf and the insensitive could have failed to hear the rock beat from the moment Blair commenced his address at the 1995 Labour Party conference. Repetitively deploying, like a vulgar stage hypnotist, staccato invocations or commands, in language drenched in birth imagery, he sought to lure us into his reverie:

> Today I place before you my vision of a new Britain. A nation reborn. Prosperous, secure, united.
> One Britain. New Labour. New Britain.
> I know that for some of you, New Labour has been painful. There is no greater pain to be endured in politics than the birth of a new idea.

And as he began, so he concluded:

> New Labour. New Britain. The party renewed. The country reborn. New Labour. New Britain.

As the 1997 election approached, Blair rolled on, having his photo-ops, as in the music magazine *Q*, clad in Next with Cherie in Versace, sharing a fruit bowl with that Prince of

Protean Perversity, that sometime saluter of the Nazi flag, David Bowie; politician and rock star, flaunting their androgynous qualities, singing their bewildered androgynous anthems, expressing the dilemma whether, these days, boys or girls should be liked, invoking moondust to dissipate confusions.

Bowie lives on. The androgynous creature whose appearance, South London accent and fluid sexuality had placed him at the forefront of the 1970s youth culture was, in November 2000, voted, by 100 current pop stars interviewed for the *New Musical Express* magazine, as the one who had most influenced them; he was named as the most subversive icon of his generation, the 'serious statesman' of rock; still our pop stars and the kids listen to his 1972 album which sparked off his huge following and which told, in the *Rise and Fall of Ziggy Stardust and the Spiders from Mars*, of an androgynous space-rock Messiah. And with the rock beat incessantly throbbing in the background, once again our false Messiah continued, during the General Election campaign of 2001, to preach his illusory regenerative policies.

Blair's Palingenetic Myth

Everyone knows, since he never ceases to tell us, that Tony Blair is the most Christian of socialists; and he can claim that under his leadership there has been a phenomenal membership growth in the Christian affiliate organisations of the Labour Party. There is no novelty, of course, in having party leaders who claim that their Christianity informs and is indeed the source of their political commitment. In my lifetime I have known and often fruitfully worked with men from Stafford Cripps to Viscount Tonypandy, whose religious faith has been the dynamic behind their good works as politicians.

Harold Wilson, indeed, always peddled the view that the Labour Party owed more to Methodism than to Marxism; that may, however, be a hyperbolic claim. From Ernie Bevin and Aneurin Bevan to Michael Foot, the party has had as leaders determined secularists. In South Wales, when I entered the Commons, there were probably as many Labour MPs who fiercely derided the chapel as there were those who found their politics in its tenets. Sometimes these neighbouring secularist MPs of mine would publicly demonstrate their contempt for Christianity. On civic Sundays, in accordance with the valley traditions which I too observed, the local MP would lead, together with the mayor, a march throughout the township preceded by brass bands and followed by the Red Cross, the Boy Scouts, the Territorials and members of the local voluntary organisations. The march always ended in the chapel for a civic service but at the entrance to the chapel these MPs, having endorsed the values of civic virtues, would ostentatiously bid their constituents goodbye and refuse to partake of 'the opium of the masses'. It was indeed among such secularist MPs that I found my firmest allies when all the churches of Britain, unitedly and in concert, sought in 1963 to sabotage my original efforts to reform the divorce laws.

Nevertheless, overall, the record shows that a particular exegetical theme has played a large part in the shaping of the political thought of many Labour leaders. It was one that perhaps owed more to the Old Testament than to the New, for the emphases and goals in early Judaism were always defined in terms of a collectivity; so that in the prophets you will find no clear ideal of personal immortality or reward and punishment after death. The highest aim, particularly of early Judaism, was a collective aim and individual salvation was subordinated to the concerns of the nation and the whole human race. Labour leaders, exposed to such an ethos in their upbringing, often transposed the notion of the priority of the collective good to their secular politics; and, much diluted, we find it echoed in Blair's rodomontade, which is so frequently permeated with reference to 'communitarianism'.

There is, therefore, no novelty in a Labour leader claiming his politics of community are informed by Christian beliefs; but there is another exegesis of Christian doctrine which, in the hands of the power-seeking politician, can be both malevolent and an abuse of its original text. It can lead, as Blair sought to do, to the almost blasphemous appropriation of the resurrection, the making of the ancient myth into a subtext of the New Labour Party manifesto. 'Easter,' Blair declared in 1996, 'a time of rebirth and renewal, has a special significance for me and, in a sense, my politics.' The myth of renewal and rebirth is a dangerous ploy to introduce into politics. It is the myth which some historians, notably Roger Griffin, have described as the palingenetic myth. Etymologically, the term palingenesis, deriving from *palin* (again, anew) and *genesis* (creation and birth), refers to the sense of a new start or regeneration after a phase or a crisis of decline. It is precisely that myth, when it has invaded the politics of twentieth-century Europe, notably in Nazi Germany, that has wreaked havoc. This is the myth which Blair acknowledges pervades his politics and which, once again, he spelt out when he addressed a Labour Party conference in April 1995:

> Today a new Labour Party is being born. Our task now is nothing less than the rebirth of our nation. A new Britain. National renewal . . . New Labour being born. The task of building new Britain now to come.

The wellhead of palingenetic myth is, of course, religious; and in Christianity the resurrection of Jesus Christ places one such myth at the very centre of the whole faith. Notions of metaphorical death and rebirth envelop the symbolism of baptism, communion and Easter celebrations, while generations of Christian mystics have elaborated intricate verbal, pictorial and ritual mythologies to invoke the reality of spiritual rebirth on a high plane of being after dying to the world of the flesh. The invocation of such myths in politics can, very exceptionally, be inspirational; but it can, and has been in my lifetime, utterly disastrous.

Only one previous Labour leader, and that was in the nineteenth century, has in his politics drawn upon the myth, and to compare Blair's impoverished presentations with the language and content of that leader's addresses, and to place them in the context of the period, brings a chastening recognition of the dangerous banalities of Blair's persuasions that we would, under his leadership, be born again in a new Britain. Given Blair's unselfconsciousness, and his illiteracy in the field of Labour's history, it is unlikely that he is aware that the leader who used the palingenetic myth inspirationally was Old Labour's founding father, Keir Hardie, a man from whom Blair would decidedly wish to distance himself. Keir Hardie was brought up by his parents in a sternly rational creed of agnosticism; but like Blair, and at about the same age – 21 – in 1877, he was converted to Christianity. His conversion never led him to peddle pap or in any way to temper his belligerence. Conciliation and consensus were no part of the interpretation he placed upon his creed; he would have had no truck with the ecumenicalism Blair constantly preaches. When Hardie became the first and lone socialist MP in the Commons, he flayed the churches for their neglect of the issue of unemployment and, when he addressed the congress of the Congregational Union of England and Wales in 1883, his speech caused uproar. He declared:

> Christianity today lay buried, bound up in the cerements of a dead and lifeless theology. It awaited a decent burial, and they in the Labour movement had come to resuscitate the Christianity of Christ, to go back to the time when the poor should have the Gospel preached to them, and the Gospel should be good news of joy and happiness in life . . . Ring out the darkness of the land, ring in the Christ that is to be.

The delegates to the congress were outraged, but as Hardie's biographer comments, to nascent socialists and to radicals 'he seemed the Messiah of a new faith destined to regenerate mankind'. Such impossible regeneration was not to be, but more than any other man he was the maker of the Labour Party that Blair would now consign to the dustbin of history. Not without resistance, some of us succeeded in having a commemorative bronze head of Keir Hardie placed in the Palace of Westminster. As Labour MPs, panting for Blairite patronage, leave the Chamber to enter the dining-room, they must pass the corner where he gazes upon them. There they would be wise to pause and see if they can dare to look him in the eyes.

Keir Hardie's use of the palingenetic myth was certainly not directed to immediate power-seeking in Parliament; he saw his role in the House as basically prophetic, with his eyes on a very distant future. He was a backbench agitator who was not seeking to persuade his fellow MPs but, rather, to address the voiceless masses outside the Commons in the slums and in the backstreets, and by his very detachment from the parliamentary games of his day, he was to beget an Independent Labour Party outside the House. His was no fantasy pregnancy, as is Blair's; his birthing was authentic.

When, however, Blair declaims national renewal and regeneration, he skates on very thin ice. We had once before in twentieth-century Britain a party emphasising above all else its pristine nature. It was the New Party founded by the extraordinary and dangerous Oswald Mosley; it was a party that soon glided into overt fascism. More than 65 years ago, in Pontypridd, South Wales, I well recall how only a posse of miners protected me from the menacing thugs approaching me as, from the floor, I challenged the eloquent call of Mosley for national rebirth and regeneration. Mosley's fascism, its essential homogeneity, resided in its mythic call; and no one who ever heard him could doubt that he used it to powerful effect.

Mosley's fascism was a British outcrop of what Roger Griffin, in his painstaking survey of the nature of fascism throughout Europe, describes as 'generic fascism'; and he identifies the centrality of the palingenetic component of fascism's permanent mythic core to explain so much of its appeal. Repeatedly we have witnessed, during the Second World War, and in pre- and postwar Europe, the Fascist vision of a new vigorous nation growing out of the destruction of an old system; and have seen how, given flawed leaders with an elective affinity to the psychological travail of their society, fascism has had the almost alchemical power to transmute black despair in their communities into a deluded and manic optimism, which takes them along the road to self-destruction.

All these fascisms offered, and continue to proffer, regeneration; they promise to replace gerontocracy, mediocrity and national weakness with youth, heroism and national greatness, to bring into existence a New Man in an exciting new world in place of the senescent, played-out one that existed before. The vague or contradictory implications of the policies to realise such nebulous goals do not necessarily diminish their attraction, because it is precisely their palingenetic mythic power that matters, not their feasibility or human implications.

When, therefore, Blair proclaimed in October 1995, 'This is a new age, to be led by a new generation. I want this country to be young again,' he induced a frisson in the politically informed remnant of my generation. We have heard that language before in the mouths of fascist demagogues. Blair's unbecoming adolescent dream of new regenerative politics acted out in rock may, although not without considerable misgivings, be tolerable, but when the dream of rebirth is elaborated into political manifestos proffering the elixir of youth, then we are placed on alert, for this was the poison offered by the Nazi and Fascist hucksters and accepted by their dupes.

Politics smeared by the detritus of Nazi-fascist mythopoeia are themselves repellent. But, as Blair and his impertinent young political pups wage war on Old Labour, there are particular reasons why we should scoff at their claims that only a 'new generation' can save us. In their trepidation, as they seek to kill off the fathers, these political adolescents boost themselves with a dangerous amnesic and, thus drugged, the courageous youngsters, manned with piss-proud erections, dare to obliterate the reality that the most radical and 'regenerative' Labour government, which brought us the welfare state, was led by old men, by a Cabinet of twenty men and women whose average age when they took up office was 61.65 years. That Cabinet had come to power after a war in which Britain, led by an old man of almost seventy, had successfully defied Nazi Germany, whose people, deluded by their cult of youth and their version of the palingenetic myth, believed themselves invincible.

Born two years after Attlee's governments had run their course, Blair irreverently brings no recall of the war and the immediate postwar years. He would have us believe that his is the first, not the second coming. With Messianic pretensions he would have us accept that his birthday had heralded the coming in the millennium year of the generation that, under his apostolic leadership, would create a new Britain made in his image. In 1997 he was promising that in his 'New Age' we would all be young again; and in pursuit of that aim, older members, often of considerable value, were regarded as ineligible for his Cabinet. No one over the age of 55 was deemed fit for such elevation; they were either dumped or, at best, shifted to become chairmen of select committees. In May 1996 leaders of eighteen prominent UK business organisations, led by the Bank of England, had joined forces to promote the value to business of mixed-age workforces, attracting and retaining experienced employees regardless of age; but Blair determined that no such mix would prevail in his Cabinet. Indeed, this Peter Pan finds it difficult to believe that he is not exempt from the ageing process. In April 2003, when his fiftieth birthday was imminent, he disclosed that he was not looking forward to his birthday: 'Fifty sounds really old to me,' he complained.

Probably as a second son with an able older brother, now a successful QC with an expertise in banking law, displaced sibling rivalry played its part in Blair's pushing aside of older members, MPs who could have been much-needed anchormen in his government. Certainly the scar of being known at his private school as 'Blair II' may well not have healed. But it is

BLAIR'S PALINGENETIC MYTH

his own narcissism, and his envelopment in the rhetoric of his palingenetic myth, that, fundamentally, prevents him from empathising with the elderly and that causes, unusually, his opportunism to fail him. Ignoring the electoral dangers of estranging voters who form an increasingly large section of the population, he has, in his government, flagrantly corroborated ageism. Apotheosising the new, eulogising the young, means denigration of the old. He has ample precedent. Seen at its worst and most evil, the politics of regeneration and the homo-sexual ideal of virile young men found its full expression in Nazi Germany; there the 'unproductive' elderly, dubbed senile, came under the shadow of Hitler's euthanasia programme. But there are other ways of destroying the elderly than sending them to gas chambers.

One of them is to create a political ethos that by exclusion demeans them. There is an inherent sickness in a dogma which overvalues youth, denies its biological concomitant, immaturity, and, by insisting government must be informed by a scale of values where to be young is the ideal, inflames intergenerational rivalry. That, as the European Commission insisted in its realistic report of March 1996 on the ageing of Europe, is precisely what is to be avoided if the Continent's demographic problems are not to result in disaster: 'There can be no doubt that the principle of solidarity between generations will emerge as a key factor in the adjustments which will have to be made'.

But when Blair continues to avow that he intends to make Britain young again, he is spelling out, in an assault on the parental generation, his own unresolved Oedipal antagonism. And the very absurdity of his intent exposes its irrationality.

The demographic reality is that Britain will never be younger; our ageing is forever. Compounding the birth rates of the 1920s and 1930s, lower than they had ever been before, is a whole range of factors – the pill, the sustaining range of advances in medical knowledge, feminism, increased male

sterility – all guaranteeing that our low-fertility and low-
mortality population cannot be magically conjured away by
political incantations. The present British population contains
far and away the oldest body of persons that has ever occupied
our islands; and the position is irreversible.

It has been said that ageism, as a specifically social
pathology, is an identifiable characteristic of late-twentieth-
century society in advanced countries; certainly consumerism
and its accompanying meretricious advertising industry
deliberately inciting or encouraging all to be self-regarding
and, by artifice and fashion, to be ever young, are a fertile field
for the growth of ageism. Reminders, within such an
environment, of the inevitability of ageing are increasingly
unwelcome; the aged become disliked for, of course, dislike of
the old is hatred of the self, the rejection of what one must
become.

How such ageism disagreeably invades politics was
unpleasantly illustrated in February 1996 when the Tory
government deliberately sabotaged a most modest Private
Member's bill that sought to prevent upper age limits in job
advertising; and although in the debate the Blairite front-bench
spokesman promised 'comprehensive legislation to make age
discrimination in employment illegal', albeit subject to
'consultation', his awareness of the consequences of present
demographic changes and future technology did not bring any
detailed pledges or detailed thought-through responses, telling
us how it is proposed to bring about the reordering of the whole
working relationship which, in the face of the radically altered
age composition of our country, has become an imperative.
Like so many other promises, that 1996 promise of specific
legislation against age discrimination remains unfulfilled by
Blair's governments.

But very much more is required than age-discrimination
legislation; attempts, outside the context of Britain's
burgeoning employment problems, to take limited action to

assist the jobless half of all men over 55, avail little, for they are but a small part of a huge problem. A Rowntree Foundation report showed that in 1996 there were then seven million people of working age who had no jobs. Political attitudes that treat ageing as a well-nigh intractable 'problem', that implicitly suggest that the most that can be done is to assess what the narcissistic young can be persuaded to forfeit for the benefit of those who cannot look after themselves and for those who have to live in institutions and those about to die, are wholly defeatist. A striking proof of the political attitudes currently adopted can be seen in candidates' standard visit during an election campaign to a sheltered housing complex or a residential care home – a practice to which I must plead guilty of having followed – which encourages the illusion that old age is little more than an object of welfare and that it is in such venues one will find the old; in reality, in my former constituency, as in most areas, 96 per cent of older people live in ordinary housing. The instruments that have been created to meet chronic problems of ageing are not able to provide the policies or actions required for the increasingly great majority of elderly people who present no 'problem' at all. But we shall have little hope of converting into legislation imaginative political thought, directed to aid a society where birth rates diminish, infant mortality has practically disappeared, and longevity prevails, if the leader of the major reforming party seems, judging by his language, himself possessed by the Dorian Gray syndrome, the denial of the ageing process and the eulogising of youth. In *The Picture of Dorian Gray*, Wilde wrote:

> For there is such a little time that your youth will last; such
> a little time. The common hill flowers wither but they
> blossom again. The laburnum will be as yellow next June
> as it is now. In a month there will be purple stars on the
> clematis, and year after year the green night of its leaves

will hold its purple stars. But we never get back our youth.
The pulse of joy that beats in us at 20 becomes sluggish
... Youth! Youth! There is absolutely nothing in the
world but youth!

The brilliant narcissist's erotic worship of youth, however
mortified, becomes a destructive and threatening doxology
when, as under Blair, it is added to Labour's canon. For such
evocations prejudice efforts to bring about the necessary
reordering of the working lives of all who wish and are capable
of employment, a reordering which indeed is a prerequisite,
despite rising national income, if we are not to live in a country
where an increasing and substantial minority suffer severe
social disadvantage when unemployment grows in homes
where no one at all is in paid work.

To speak of making Britain young again is therefore a
dangerous evasion of the challenge that demographic and
technological changes now set us. Worse, importing such a
vocabulary into political discourse compounds the very
problem it is claiming to resolve; 'senile', 'geriatric', along
with many adjectives, as Peter Laslett in his constructive works
on ageism has long since pointed out, although originally quite
innocent of an insulting meaning, are now standard epithets of
abuse. Such pejorative views demean the elderly and are part of
the stereotyping process by which attributions can be given to
each and every member of an older generation, even although
they are applicable only to an afflicted minority. Possessed by
his palingenetic myth, Blair, not content with denigrating Old
Labour, must depict Britain itself as age-encumbered; despite
having spent three of the first and, as for all of us, perhaps the
most formative five years of his life in Australia, no
affectionate evocations of the Old Country come from Blair.
Always he repeats his mantra, New Britain, New Labour, all
must be young, neoteric and pristine. Blair, in these
declarations, is neurotically displaying what Jung has termed

the *puer aeternus* (eternal youth) syndrome, in which the individual refuses to accept his own mortality; ageing and finitude are denied, a notion highly acceptable to an electorate increasingly doubtful that eternity is to be found in a heavenly afterlife.

Blair fears age and would deny its encroachments. When his fiftieth birthday approached in 2003, he blurted out to an interviewer: 'I must be honest with you. I've been dreading 50 . . . Funnily enough I don't feel 50 . . . I feel great physically. I do more exercise today than I've done since I was at school,' he protested. He works out early in the morning or in the evening using the running machine in the gym at No.10 Downing Street, plays tennis, and football too when he can. When, in 2003, he took a winter break in an Egyptian hotel and found there many Italians, he assembled them to participate with him in a five-a-side match. Recently he clearly regarded it as an insult, not a compliment, when, on being asked to play tennis near Chequers, someone told him: 'You play quite well, you can join our veterans club.' For him, veteran is a pejorative, and age is a disease, never an opportunity. He responds to the ageing process not as a mature man but as an empty-headed pretty actress fearful of losing her good looks.

In political terms, to sustain such conceits means nothing must ever be seen to be stale; ripeness, maturity, are menacing. Blair mourned as 'tragic' the second enforced resignation of his *doppelgänger*, Peter Mandelson, from government in January 2001; but it was Mandelson who, in constant press interviews and with his mentor's approval, defended notions of permanent revolution, of constant and never-ceasing questioning of the present. Modernity for the Blairites has long since ceased to be a means to the political end of facing the electorate with internal structures brought up to date; it has become doctrine. Charlotte Raven, in an *Observer* article, insightfully commented:

modernisation, that procedural strategy turned pseudo-philosophy, is quietly becoming a doctrine. Under Kinnock's custodianship, you felt that it was genuinely the means to a proper political end. But then, having done all its work within the party, it should, logically, have evolved and been replaced by a concern with what to do with the success it was supposed to facilitate. Instead it has stretched its neck wider . . . It is no more the conveyance, but the destination – the route map which has ended up at the Grail. And, scariest of all, they've started to believe in it – as if it was ever anything at all.

An ageing Mao almost wrecked his country with a cultural revolution in which everything old and traditional was to be destroyed; his denial of approaching death was projected on to society which, at his command, was to be born anew, and thus he fantasised he too could will himself to be young again. We, of course, are in no danger of Blair's born-again farrago inflicting Mao-like turmoil upon us. His psyche is too striated with inhibitions that compel him to avoid serious conflict at all costs. Sensing the fatal flaw, this incapacity for action to correspond with his doctrine, Raven, quoting Blair's 'I want us to be young again', pertinently adds: 'If the modernisers' case signifies anything, it's this semantic incoherency, nostalgia for a future which they wish for but cannot create.'

The history of the British Labour movement provides us with few examples of leaders afflicted with this psychological flaw; but there have, however, been not a few of this genre, into which Blair chasteningly fits, among past European socialist leaders who, more burdened than British leaders by ideology, usually with some version of Marxism, made strikingly visible, when in office, their total incapacity to match political action with their political theory.

The classical example, often cited, is Otto Bauer, one-time Austrian Foreign Secretary and leader of the Austrian socialist party, whose theorising so entranced Léon Blum that, when Bauer died in exile, Blum, as French Prime Minister, had him buried with all the ceremony of a state funeral. Freud had treated Bauer's father and then, made aware of the bizarre family background by unravelling the perplexities of Bauer's sister, discovered the aetiology of hysteria. Otto Bauer's own hysterical personality shaped his seductive and dangerous political style; it was a style that proved fateful to Austrian democracy, combining as it did a militancy of language with an almost total absence of deeds. As Blair, possessed by a palingenetic myth that he has turned into a governing political doctrine, so often notoriously evades committing himself to legislative details telling how his doctrine would be applied, we are uncomfortably reminded of characters like Otto Bauer.

These reminders become even more insistent when one notes the conclusions of clinicians, like the American Alan Krohn, who have provided us with modern definitions, wrested from their clinical work, of the hysterical personality. Such a personality, it is suggested, may be something of a pace-setter:

> Though the hysteric remains within the bounds of convention, his sensitivity to the ambience of his culture makes him sensitive to emerging cultural trends just before they enter the main stream of the social ethos. In art, sports and popular intellectual pursuits, and even more in such visual, exhibitionistic areas as fashion, interior decorating and cocktail-party conversation, the hysteric frequently allies himself with what is coming into vogue . . . . the hysteric promotes modest, minor change that rarely challenges anything basic to the society. The changes they respond to and try to be early participants in are more of style than of ideology, though . . . the former has at times tried to pass as the latter. The hysteric, in his excitement and participation in changes of style, can help a society foster the illusion of change, promoting a sense

of self-satisfaction that things are moving ahead, without really disrupting and reconstructing anything important. These changes which the hysteric is inclined to usher in need not necessarily be completely trivial. However, even if the changes have substance the hysteric will strive to embody them only if their divergence from what has come before is slight. The hysteric enjoys change, but only as he enjoys sexuality to flirt with it but to remain safe from it . . .

Such observations are made after explorations of the early family experiences of those displaying these traits, experiences which can be found to be suggestive of the impingements within Blair's early environment. Certainly one persistent strand in the cluster of behaviour patterns that marks out the hysterical personality is the failure, after engagement in heavy petting with the idea, to proceed to consummation.

One reckless proposal, fortunately never consummated but richly illustrative of the pathogens endemic to Blairite 'new' thinking, was the anti-older generation scheme eagerly put forward by Peter Mandelson before the 1997 General Election; this has never been acted upon – unsurprisingly, since Mandelson's enthusiasms, be it for the Dome or Stalinist communism, are short-lived. He is the man who, as a young communist, fiercely defended Brezhnev's invasion of Czechoslovakia and whose crusade against those he suspects of 'Old Labour' tendencies, always reminded me of a converted revivalist warning against all the sins of which he has grown tired. One of his sudden conversions as a young man, after a short sojourn in Tanzania where he appeared to have found God, was from Marxism to Christianity. His belated conversion presumably lingered on in the proposal he put forward, in an uncomfortable moralistic guise, for a public dowry to be made available to those committing themselves to permanent cohabitation with a partner; his scheme is worth recalling for it is unusually illustrative of the bias and shallowness of the 'philosophy' that has enveloped Blair's government.

Proposals of the nature that Mandelson put forward have a long and disreputable tradition and are unpleasantly reminiscent of right-wing, neo-fascist or fascist policies, where preoccupation with the need for national regeneration meant that population and family policies were ever conjoined. France, even before Pétain, in 1939, had a revised *Code de la Famille*, which enshrined, in laws that encouraged marriage and provided subsidies, the traditional apprehension that France's national grandeur would be subverted by under-population. In Italy Mussolini's regime was indeed founded on a palingenetic vision; the dictator's pronouncement as he denounced falling birth rates included constant mention of a 'spiritual renewal' of the Italian people, and the 'rebirth' of a 'young and fertile race' the delivery of which he sought to facilitate by subsidies rewarding prolific women for performing their patriotic service to the nation. And in some ways, in Nazi Germany, Mandelson's dowry scheme was pre-empted. Side by side with an evil 'eugenic' programme aimed to ensure a rebirth of an Aryan race, purified of tainted blood, came incitements to the racially pure to increase their numbers. The Nazis were particularly proud of their marriage-loans system. The Nazi scheme gave couples interest-free loans of up to 1,000 Marks, the repayment of which was cancelled when they had their fourth child. Issued in the form of coupons for household goods, the loans were initially given on condition that the future wife who had worked for at least six months prior to the wedding gave up gainful employment after marriage.

Mandelson's dowry scheme was not a copycat of the Nazi dowry system. That scheme is to be differentiated from Mandelson's in the method used to finance its cost; inspired by French legislation, the fund to pay the loan was partly financed by the revenue from a 'celibacy tax' on unmarried men and

women, a method of fundraising that would certainly not be
personally advantageous to bachelors like Mandelson. His
proposed method of fundraising was far less equitable, and one
that unsurprisingly emerged from the youth culture that the
palingenetic mythology corroborates. He urged a form of
generational tax law on 'empty nesters' in their sixties who,
having worked for decades to rid themselves of their mortgage
were, he complained, enjoying 'reasonable incomes with low
outgoings and are sitting on significant equity capital', which
should be mobilised 'to give young people a better start to
married life'. This man, lacking in-laws and children, would
have legislation creating the flexibility to release this equity,
legislation clearly seen – to all but those lacking sensibility – to
provoke guilt or resentments if the parents failed to take
advantage of its provisions.

There were other peculiarities about Mandelson's scheme.
All the neo-Fascist and Nazi family funding schemes had a
clear and unequivocal goal: young marriages meant more
births and thus assisted national regeneration. Mandelson,
perhaps embarrassed by his lack of marital status, was less
explicit; nevertheless, birth production was part of the goal of
his dowry plan; it would 'make life with a new baby so much
more bearable' and, he claimed, the dowry would reduce 'the
anxiety, frustration and tension at a testing moment in any
relationship'. Parenthood seemed to be viewed by this man not
as a blessing but, if not a curse, certainly as a penalty that a
State-endowed dowry should mitigate. It is a view that is not
out of kilter with his ambivalence about marriage itself, for
that is not presented as a good in itself but merely a useful
indicator, affording 'the simplest test of eligibility' for the
dowry; and in his book, as in his surrounding interviews, he
looked forward to the proposal being extended 'to couples
who affirm a long-term commitment to each other but for
reasons of their own reject the form of marriage'. In his
order, homosexuals in long-term relationships and cohabiting

heterosexuals should, ideally, not be excluded; and, more, to further the overall scheme, the old should pay for all this by tightening inheritance taxes.

That so jejune a scheme, one which was replete with generational bias, so likely to attract mercenary and unstable couples and so calculated to provoke resentment – because qualification for the dowry would bring financial means tests and evaluations of permanent 'commitment' by bureaucrats – was seriously put forward by someone who continues to have a malevolent influence over Blair, and upon whom he is so unhealthily dependent, is dismaying. Most of my parliamentary life was spent in reforming laws impinging upon human relationships, and I know how delicately one must tread if, in the end, such legislation is to be healing, not disruptive. But even if one discounts some of the personal dilemmas that were reflected in Mandelson's inept proposal, the whole ill-thought-out notion remains unhappily illustrative of the Blairite's fatal attraction to the inchoate: always the canvassing of an alleged New Idea, never the detailed signposting of the route to its fulfilment.

Lacking such signposting, Blair's first government lost its way. In the run-up to the 2001 General Election the message was, rather, that the trail would soon be picked up. Repetitively and firmly we were told that Blair stood for the future, a future which he indeed made into a proposal in itself; and this future – a reborn Britain – was to come about like a 'happening'; it was implied that only the querulous and unimaginative were spreading doubts about the efficacy of this spell within his palingenetic myth-making. And such dissenters Blair's aides confidently believed could be dealt with by the leader's speech being accompanied by a briefing for journalists stating the new initiatives catalogued in his address, notably 'a new type of politics, no promises which we cannot deliver'. So the future was to come about with the new promise, a promise not to promise, an innovatory and brave pre-election pledge calculated to lend an air of credibility and realism to his fantasy.

Such a political environment inevitably has beckoned in yet more disenchantment, to add to that already being experienced, for government by dream must collide with reality. The creation of this political environment has, too, other inimical effects; it not only incites ageism but it sabotages the constructive work of those like Peter Hildebrand, the psychoanalyst who for twenty years conducted at the Tavistock Clinic a workshop on the problems of the second half of life. Rebelling against the oppression of the predominant youth culture which Blair's political expositions reinforce, it is possible to see ageing as a creative process, not as an arrest, in the course of which, despite having to cope with new pressures on relationships, as well as old conflicts, and despite increasing physical limitations, rich and fulfilling possibilities are offered for exploration and discovery of the latent and unfulfilled aspects of ourselves.

The years between the early fifties and old age should not be regarded as a mere postscript; to do so at a time when the post-parental phase of robust health has been so greatly extended, and when for the first time men and women can look forward to thirty to fifty years of productive life after their children have reached adulthood, is, when expressed by Blair in his paeans of praise for the new and young, wholly inappropriate to today's societal needs and is as presumptuous as it is destructive. Blair once told the Chief Rabbi that he was reading through the Bible and that he had reached Ezekiel; in that event, he has certainly overlooked the Fifth Commandment.

The deficit in Blair's programme is the lack of wisdom; he accelerates the change that has taken place in recent decades – the abandonment of the wisdom of the elders and their capacity to make a worthwhile contribution. The pace of technological change, leaving so many older people feeling they are immigrants in a strange land, encourages the notion that they are to be regarded as surplus; but the Internet provides information, not wisdom. I am only too conscious at the age of 86 of how the raw speed and effectiveness of much of the thinking of the young, as part of the natural process, decline with age; but this is often amply compensated for in the ageing individual by the capacity to scan the field and arrive at solutions by using a process of lateral thinking, a capacity that tends to evolve in response to the gradual and sometimes imperceptible losses in the ageing process.

Hildebrand has neatly illustrated this trend in telling of that brilliant tactical thinker the first Duke of Wellington. When the Great Exhibition was opened, the vast Crystal Palace was plagued with a completely unforeseen infestation of the common London sparrow, which threatened to lay a thin layer of mess and untidiness over the whole sparkling edifice and its contents. Those responsible for the Exhibition were close to despair, with the result that Queen Victoria decided to consult the Duke, who was then in his eighties and regarded by her as the repository of all wisdom. On this occasion his tactical genius gave her the immediate and sensible answer that Prince Albert and the scientists and engineers had not been able to discern: 'Sparrow-hawks, Ma'am. Sparrow-hawks.' The Duke had seen through to the heart of the problem and found the answer that had escaped the scientists.

If the maximum available benefit is to be obtained by our society, then the zeal and energy of the young need to be tempered by those whose age often brings them greater detachment, a talent to stand back from the fray, above the immediate battle, and enables them to bring a sense of balance and authority. It is a need that exists in the boardroom, in the deliberations of trade union executives and university councils, and most obviously in our politics now so replete with a sense of expediency forever practised on a day-to-day level. It is because Blair senses the growing public distaste for this present form of government, its venality matching its opportunism and desperate improvisations, that he claims he is bringing a 'new type of politics'; what in fact he has proffered is the oldest type of politics: the politics of the shaman whose magic the credulous believed could control good and evil and whose incantations could quicken the dead. But there is no dodging ageing and death; and no one and no nation can be born again.

Even as age cannot long be disguised by cosmetic and surgeon, so too the politics of the pristine, of the new, cannot long be sustained; its blemishes will soon emerge. Mature democracies and older people alike must accept their losses. In Britain's case, its loss of empire and military and economic power has to be mourned even as a once-beautiful woman must mourn. Recapturing youth is a foolish and vain quest and it is irresponsible to plead, as Blair is doing in political terms, its possibility.

There are more positive responses open to ageing; and if those responses infuse the body politic, as can occur through more emotionally mature leadership, then out of the acknowledgement of loss and out of the mourning, there can come a creative liberation. George Pollock, the American analyst who has contributed much to an understanding of the potentiality of ageing, has spelled out what he has called the mourning liberation process:

> The basic insight is the parts of the self that once were, or that one hoped might be, are no longer possible. With the working out of the mourning for a changed self, lost others, unfulfilled hopes and aspirations, as well as feelings about other reality losses, there is an increasing ability to face reality as it is and as it can be. 'Liberation' from the past and the unattainable occurs. New sublimations, interests and activities appear. There can be new relationships with old internal objects as well as new objects. Past can truly become past, distinguished from present and future. Affects

of serenity, joy, pleasure and excitement come into being. Narcissism may be transformed into humour, wisdom and the capacity to contemplate one's own impermanence.

Pollock may be too optimistic, and the ideal he claims is possible may only rarely be achieved; but it is a goal that can be set before a society as before an individual, and the politician, like Nye Bevan, who never ceased to affirm that the achievement of societal serenity was the purpose of his politics, had an understanding of the developmental process that can operate in the body politic. Anabolic and catabolic forces are forever driving within our society, and which of these competing forces triumph is extraordinarily dependent upon the available leadership. When Blair discards and mocks Old Labour, and invites us to become engulfed within his palingenetic myth, he is retreating from adult politics; youth is a beginning not an end, and to make, within our politics, by sound-bite, posture and sloganising posters, an apotheosis of all that is young and new is both dangerously regressive and pusillanimous.

By the year 2000, however, the aged had had their fill of Blair's provocations; their stoicism and past allegiance to Labour were stretched to the limits when he and his young pups, while boasting of Britain's thriving economy under New Labour, threw them as a morsel a derisory 75p increase to their pensions. The storm burst and at the 2000 Labour Party conference, Old Labour, led by the redoubtable former trade union leader Jack Jones and the indomitable Barbara Castle, mobilised protests and gave Blair and his acolytes the verbal thrashing they deserved; whimpering and frightened, they offered immediate placatory pensions. But the bitterness increases as Blair, singing his Wildean tunes eulogising youth, now plots to relieve his generation of further fiscal burdens by forcing the elderly to work until they are seventy or face vastly reduced pension payments.

Technology and demography ensure that never in British history has there been a greater need to capture a totally

different mood, so unlike Blair's, of Robert Browning; it is the
mood which is required to envelop our politics:

> Grow old along with me
> The best is yet to be
> The last of life for which the first was made.
> Our times are in His hand
> Who saith, A whole I planned.
> Youth shows but half; trust God; see all; be not afraid.

The Hermaphrodite and the Androgynous: The Distinction

Blair has lured the voters even as did the Pied Piper of Hamelin who cheated the spellbound children of their adulthood and led them back into the womb-mountain, for the leadership that Blair provides is that of androgyny, one that infantilises the electorate; its identity is vague, ill-defined and free from the burden of adult and gender choice.

If we are to be alerted to the hazards such political leadership provides, then we must discern the distinction between the debased charisma it exudes, one to which a confused and immature electorate responds, and the charisma of leaders, of whom Gaitskell and Bevan are contemporary British examples, possessed of hermaphrodite charm. Even a slight excursus into the history of the influences exercised by hermaphrodite leaders and myths illuminates how different is their spell from that exercised by the androgynous, and how each spell can have entirely different political consequences.

The prototype of all those exercising hermaphrodite leadership is to be found in the man who is so often described as the first individual in history, the Pharaoh Akhenaten, living fourteen centuries before Christ, a ruler who in all the various images exhumed by the archaeologists is depicted as effeminate, lacking a phallus or, more usually, with an explicit hermaphrodite anatomy. When, as in the Royal Academy's African art exhibition of 1996, we are left only with a remnant of this extraordinary leader which is confined to his face, still we are ensnared by his seductive and sensuous lips, as we may well be, for he has, as no other man, captured the imagination of the most austere of Egyptologists, as well as men like Freud, who regard him as perhaps the greatest man that has ever lived. The revered Egyptologist James Breasted wound up his classic study of Akhenaten's reign in these words:

> There died with him such a spirit as the world had never seen before – a brave soul, undauntedly facing the momentum of immemorial tradition, and thereby stepping out from the long line of conventional and colourless pharaohs, that he might disseminate ideas far and beyond the capacity of his age to understand. Among the Hebrews, seven or eight hundred years later, we look for such men; but the modern world has yet adequately to value or even acquaint itself with this man who in an age so remote and under conditions so adverse, became not only the world's first idealist and the world's first individual, but also the earliest monotheist, and the first prophet of internationalism – the most remarkable figure of the Ancient World before the Hebrews.

The typology of Akhenaten has thrown attempted medical diagnoses of his physical condition into confusion. The assertion that he suffered from a disorder of the endocrine system, that there was a malfunction of the pituitary gland, and that the indications are that the peculiar physical characteristics which all his depictions reveal are the result of a complaint known as Frohlich's syndrome, have been subverted by the fact that Akhenaten, uniquely among the pharaohs in having himself represented as a family man, seldom appears except in the company of his wife and daughters. The physicians cannot resolve the dilemma: how can so uxorious a husband and so philogenetive a parent have suffered from Frohlich's syndrome, which would have rendered him impotent and passive except for a short period in adolescence before the full onset of the disease?

Perhaps Akhenaten did have some physical characteristics suggestive of the hermaphrodite, but the manner in which he directed himself to be depicted, where all such characteristics are heavily emphasised, sometimes to the point of caricature, sometimes grotesquely, clearly meant he was determined that his self-perception and his people's perception of him should be that of a leader possessed of the powers of the hermaphrodite; those powers he exercised in a staggering manner against the Egyptian establishment and priesthood, precipitating a revolution in thought, notably in his insistence on monotheism, that reverberates down the ages. Indeed, if Freud's conjecture in the most arresting of all his works is correct, the original Moses was himself an Egyptian follower of Akhenaten.

What is clear beyond peradventure is that the later chroniclers, in the biblical Books of Moses, had wholly absorbed, in telling of the god of the Hebrews, the notion of an hermaphrodite organism which has explicitly male and female sexual reproductive characteristics; for woman as well as man, Genesis insists, was created in the image of the god who evidently contained both elements. And being so created, Eve springs from Adam's rib. This concept of a primal divine hermaphrodism, found of course in the creation account of so many cultures, arises from the wish to believe that the Ultimate Being is a unity in which all present pairs of opposites, including the sexes, are contained. Ancient myths abound in tales of a time when the eternal male, Father Sky, and the eternal female, Mother Earth, were locked in unending embrace; there was neither duality nor multiplicity, only one hermaphrodite condition. It was only later, when the cosmic egg was broken, that creation took place. The sexes were separated, and have ever since longed to be reunited, each in the other.

The Greeks, less coy than the Jews, were more explicit in telling of humankind's nostalgia for the once-upon-a-time when man and woman were one. In their art, as in the statues of the Graeco-Roman epoch, they often projected on to the mythological figures, whom they regarded as harbingers of their destiny, fully developed female bodies with pronounced male sex organs. Far from denying sexuality, such depictions emphasise its presence; we witness in the marble portrayals both the eternal wish expressed in the mythic idea that once man and woman were one, and an acknowledgement that all human beings are potentially bisexual. The hermaphrodite affirms sexuality and the dictionary definition of hermaphrodite, which presents androgyny as its equivalent, is misleading, for the androgynous, contrariwise, wishes to negate sexuality, to deny, by blurring, any gender whatsoever; male and female are to be neither separately defined nor explicitly conjoined.

In our present day, androgyny, as exhibited by our pop stars and fashion models, is a retreat from genitality, which is adult and carries therefore the threat of responsibility; however attractively displayed or packaged, retreat, defeat and deadness are endemic to its condition. In politics the charisma of the hermaphrodite leader can lead followers to catastrophe, but as a weapon in the hands of a leader retaining a firm hold on reality it can be inspirational, and a resultant benign dynamic can arise within his society. No such hope can be wrested from an androgynous leadership; the conservatism inherent in its nature, the ebb-tide ever dragging such a leader back to the magic islands, to the imagined security of the womb, overrides all the over-determined protestations that, with him, we can face the future.

The terrible accusation that can be made against such a leader, far worse than any that can come from a ministerial front bench, is that involuntarily he is a practitioner of the politics of perversion; for politics too is an arena where, to a greater or lesser extent, perverse elements which may feature in the lives of people suffering from various forms of disturbance may be acted out.

Androgyny is a dangerous quality; by its very nature shirking full consummation, it sometimes expresses itself in perversions in the clinical sense, often finding the fetish more attractive and safer than the woman. A distinction, however, exists between the true pervert and those who, like the vast majority of people, from time to time indulge in fantasies, usually sexual, which deviate from the culturally accepted norms; indeed, for many of them the most they do is put their fantasies into occasional practice in their foreplay.

While the true pervert's deviance is a persistent and constant form of aberrant sexual behaviour, androgyny, carrying with it perverse elements, can pervade the global structure involving the individual's whole personality, and find its expression in activities which fall far short of, and are to be differentiated from, those which are correctly given the diagnostic designation of perversion. I believe Blair's politics to be riddled with such elements; and that the consequences of such politics to our society can be far more dangerous than the activities of the true wretched clinical pervert, often indulging his practices alone, and always confined to sexual deviance.

Politics of Perversion

To allege that we are being enveloped in the politics of
perversion is a serious charge; and, if it is to be sustained, we
must turn to the clinicians whose case-books bulge with the
histories of perverts, and then ask whether our surmise is
validated by their findings, and whether, without extravagances, we can suggest that in many respects the politics we are
being invited to practise are analogous to the pervert's lifestyle,
and stem from similar sources.

The task we set ourselves is fraught with difficulties, not
least because of the disgust and outrage which can be provoked
by the very mention of the word 'pervert'. Our protestations
that we must always distinguish, as do the psychoanalysts,
between true perverts and those who may show what is
described by the psychoanalysts as 'sub-clinical perverse
elements' in character structures are irrationally brushed aside.
There comes into existence a quaint notion that psychiatric
research into those elements should be based on the less prominent members of the human race, exempting the prominent, the
great and the sublime. Such a reaction is understandable, as the
tabloids daily confirm Schiller's poetic aside: 'The world loves
to blacken the radiant and drag the sublime into the dust.' But
a path can be steered between tabloid scavenging and, in the
genuine public interest, a necessary scrutiny of our political
leaders: 'There is no one so great,' Freud wrote when justifying

his scrutiny of Leonardo da Vinci, 'as to be disgraced by being subject to the laws which govern both normal and pathological activity with equal cogency.'

There is a further difficulty, however, in surveying the operation of perverse elements in the politics of the leaders and the led. Perforce the starting-point of such a survey must be a search for the origins of the true pervert's startling deviations; and it is at first disconcerting to find that among those who have gained an expertise in the treatment of perverts there is a tendency, particularly as between psychoanalysts in Britain and those in France, to take up differing vantage points as they focus upon the first precipitates of a pervert's condition. All the psychoanalysts, however, share a common view that the bizarre practices of the pervert constitute a regressive attempt to shield himself from a reality that he finds too threatening to tolerate.

In Britain the emphasis of the psychoanalytically orientated psychiatrist is upon the stratagems that the pervert has invented to protect himself from the retaliatory action that he fears will be evoked because of his aggression, aggression which is at large and liable to bring about his annihilation. In France, psychoanalysts, and particularly the remarkable Janine Chasseguet-Smirgel, have a different focus. The disclosures of their patients have taught them that the pervert, fearful of further libidinal development that would take him into full genital relationships – which he regards as terrifyingly threat-ening – retreats from unbearable truth to find his shelter in practices that have an accompanying fantasy of a perverse world where orifices are indistinguishable, where there is no distinction between the vagina and the anus; it is the universal anal-sadistic world of the Marquis de Sade, an imagined world where all reality has been pounded into an undifferentiated non-threatening mass. There, the pervert, wallowing in this mire, opts to be bogged down rather than reach an adult world where, unlike in the pervert's fantasised world, differences between the sexes and generations prevail.

Neither British nor French analysts, however, in any way categorise the pervert's practices as conduct totally outside the range of experience known to most people; the British analysts stress that some of the pervert's longings can be a component of the most normal of loving desires, and Chasseguet-Smirgel sees perversions as 'a dimension of the human psyche in general, a temptation in the mind common to us all'. There is therefore substantial congruity between both viewpoints; and the clinical evidence yielded by both means that we can expect that perverse components within a political leader's propaganda can, at an unconscious level, find a resonance throughout the whole community. In my view, those resonances are being teased out by current presentations of Blairite policies within which we find distressing analogues of the desperate efforts of the pervert who gains, within the fantasies accompanying his tortuous practices, temporary relief from his anguish. To recognise those analogies, it is wiser to adopt the viewpoint of both schools of psychoanalysis separately, although, since both are based substantially on the bedrock of classical Freudian theory, doubtless at some future time the metapsychological theory may evolve harmonising their present differences.

Psychoanalysts in Britain who treat perverts have come to recognise a particularly important complex of interrelated feelings, ideas and attitudes which they refer to as the 'core' complex of perversion. The late Dr Mervin Glasser, the dedicated consultant psychiatrist who at London's Portman Clinic treated so many perverts and brought illumination to the nature of the complex, told us:

> A major component of the core complex is a deep-seated and pervasive longing for an intense and most intimate closeness to another person, amounting to a 'merging', a 'state of oneness', a 'blissful union' . . . This longed-for state implies complete gratification with absolute security against any dangers of deprivation or obliteration and a

totally reliable containment of any destructive feelings towards [the other person, usually the mother or mother surrogate].

The case histories Glasser used to illustrate the components of the core complex have a familiar ring. When, for example, he told of a transvestite imagining himself crawling up the birth passage and curling up snugly within the womb, we note the correspondence between that fantasy and Blair's dream of a blissful union, of a politics without discordance or schism; and we note too how similar are the yearnings of the transvestite to those embedded in Blair's favourite rock music, which is replete with the bliss of an imagined pre-natal condition; and, no less, we see equivalences between the transvestite's 'merging' and the return to the womb which is the precondition for the fulfilment of the palingenetic myth governing Blair's politics.

But it is when we turn to the psychoanalyst's search for the origins of the true pervert's compulsive need to escape from reality, from the dangers he feels in the external world, that we begin to understand that the acts of the pervert are not what they seem to be, and that in most cases they conceal their real nature rather than reveal it; for the perversions and the accompanying fantasies are in place as a shield to protect him from the consequences of the unconscious violences which seize him and which, if released, would destroy him and others.

When we grasp what Edward Glover (the doyen of the last generation of British psychoanalysts) asserted – that the pervert's wayward behaviour is 'a defence against an over-charge of unconscious aggression and/or sadism' – then I believe we find lit up for us the darkest crevices of the perverse elements within Blairite politics. Blair's placatory style, his need to have consensus by diktat, his concentration on the 'middle ground' and his avoidance at all costs of 'extremism', his attempts to outlaw Old Labour, which insists that all the gains for ordinary people have come about, not by wooing, but by struggle and by fights which must be sustained, help us to begin to appreciate that his approach is determined by a force in respect of which electoral advantage is little more than justification for his own perverse political compulsions.

Always a distinction must be made between a true perversion and the perverse elements that may appear in the lives and ideologies of those to whom the diagnostic designation, with all its pejorative and sometimes criminal overtones, most certainly does not apply. But with that caveat again made and emphasised, I nevertheless believe that Blair's fear of political confrontation with those who would deny him consensus, can be understood better if we acknowledge that his fated mishandling of his own unconscious aggression is akin in some respects to what we see erotically endured by the true pervert.

When under Glover's chairmanship and tutelage I served for so many years on the Council of the Institute for the Scientific Treatment of Delinquency, I needed no persuasion from him to accept his view that the perversions were indeed a defence against an overcharge of unconscious aggression, for as a newly qualified solicitor I had found myself not infrequently defending perverts who had offended against public order; and they had taught me what Glover explicated. I still recall my shock when, after successfully persuading the court to inflict a non-custodial sentence on a pervert and after, outside the court, I had counselled him to confine his practices to the private domain, he peremptorily walked away from me, saying he could not do that for, if he stopped, he would kill someone. A few years later I heard that in another city he was charged with attempted murder; his perversion, stifled or inadequately realised, had proved too frail to contain his violence.

On another occasion, by which time I had gained more professional experience, the replies I received when questioning a perverted murderer client about his motivation gave me less surprise. He was engaged in his perversions in a bath with his colluding wife when he suddenly desisted and proceeded to cut her up in little pieces. When I asked him, in his cell, why he had slain his wife, he replied tonelessly: 'I had to. If I hadn't killed her, I would have killed myself.' He was being truthful; the self-lacerations that he would have inflicted when even his perversions could not protect her from his aggression had been unleashed upon his wife. Such dramatic presentations of the link between unconscious aggression and perversion may only exceptionally come to the notice of a criminal lawyer, but they are evidently commonplace within the experience of clinicians. One psychoanalyst has written:

> When one works, as I do, psychotherapeutically with both delinquents and sexual deviants, one may observe how the patients may be graded on a continuum ranging from violence to true perversions. In some instances one may actually observe the process of sexualisation taking place before one's eyes, so to speak, in the course of the treatment.

The terrible violences that can result when the barrier of the pervert's defences is breached must not, however, mislead us into believing that the true pervert is someone utterly different from ourselves, that he does not belong to the human race. He goes as a babe through the same developmental stages as we all do; but the tragedy of the pervert is that the dilemmas from which the majority of us escape, carrying only perverse elements of greater or lesser strength, remain raw and wholly dominant in the pervert's adult life.

The developmental stage of infant life in which the psycho-analysts tell us the adult pervert remains can, without, it is hoped, lapsing into excessive distortion or oversimplification, be succinctly depicted. Our initial intense need as babes for the mother creates a wish to merge with her, but that wish carries the implicit concomitant of the loss of a separate existence as an individual – annihilation. To avoid such a fate there is an intensive aggressive reaction aimed at self-preservation and the destruction of the mother; but such a destruction would lead to the loss of the mother, to total abandonment, so the babe's woes are compounded as the anxiety he felt that he would be annihilated by merger is now supplemented by his anxiety that he would be abandoned. The force of the aggression that he feels because he is thus trapped in an impossible dilemma is not to be minimised, and it is that aggression that we find can be released by the adult pervert who has never resolved the original Catch-22 situation.

Although the babe cannot extricate himself from the predicament fortunately the mother can and does come to the rescue for most of us. It is her ministering to our needs that helps us on our way. Gradually, as her mothering endows us with the confident self and diminishes our fear of individuation, the wish to merge becomes less insistent. Gradually the confidence grows that the mother's temporary absence does not mean abandonment; and so, the fortunate babe's aggression is increasingly tempered and the consequent anxieties lessened.

The adult pervert, however, has not been so saved. The mothering he received was defective, and failed to resolve his dilemma. Glasser has authoritatively told us of the mothers who bequeath so wretched a legacy:

Frequently we have no objective information to corroborate the patients' depiction of their mothers, but one characteristic features so consistently in the accounts the true perverts give that one is safe to assume their veracity. This is that she has a markedly narcissistic character and relates to her child in narcissistic terms . . . Her narcissistic over attentiveness, in treating him as part of herself, reinforces his annihilatory anxieties and intensifies his aggression towards her. Her neglect, emotional self-absorption and insensitivity to her child's needs will both frustrate him and arouse abandonment anxieties and again intensify his aggression towards her.

The psychoanalyst categorises the characteristics of the mother who creates the true pervert, but even when the characteristics of the mother appear in less florid form, but when the mothering is less than good enough, then the imperfections that prevent the mother from empathising with the babe and adequately meeting his emotional needs mean that the babe, when he reaches adulthood, will be likely to have far more perverse elements within his psychic life than an adult whose infancy was happily blessed; and the most significant social consequence is that such an adult will have greater difficulty in handling his own aggressivity.

This is the handicap maiming Blair's politics. The true pervert is attempting to prevent his unconscious aggression surfacing, destructively imploding and exploding. By his sexual deviations he attempts to quench the annihilatory anxieties that came from the threat when he was a babe that his enveloping mother would fulfil his wish for merger, and his abandonment anxieties, which stem from his fear that the destruction he wished to wreak upon the narcissistic mother denying him individuation would leave him abandoned. However, a mothering less starved than one which results in the true pervert, but one which nevertheless is similar if less defective than such mothering, can result in an adult finding himself compelled, in self-protection, in a bid to keep under control the aggression which in more normal development may have been benignly assimilated, to use stratagems, albeit more subtle than the pervert's; and it is my view that Blair's consensus by diktat politics is such a stratagem.

Not for nothing was the gibe deservedly made against him, as he sought Conservative votes, that he should be renamed 'Tory Blur'; he desperately needs his consensus, one from which aggression is proscribed and conflict banished, even as the true pervert needs his bizarre sexual deviations. Blair's biography, personal and political, tells us of a man struggling with unconscious and unassimilated aggression; but the consequent perverse elements are not expressed in sexual deviance. They are seen in his incapacity, like his mentor Macmurray, to tolerate ambivalence, in his constant display of rock-womb yearnings, in his immersion in the palingenetic myth. The impress of his mother's narcissism is as firmly delineated upon him as it is upon a true tragic pervert; and the perverse elements finding expression in his politics have a similar object to that of the true pervert, to hold down unconscious aggression which threatens to escape; when, despite his efforts to repress it, that aggression *does* escape, it is untempered, out of control, overwhelms rationality and sweeps him along as it did when he became the cheerleader for the fraudulent war against Iraq. The faulty mothering which initially left his belligerency so inadequately mortified has, through his early traumatic experiences, been repeatedly recharged and been only half stifled, not least during the period when his father, dead but alive, would look at his son with eyes which the boy would almost inevitably have regarded as accusatory.

There will be those who demur, and protest how can it be suggested, given the scant information available, that Blair's mother, although courageous, had in all probability a markedly narcissistic character and related to her baby in narcissistic terms; but the trained clinician treating his adult pervert usually and similarly lacks objective information to corroborate his patient's depiction of his mother. However, the clinicians have, by noting the common features of their pervert patients' depictions of their mothers, collected sufficient material to build up and to test their hypotheses and the validation of those hypotheses comes in the success or partial success of their therapy.

The therapist, it is true, has the advantage of the consulting-room or the couch; but Blair is no shrinking violet. Lacking reticence, this actor, composing his scripts or choosing those he finds congenial to his temperament, provides almost daily a plenitude of material unlikely to be so readily proffered by a patient to his therapist and, within that material, with a constant presentation of consensus politics, we see the same desperate urge to maintain psychic stability as possesses the pervert whose practices are his attempts to contain the violences which he fears would otherwise break out against himself or others.

Both the pervert and such politics are reaching out for what psychoanalysts have described as psychic homoeostasis, akin to the physiological concept of homoeostasis, the tendency of organisms to maintain themselves in a constant state. But the capacity of the individual to adapt to the demands and disturbances that arise from clamorous internal needs and from those made by the external world is profoundly affected by his earliest upbringing; and, handicapped by a particular upbringing, the pervert's mistaken efforts to achieve homoeostasis are wretched and precarious, and so are Blair's.

The precariousness of Blair's imperfect homoeostasis is reflected, in political terms, in his ceaseless efforts to impose a discipline upon his party members, to silence any who criticise his stances for his psychic homoeostasis is fraught with all his primal and subsequent traumatic anxieties. In June 1996 the *Observer*, well primed by Blair's entourage, was able to report under the headline 'Blair tightens his grip on party':

> Labour MPs judged below standard or disloyal may be barred from standing as official candidates after the general election under new proposals to be canvassed by Tony Blair . . . Labour's leader will also seek a tighter rein on parliamentary candidates by urging local parties to choose from a list drawn up by Labour's National Executive.

Blair has not succeeded in reaching the objectives reported by the *Observer*, but how determinedly he strives to attain those objectives was well illustrated when, late in 2000, he tried to persuade, by offering the inducement of a peerage or a place on a quango, some 25 MPs who intended to retire to delay their declaration to quit until after the announcement of the General Election date; then, the rules dictate, the shortlists become centrally controlled, making it easier for favoured Blairite candidates to win selections.

When the journalist Hugo Young attributes, as he does, Blair's 'iron hand' to a fear that any expressed dissension will be exploited by those manning a hostile media, he is surely mistaken. Blair can, when he wishes, well accommodate the media; he has no difficulty in having a rapprochement with Murdoch or lunching with the editorial staff of the *Sun*. What Blair fears is not the press, but himself.

Press criticism he can often temper or quench, but not his own neurotic fears. It would be difficult to believe he was not privy in the summer of 1999 to the intervention of Alistair Campbell, his press secretary, when an attempt was made to suppress a commissioned article I had written for the *New Statesman*. The article claimed that Blair's aggressive enthusiasm for battle in the Balkans was a displacement of the suppressed and unreleased unconscious aggression he had felt as a child towards his father. The article was warmly accepted; it was to be published in the next issue – but then came some curious telephone calls to me, both from the editor and the foreign editor of the journal. I was told they had learned that Blair's father was seriously ill, that in effect, Tony Blair was on a 'Red Alert', and that it was felt that it would be tasteless to publish the article in a week when Blair might be so bereaved; I, of course, concurred and it was agreed that the article should be held back and the situation be monitored in the coming week or two. But I mistrusted the tale, used my own sources, found Leo Blair was in robust health and just back from an Irish holiday, that my article had been seen by Downing Street and that Campbell had been prompted to intervene and invent the whole story. To kill the article, they were prepared to kill off the father. Disgusted by such unseemliness, I gave the article to *Tribune*, which published it on 18 June 1999; *Tribune* explained the Downing Street intervention. This was an occasion when no denial from No. 10 followed.

The fact is that what Blair cannot accommodate is Old Labour's insistence that working strictly within the parameters of the prevailing economic system means Britain will never have the changes it needs. In his eyes that is heresy, for acceptance of that doctrine would affect the consensus he has built up, one which, despite all the posturing and rhetoric, has left the electorate believing, on good grounds, that there are few policy differences between any of the political parties. It is a heresy which, if adopted, would upset Blair's precariously poised homoeostasis, one that is so brittle a container of his free-floating unconscious aggression. Traditional Labour is, therefore, more of a personal than a political threat to Blair; and because, fraught with anxiety, he finds it so threatening to his personal intactness, all his considerable unconscious aggression is released against those who show the slightest tendency to deviate from his contrived consensus. Then we see him as Robert Harris, the novelist and journalist, has described him: 'He is emerging as the most ruthless leader Labour has had, imposing a revolution on his party like Thatcher did on hers.'

But this is a 'revolution' to serve Blair's compelling needs, not those of the party or the country. Blair's near paranoiac concern that his homeostasis remains in place demands that all must join in consensus, that policies must nearly always respond to the prevailing majority, always be adjusted so as never to offend. Authentic leaders, however, lead; they do not follow; and no MP, whether back-bencher or leader, should act as a seismograph passively registering the temporary prejudices of the electorate. No promised land can be reached by following the directions given by pollsters. If Moses had responded to opinion polls, he most certainly would not have crossed the Red Sea.

No pervert has ever been more articulate than the Marquis de Sade. By recording his sadistic fantasies he has obtained the deserved accolade of having his name perpetuated in every European language. The French analysts, unsurprisingly, have often turned to their fellow countryman to assist them in their divinations of the precipitates of the symptoms presented to them by their pervert patients; for Sade's Code of Laws, in his *120 Days of Sodom*, sets out with astonishing clarity the rules that must govern the life of a true pervert. Those rules, and the resultant exegesis made by the French analysts, help us to understand the significance of the widespread renaming of Blair. There are more than vestigial traces of Sade's doctrine in 'Tony Blur's' policy presentations.

It must be remembered that Sade's singular imaginative achievement was his creation of a fantasy world where all differences were annihilated; in his perverse universe any notion of organisation, structure or division was suppressed. The goal of the Sadeian hero is the attainment of a complete merging; he is man violently assaulting nature, eradicating the essence of things and thus instituting what he describes as the 'absolute mixture'. Always, in playing on his constant theme of sexual intercourse, the protagonists he depicts are engaged in group sex, men and women, children and old people, virgins and whores, nuns and bawds, mothers and sons, uncles and nephews, noblemen and rabble: 'All will be higgledy-piggledy, all will wallow, on the flagstones; on the earth, and, like animals, will interchange, will mix, will commit incest, adultery and sodomy.'

In Sade's world all the barriers that separate man from woman, child from adult, mother from son, daughter from father, brother from sister, are broken down; and in elaborate permutation of erogenous zones, all of them are made interchangeable. 'Mixture,' Chasseguet-Smirgel has written, 'would be considered the heading under which the whole of Sade's fantasy world is played.' And to obtain that mixture he conjures up a vision of a devouring digestive tract, an enormous grinding-machine, where all that is taboo, forbidden or sacred is disintegrated and reduced to excrement. The world of differences would be wiped out and in its place would be a world reduced to faeces.

Sade's literary capacity as a pornographer may be unique; but the perversions he describes tease out responses in the thousands who continue to read him, for possession of perverse elements within the psyche is the common lot of mankind. When those elements play a considerable role in the cast of mind of a politician, then his outpourings can often deserve to be dismissed as 'mush'; there is not an immeasurable distance between Sade's faecal mixtures and Blair's 'Blurism'. That policies are so diffused, so lacking in definition, is because such a presentation is endemic to Blair's temperament; a distinctive detailed display of his political wares, each separately to be viewed, is at all costs to be avoided.

'Bubble 'n' Squeak' was therefore an apt heading to be given by Roy Hattersley in his review of *The Blair Revolution*, co-written by Blair's principal aide. As a political sophisticate with ministerial experience, Hattersley impatiently rejected the mushy *mélange* proffered to him by Peter Mandelson. He vigorously condemned a work he regarded as 'banal', 'pretentious' and, above all, 'confused', 'reducing ideas to vague generalities' with passages of:

> pure gibberish. The Blair Revolution – wanting Labour to be a 'synthesis' which unites the Left and Centre rejects ideology and replaces it with banalities.

Hattersley's gibes are well deserved, for Mandelson's idealisation of Blair's penchant for 'synthesis' is analogous to

Sade's idealisation of his doctrine of faecal 'mixtures'. Sade's eulogies to the fudges he fantasises took him to a lunatic asylum. Blair's fudging, however, helped to take him to the premiership. A *Times* editorial just before the 1997 election deservedly mocked Blair's enthusiasm for the lead singer of the rock group Blur, accurately commenting: 'His much publicised wooing of Damon Albarn has already won him the nickname "Blur", a hard prod at his soft focus vision'; and that blurring has persisted throughout his premiership. It is that 'soft focus vision' that has led him to make formulations which have become so indistinguishable from Tory policies that he can continue, as he did in a May 1996 *Observer* interview, to offer 'moderate' traditional Tory MPs a safe haven, promising them legislation and policies that they would be able to support; that indeed is one promise of his six-year premiership he has kept.

What, then, are the ultimate sources of this extraordinary Sade-like desire to deny differences which finds expression in Blair's fudging? Only the naive would be content to explain it away as mere political tactics, that Blair is just a skilled player of the usual game of equivocating politicians. His political history and its persistence deny such an interpretation. An elucidation of the motivation of those who have such a compulsion to smudge tells us, yet again, of the perverse components that are so embedded in Blair's political outlook. It is Freud's essay *Fetishism*, published in 1927, that gives us the clue we require to understand why a compulsive need can arise to deny or belittle differences. Freud explains that the fetishist never, when a little boy, came to terms with his frightening discovery that a significant anatomical difference exists between the sexes; a fetish assists him, for 'the normal prototype of the fetish is a man's penis', and holding on to his fetish enables him to engage in his sexual proclivities while still maintaining the illusion that at one stage of our early development is, Freud tells us, common to all men, that the mother is like the son, that she has a penis. Initially, little boys, horrified at the sight of a woman's genitalia, deny what their eyes are telling them for they interpret it as an intimation of the retaliatory castration by the father that could await them if they acted on their Oedipal desires. For most, the Oedipal phase is worked through and the reality of the differences is reluctantly accepted, but the pervert has carried his initial horror into adulthood. Some indeed, as the casework material presented by psychoanalysts reveals, persist in denial by having fantasies about a phallic mother or, more usually, fantasies where blurring and merging themes predominate as they attempt to deny the uniqueness of each sex and to pretend that men and women are one. None of us, however, escapes unscathed from that early frightening experience, and perverse components can often be observed at work when we see some adults forever recoiling from the unequivocal, always attempting to build bridges over the unbridgeable.

When the infant has sight of and becomes aware of his penis-less mother, we see at their most exotic the vain attempts to deny differences; but the child analysts point out that even before the baby is shocked by his discovery, he has already had premonitory experiences which have caused him to struggle against acknowledgements of separateness. From the beginning the suckling babe experiences anxiety when the breast disappears, and the analysts postulate that in order to create internal harmony and psychic peace, he therefore continuously fantasises about the constant presence of the breast and thus, blurring and merging the bodily boundaries between mother and child, he psychically avoids the pain of separation.

More, a little later, the toddler enters a psychosexual stage when, despite the pleasure he experiences because of the stimulation of the rectal nerves when he expels his faeces, defecations are nevertheless accompanied by considerable anxiety; for he fears that the production of faeces represents a dismemberment or loss of body parts. In order to avoid that anxiety, he seeks to annul the experience of loss by retaining faecal products in his rectum; thus, by clinging to his faeces, he makes his bid to avoid separation and so forestall the coming into existence of the dreaded unacceptable difference between himself and the faecal stool.

No one chooses to become a pervert and no one chooses to retain perverse components in his character structure. Our choice is determined for us in our mother's arms; the mother who is able to give a babe a profound sense of security leaves him equipped to face reality and gradually to acknowledge without fear that a separateness exists between him and the mother. Similarly, the mother who encourages the infant on the pot, praising his productive efforts, diminishes his fear of bodily loss and enables him to have the courage to distinguish between his creative faecal products and his own body. When the babe is a little older and with horror discovers his mother has no penis, it is not inevitable that the child will later become an equivocating adult, taking refuge within a notable and protective mindset shielding him from any recall of the primal revelation of distinction. Whether that occurs or not is largely dependent on the structure of the family system within which the infant finds the Oedipal drama being enacted. The Oedipal wish to possess the mother and supplant the rival father is an impossible wish which, in some way, we must relinquish. The incestuous choice must be forfeited, for if pursued we fear a terrible retaliation. Every boy has to pass through this Oedipal phase when he concentrates sexual wishes upon his mother and develops hostile wishes against his rival father; but how he lives through and later emerges from this traumatic and conflict-ridden phase, a time when the aspiration of the child crumbles under the impact of retaliatory castration fears, depends on the response of the parents.

If the parents respond positively to the primary affectionate and competitive assertiveness of the child, then the Oedipal phase need not be wholly dominated by unassimilated lust and hostility and all the accompanying fears such emotions bring. But if the child has a mother dutiful but too narcissistic to relate sufficiently positively to allay the child's anxieties, and if, too, she is a submissive wife in a household ruled by a domineering unempathic father, then inevitably the sight of a mother without a penis has an unmitigated and more powerful and lasting effect.

The provocations of the feared father stir up the child's hostility; and the stronger that hostility is, the greater is the fear that in retaliation he will be castrated, that he will lose his penis, as he imagines has been the fate of his mother. The potential pervert cannot tolerate the visible depiction of the fate he fears and still, as an adult, denies in his practices and with his fetishes the anatomical differences between the sexes. He is an exceptional product of his early environment, but any child brought up in a household with a similar scenario, as Blair was, is vulnerable and, although avoiding the true pervert's fate, may carry into adulthood embedded in his personality perverse components expressed in a marked distaste for differentiation and a strong preference for the ill-defined. Definition is too evocative of the horrors and fears occasioned by his primal discovery.

The appeal of androgyny, lacking any explicit distinctive male and female genital quality, is, of course, that it cloaks that original discovery; the penis and vagina are covered over and the pain of making a distinction is therefore dodged. Such evasions can find a political expression. The masking of political decisions by an androgynous leader should therefore be seen for what it is, not as a temporary political stratagem but as a psychopathic phenomenon that will not cease when the immediate political tactic has served its purpose.

As an androgynous Opposition leader, Blair successfully proffered a blurred manifesto to a colluding electorate which, weary of Tory sleaze and the Tory internal strife, wanted change but no pain. But neither the leader's temperament nor the problems to be overcome disappeared when, under Blair's governments, the vague aspirations were, predictably, not converted into defined legislation. And since Blair's psychological problems remain in place and, by default, he gained a second term in office, we are finding as inadequate a response to the real challenges facing Britain as characterised New Labour's first administration.

Soft on the Causes of Crime

The Queen's Speech of December 2000 announced the coming of five anti-crime bills; Blair was determined that the growth in, and the fear of, crime was to be an issue playing a substantial part in the 2001 General Election. It was an issue that Blair handled to his considerable political advantage when, as Shadow Home Secretary, he encapsulated his approach in a notable sound-bite, 'tough on crime, tough on the causes of crime', a comment which straddled both the populist clamour for punishment and the desires of the informed reformists anxious to direct attention to the aetiology of criminal behaviour.

As usual, Blair was attempting to reconcile the irreconcilable for the consensus slogan, although seductive, is flawed. 'Tough' yields to the anger and frustration felt by a community threatened by an anti-social minority but reinforces the illusion that harsh punishment will bring us greater social peace and distracts attention from genuine exploration of the roots of crime; there is no seamless compatibility between advocating both harsh punishments and a focus on the causes of violent crime. Indeed, although greeted with understandable incredulity on the part of those whose bitter experiences of the criminal is limited to being victims of crime, the fact is that punishment is often a lure, not a deterrent, for a considerable section of the criminal caste; and when one explores this bizarre phenomenon, a lead is given directing us to the source of so much delinquent behaviour among the young.

During the last debates in the Commons on the abolition of capital punishment, it fell to me after Sidney Silverman, the renowned abolitionist, had died, to steer the House to an acceptance of the proposition that the temporary suspension of state strangulation should be made final; and during those debates I repeatedly drew attention to the phenomenon of criminals who had become criminals through a sense of guilt engendered in their childhood. I had found that among the murderers whom I had defended there were those who positively resented my efforts to save them from the gallows; they had killed to die, and indeed more than one-third of murderers, when hanging was in place, pre-empted the court's judgement and killed themselves.

These murderers seeking their death sentences were exhibiting the same syndrome that was often presented to me by criminals facing lesser charges who, if I obtained their acquittal, were resentful but, if convicted and given long sentences, would write me long letters of thanks praising my spirited efforts to defend them and never reproaching me for my lack of success.

In those days, as a young solicitor, the accused pariahs of the city of my birth thronged my waiting-room. I would note how soon after the arrest of one of these habitual criminals, his stance and physical appearance improved. His furtive, hangdog look would seem for a while to slough off him. He was no longer as lost as before; he had indeed been found by courteous police, then less brusque than today, had been questioned by the attentive probation officer and had acquired a solicitor who displayed interest in him. He was Somebody. And, when the great day of the trial came, he stood in the very centre of the stage in the elevated dock. Here the stipendiary magistrate, the prosecuting solicitor, the clerk, the evidential rules and indeed the whole process, as well as his own advocate, protected and respected him. In many courts he was addressed as 'Mr' and when he gave his wild fanciful account denying his guilt, his absurd and improbable story was treated with total seriousness. Until sentence was pronounced, for that brief interval, he was a person. Then, thrust back into prison, he lapsed once more into his bewildering anonymity – his name taken from him and a number substituted, garbed impersonally, a nobody, utterly confirmed in his lack of identity.

Yet few of these men really wanted to be acquitted. On the contrary, when I succeeded in persuading the court that the case was not proved beyond reasonable doubt, the client would at most mutter a surly and ungracious thank you. These were the ones who were neurotically burdened with a sense of guilt for the childhood crimes they had committed only in fantasy, who staggered inexorably, like doomeded characters in a Greek tragedy, towards the punishments that they demanded as their right. Lacking the imagination of a Lawrence of Arabia to justify the flagellations for which they ached and which alone could bring temporary relief, such men commit the most petty and stupid of crimes to ensure that the blows of society will fall upon them. To guarantee that their claim for punishment should not be overlooked, some indeed all but leave their visiting-cards behind when they commit their offences. And not infrequently some immediately rush off to the police to enjoy the agony of confession, a few even selecting and insisting on seeing a particular officer in whose presence their self-abasement must be conducted. A very large number, on being challenged, readily offer an incriminating statement which they sign and later repudiate, often suggesting that they have been threatened or beaten into submission by the police. The hapless and embarrassed policeman has in fact only exceptionally yielded in this way to their masochism and in the witness-box tries to step out of the fantasy role which his determined victim, with exquisite delight, projects upon him. The charade is maintained until the very end of the trial and the plea of Not Guilty is insisted upon even after conviction; for this is the only way in which the last remnant of self-respect can be maintained. But the defending solicitor who cheats the accused out of his punishment is not loved. It is true that the accused requires someone to present the denial of his guilt with fervour, so that the shameful need for punishment can remain private, but the most terrible denouement is to be acquitted. Fortunately for him, the whole process of a trial in Britain is so constructed that the sadism of the court and the masochism of the accused, though most amply assuaged, are most decently concealed.

Of course, only a minority of offenders – although a more significant minority than is usually conceded – can confidently be said to be criminals through a sense of guilt; but it is one of the sources of criminal behaviour that particularly mocks the ill-informed view that punishment must necessarily act as a deterrent, and it does direct our attention to the unresolved childhood problems that play so significant a part in adult criminal behaviour.

It is a syndrome, however, that certainly does not stand alone as a warning to those who declare themselves to be 'tough on crime'. Infuriating as it may be to those who believe in longer and longer sentences, it is a fact, well-established clinically, that for some criminals harsh penalties are a provocation. I have often encountered criminals whose responses have made it clear to me that the essential dynamic behind their criminal behaviour was defiance, with the excitement of breaking the prohibition against burgling a house or sexually assaulting a woman being far more important for them than the actual gaining of stolen goods or experiencing the tumescence accompanying their assault. Dr Mervin Glasser, the clinician whose death in 2000 brought to the end a lifetime's work exploring the psychodynamics of criminal behaviour, in writing of sexual crimes, told us:

Careful exploration of the dynamics of the offence will reveal that the pleasure comes as much, if not more, from the excitement of defying the prohibition as from the sexual acts themselves. Criminals know this 'dicing-with-death' thrill very well, even having a term for it, namely the 'adrenalin factor'.

One of the many problems that society therefore has to face in dealing with criminals is that some of them gain their kicks from the knowledge that their deeds are forbidden; for such criminals, the more their deviant behaviour is universally and intensely forbidden, the more attractive is the offence. Since objective scrutinies reveal that punishment can sometimes provoke and attract crime, we are entitled to question the motivation of those who, irrespective of the evidence, remain so possessed by a drive to punish.

All the many Commons debates on penal issues in which I participated, and all the years I spent, often fruitlessly, as a member of the Home Office Advisory Committee on the Penal System, taught me how difficult it is to gain acceptance of the truism that our failure to handle crime arises from our failure to handle ourselves. As Freud put it so tartly, 'the law does not forbid that which man is not prone to do'. Therefore, 'Thou shalt not kill' or 'Thou shalt not covet thy neighbour's wife' are not merely abstract dicta, general, or spontaneously invented prohibitions against the deeds of some few unknown and as yet undiscovered evil men. On the contrary, these are commandments issued for the 'average' man with the 'average' propensity. As the American psychiatrist Gregory Zilboorg once commented:

Cain was not a unique perverted deviation of manhood, and Abraham was not a unique, evil father who in order to flatter the Lord was ready to butcher his son. In other words, the average man is the carrier of the very impulses which are called criminal when they are acted out.

The anxiety, often although not always disproportionate, that crime causes, can spring from our capacity to identify with the criminal's impulse and our fear that we may be tempted to give vent to those impulses within us which are usually inhibited. For millions the temptation can be dampened by reading detective stories and viewing televised murder mysteries; but the anxieties of some, like former Home Secretary Michael Howard, can be quieted down only in sudden unconscious denial of any similarity with the criminal; then, through repressive penal policies, they hurl themselves upon the criminal with all the power of their displaced aggressive, punitive, destructive hostility.

Howard epitomised all the qualities of the hang-them-flog-them brigade. I always found him to be a ninny; the first time I sought to engage him in conversation when we were leaving a committee together he behaved like a frightened rabbit caught in the headlights and he literally then, and subsequently, scarpered away from me the moment it seemed we would encounter each other. His growing reputation among many as the worst home secretary of the twentieth century is well deserved. His desperate, over-determined macho display was, in my opinion, one of the symptoms of his incapacity to come to terms with his own unconscious aggressivity, which he hurled upon miscreants even as the Mrs Grundys of this world lament and condemn the sexual peccadilloes of those they envy.

What is humiliating to those of us belonging to Old Labour has been the sight of New Labour's me-too-ism. Howard's April 1996 white paper casting aside the accumulated evidence that prison should, in the interests of our society, be used as a last resort and that crime was closely related to social deprivation, was substantially left unchallenged by Her Majesty's Opposition. It is painfully ironic that it was left to the

Lord Chief Justice and his fellow judges to declare that Howard's white paper proposals constituted 'a perversion of justice', a condemnation using language accurately describing the nature of those proposals.

But no such unequivocal condemnation came from Labour's front bench. How could it? Fearful that a frontal attack on the proposals would subvert the leader's affirmation that he was 'tough on crime', his satrap Shadow Home Secretary was dumb; only the judiciary sought to stem the tide of populism that penal issues can rouse. And now, while the judiciary still endeavours to stem that tide of populism, Blair and Blunkett together continue to peddle the illusory belief that custodial punishments will act as effective deterrents. In April 2003, Blunkett announced yet another emergency building programme, one intended to provide more than 1,000 extra places by 2005 at a cost of £138 million; in vain did penal reformers protest that the building of the new prison cells would make little difference to the yawning gap between available places and the spiralling numbers being jailed, and that the same money spent on developing effective community sentences and remedial treatment would have a much greater impact.

It is easier to go with the tide, and a leader who, as has been repeatedly stressed in this book, is so troubled in coming to terms with his own aggression is far more comfortable in joining the chorus of condemnation of the anti-social delinquent than in daring to focus on the epicentre of the eruption of criminal violence which we are witnessing. That epicentre, whether one surveys the desolate inner city areas teeming with unemployed youth or the drug scene of children of dual-earning parents, is within our crumbling, stress-ridden family system. If there is a diffidence in probing the disorders to be found there, it is because such an exploration, as a preliminary to a salutary response, means that we often consequently have to confront our own disorders; and that is discomfiting. It is so much easier to deny our own disarray and then vengefully to lament the visible and dangerous expression of our turbulence in others.

Once I came so dangerously near to that epicentre of crime that I could not escape without being scorched. When I insisted, as a member of the Home Office Advisory Committee on the Penal System, that the issue of conjugal visits for very long-term prisoners should be considered, I assumed that those prisoners were suffering the same sense of deprivation as so many of us did in wartime when serving overseas on isolated postings in desert or jungle. However, as I moved through our maximum-security prisons discussing the issue with the possible beneficiaries, I found the suggestion strangely causing as much consternation to them as it did to the Home Office officials. The men I was meeting were, for the most part, professional criminals, thoroughly committed to a life of crime, who had mixed freely among the criminal underworld; most of them were physically tough and vigorous, and under 35 years of age; they had committed homicide or near-homicide in pursuance of robbery, and were violent and ruthless. Many of their crimes were ambitious and daring; jewel thefts and massive wage snatches were part of their way of life. Yet these desperadoes, including some of the train robbers, beneath their bravado quivered like jellies when one discussed with them the possibility of conjugal visits.

It is not easy to discuss sex, within a prison environment, with an inmate. Apart from the obvious difficulty that the prisoner speedily discerns the sexual viewpoint of the enquirer, and so gives distorted but acceptable replies, there is also the danger that genuine confidences in this domain can become a sort of sexual complicity between the subject and the investigator. The complicity can be experienced as embarrassment or pleasure and, in either event, the confidences may bear little relation to reality. The investigation, insensitively conducted, can indeed falsify its objective and I fear that initially, unaware of what dangerous ground I trod, I proceeded most clumsily.

I was therefore taken aback to find that most of these men proffered to me all the arguments against conjugal visits that I had heard less skilfully assembled by their jailers. All the practical difficulties of arranging conjugal visits in conditions that combined security with decency were elaborated upon to me by these prim thugs; and they were certainly not slow to damp down my liberal reforming zeal by pointing out the consequences of many fatherless children likely to be born. The tension I sensed when the matter was broached, and their eagerness to shift the conversation to other minor grievances, when seen as a recurring pattern, put me on guard and eventually gave me more insight into their problem.

I was, in fact, cheating and they did not like it. The rules of the game were well understood by them and the prison authorities and I was not observing well-established regulations. A conspiracy existed between jailer and jailed; the prisoner was reduced to his desired level of a pre-pubertal child and, in return, he received tranquillity. The pretence that it was his confinement not his fear that prevented an adult sexual attitude was under no circumstances to be commented on; while, in the maximum-security blocks with walls covered with pin-ups, these gangsters swaggered and boasted of their past criminality, they had the excuse that only the prison walls prevented them from being great lovers. The truth was otherwise; the overwhelming majority of them had had no regular relationship with any woman at the time of their arrest.

In the prisons they were back in childhood; even as, when infants, the father was the law imposing his will upon them, so now as adults, on the occasion of transgression, they were subject to an all-powerful authority. And they were accepting their quiescent sexuality with relief, for these were flawed men. All of us must, after puberty, break through parental authority to become sexually mature; but to achieve such adulthood means a successful revolt against the father. But we rebel successfully only if we can do this without excessive fear; and these were men who feared freedom.

They yearned to shelter behind an authority, behind the prison's walls, renouncing their maleness in return for protection even as they had, out of terror, subjected themselves to parental authority. For all these killers and brutes came from rejecting, disordered and deprived homes and these miserable men had received no love to temper the fear that we all must overcome to replace our own fathers. It is not surprising that the talk of conjugal relations disturbed them; they knew it was not sex of which we spoke, but of the constrained freedom of adulthood limited by obligations of family, friends, work and society, and this was the type of freedom which frightened them out of their wits. Onanism was their preferred choice; they wanted to be left to their childish sexual activities.

Almost all these damaged men were the products of a brutalised childhood, cursed with violent fathers or a series of intimidating surrogates who from time to time lived with their unmarried or deserted mothers. And as long as the incidence of such precarious family units increases, so, despite all the growth in the number and length of custodial sentences, will the number of criminals abroad multiply in our society. We can fill our stinking jails so, as now, they contain more prisoners than ever before in our history and we can embark on building more and more jails, but unless we address ourselves to the abject failure and incapacity of hundreds of thousands of frail family units to socialise their children into law-abiding citizens, we shall end up beleaguered, as in many parts of the United States, in our own homes.

Thousands of children from low-income and single-parent homes are presently being expelled, because of their uncontrollable violence, from schools in the deprived urban areas; they are being left to roam the streets to begin their careers in crime. To respond to these kids' dilemmas and all the havoc they create in their neighbourhoods with 'lock them up', 'curfew' and 'tough on crime' slogans is sheer self-indulgence; they will as adults return in kind the hostility we direct at them.

Not all crimes are spawned in our run-down, working-class estates; nevertheless, the bulk of crime does come from our lumpen proletariat, a class which is growing, not diminishing. The number of people in Britain classified as 'very poor', as the Joseph Rowntree Foundation December 2000 report made clear, has increased by half-a-million since 1997 when Labour came to power; and during that same period, the number of children in Young Offenders institutions has continued to increase; 4,000 children between ten and sixteen years of age spent time in custody in 1999.

It is, of course, not only the children of the poor who are vulnerable and who in turn will make us vulnerable; the equation is not necessarily a simple one between poverty and crime. The children within the dual-income family are often as much at risk and as emotionally abandoned as the truants on the streets of the inner cities. Home-making and child-rearing are more important than designing computer software or marketing box files, and a country that wants to feel safe needs to re-evaluate the worth of unpaid domestic work, whether done by women or men, and then be prepared to pay the cost that such a recasting of our societal values would entail.

But such a recasting requires the reshaping of the economy; it needs a defiant government prepared, as was the Labour government of 1945–51, to challenge all the inimical vested interests which New Labour in government so readily now accommodates. Those of us left who were brought up in the 1930s in distressed areas like South Wales know how profound were the changes in the quality of life that came about for millions as a result of the legislation of the first postwar government; and now, when comparable drastic changes are required, we should recall that those changes were not achieved by accommodation. Even the most benign of changes, like those heralded by the National Health Service Act, were opposed in the Commons by the Tories, who echoed the initial and almost unanimous opposition of the medical profession. No quarter was given or received as postwar Labour created the welfare state and put heavy industry and the utilities under public control.

At the least, a genuine response to the growth of crime requires massive investment in the inner cities, augmentation and considerable funding of all our family support services, including adolescent units staffed by child analysts and psychologists, far more teachers appropriately trained in the laggard overstretched schools in problem areas, social workers who have received far more rigorous training than at present, screening and shaping of those working in our children's homes, costly retraining of prison officers so that they could become rehabilitation carers and not turnkeys, and a recognition that a parent should, by subsidy and tax relief, be enabled to remain at home during the child's early years.

Such programmes have to be paid for and that means a redistribution of wealth, a readiness to strip the City of its fiscal and other privileges, and a frank acknowledgement that financial sacrifices will have to be made by those well able to bear them. It means the breaking-up, not the creation and sustaining, of a governing consensus that exacerbates our present ills, and excites the growth of violent crime. It means a programme which, by temperament rather than by ideology, Blair is inhibited from enacting.

Fellow-feeling of the Unsound

During and after the 1992 US presidential elections Blair and his young political pups became intemperate disciples of Clinton and his advisers. Dazzled by Clinton's electoral success and interpreting the victory as a triumph for the tactic of abandoning traditional interest groups, rust belts and rainbow coalitions, and appealing to middle suburban America, Blair, despite vigorous protests by John Prescott and 'Old' Labour, imported a copycat campaign and proceeded to Clintonise the Labour Party. 'New' Labour was to follow in the wake of 'New' Democrats.

By 1994 the Clinton programme was in complete disarray; a disenchanted electorate, viewing the shambles, returned a hard-right Republican Congress which proceeded to dismantle all the social and welfare gains made by liberal America over the last generation. Clinton's domestic débâcle had been total and Blair, seeing his admired mentor's dissolution, was temporarily nonplussed. His biographer John Rentoul concedes: 'Blair's response to Clinton's failure was weak and unconvincing.' Blair, says Rentoul, 'implied that the President lacked the determination to pursue New Democrat policies in office . . . you don't run on one basis and govern on another'. As Prime Minister, that was precisely the course Blair was to follow, for

the inhibitor that crippled Clinton's 'determination' was of
similar order to that which maims Blair.

Blair did not dare, in 1994, to diagnose the cause of Clinton's
speedy retreat for that would bring him too near an insight into
his own dilemma. Blair and Clinton have indeed much in
common. It is not, however, simply – as one Tory back-bencher
tartly commented – that 'Blair is Clinton with his zip done up'.
What they share and what has been so determinant in their
conduct of public affairs are the unmetabolised early traumatic
experiences which both endured and with which neither has
successfully come to terms.

In Clinton, Blair found a fellow-sufferer, a carrier of the
virus that cannot tolerate a seriously conflictual political
environment, for that evokes the agonising pains of unendurable early years. The irony, of course, of those politicians
afflicted with the virus is that they provoke the very conditions
that they desperately wish to avoid. So often unconsciously
they recapitulate on the political scene the endless conflicts of
their early childhood; and then, having raised the storm, cannot
face the tumult.

Clinton never escaped in his politics from this compulsion to
re-enact the searing and violent domestic quarrels between his
alcoholic stepfather and his self-willed and hot-tempered
mother. In his private life, fellatio has been such a re-
enactment; there he found the pleasures of the earliest pains of
his childhood for, such is our biological endowment, pain and
pleasure are never far apart. And perhaps no physical act can
more nicely bring together, for both parties, a greater simultaneous release of sadism and masochism. But, as in his private
Oval Room antics, so in the public determinations that took
place in his sanctum; there, as in every other public office he
has held, he became the centre of extraordinary controversy.
Even as he was forever declaring his distaste for conflict, he
provoked it, continuing to feel that he must be, as he has said in
his own words, 'conflict adverse'. He sought to work out this

feeling benignly – as in his interventions in Northern Ireland and in the Israeli-Palestinian disputes. But he was entrapped; out of conscious control, he was destined to create turbulences which he then feared to withstand.

To the odd exemplars within his pantheon, from Macmurray to Jagger, Blair, moved by his penchant for narcissistic choices, readily added Clinton, the man whose appalling childhood has so maimed his decisiveness; in Clinton, Blair found a man whose early traumas exceed even his own. Clinton's father died before the son was born; and the third man the mother then married was a violent alcoholic, ready to display and use a gun in the domestic brawls which were part of the sado-masochistic background to Bill Clinton's childhood. By the time Clinton was fourteen years old, the growing son, to protect his mother, was breaking down locked doors to gain entry into rooms where the stepfather was beating up his wife; at fifteen, Bill Clinton was swearing a deposition against his stepfather after calling the police to the home to arrest the violent man; but the mother, within three months of divorcing him, remarried him. Clinton was fated to be brought up in a household in almost constant disarray, where a minor disagreement could speedily explode into violence.

And that recall dogged him in all his political dealings. An immature electorate, thirsting for 'strong' leadership, within a year of his election had turned on him as awareness grew that rather than confront, rather than face down the vested interests assailing him, Clinton would concede. His self-acknowledged 'conflict adverse' temperament left him fair game for his challengers; it was precisely because of what they perceived as his wimpishness that the Republicans, overreaching them-selves, challenged him in 1996 over the US budget deficit issue. Their divisions, and the tactics of Clinton's advisers, temporarily disadvantaged them, but in the end the substantive issues were decided as the Republicans demanded. Clinton, aided by his populist foreign adventures, had his second term but it was largely on Republican terms. And when the time came for him to depart, there was so little to distinguish the parties that the electorate, with the aid of a disgracefully partisan Supreme Court, and despite low unemployment, plummeting crime, unprecedented economic growth and all the advantages of incumbency, handed over the reins to atavistic America. After all the brave words uttered in Clinton's first presidential election campaign, after enjoying two terms in office, the world found the most powerful nation on earth firmly in the grip of corporate America.

That was Clinton's legacy and it sprang, above all, from his fear of confronting the powerful. The new president's father, George Bush senior, once advised us to read his lips; but in the case of men with personal biographies such as those of Clinton and Blair, it is not their lips we should read but their persistent smiles. Both are nervous smilers, the smiles of men with an almost pathological fear of offending, hiding the anger behind their smiles, fearful of venting their rage. The frequent inappropriateness of their responses found in their countenances is what we can expect from them when they are faced with the political choice fight or flight; always fearful of triggering off the destructive power of their early traumas, too often their response is excessively placatory, desperate to create a consensus when it cannot, or should not, exist.

Still smiling, in December 2000 at Warwick University, the two men, accompanied by their wives, joined together in a mutual admiration society bade farewell to each other. Absurdly, Blair declaimed that the kinship between them reflected the kinship between the American and British people. The use of the word 'kin' jarred; there is no consanguinity between the Hispanics and Asiatics of California, the Cubans in Florida, the blacks incarcerated in the maximum security prisons of mid and southern America, or the Jews of New York. But that there came into existence a warm emotional friendship between the two men, there can be no doubt; it was based on fellow-feelings of the unsound, each man unable to handle his basic instincts: Clinton, notoriously in trouble with his sexuality and Blair with his aggressivity.

The consequences of that relationship for Britain, and indeed Europe, have been dire. It has been little remarked upon, but I have no doubt that when future historians review the last decade of the twentieth century they will find in that unhealthy relationship the source of one of the greatest missed opportunities our continent has ever experienced. When Blair became leader of the Labour Party and later Prime Minister, Neil Kinnock, to his credit, privately used all his endeavours to persuade Blair to establish a rapport with the socialist leaders in Europe; and, through the meetings which Kinnock set up, it began to look as if Europe could be re-shaped into a demo-cratic socialist continent. With Jospin in power in France, with a left-centre coalition in place in Italy, with a zealous German finance minister, Oskar Lafontaine, dominating Germany's political scene, the stage was set; but it was not to be. Blair cooled, even as his relationship with Clinton warmed. Blair, so ready to give public support to Clinton when the president was squirming amid personal scandal, extended no aid to Lafontaine as reactionary domestic and international forces bore down upon the socialist minister, and in March 1999 those forces succeeded in bringing about Lafontaine's removal. The moment that could have been a turning-point in Europe's history came and went; and now the swings to the right-wing in Europe have led to the dubious Berlusconi presiding over Italy, and to Chirac, a man whose private financial affairs are as murky as his public dealings, ruling France; the great opportunity has, tragically, been lost and is unlikely ever to return.

When a rallying call to Europe came from Blair, it was to be for another cause. With Robin Cook acting as his satrap, he released all his bottled-up aggression against Milosevic and incited Europe and the USA to embark upon a Balkan war, one that was illegal by any international rules of law, and one that was to show up Western humanitarianism as a sham, a cover for the exploitation of foreign affairs for domestic ends; one that, without fear of effective retaliation, could be used as an exquisite vehicle to carry Blair's aggression.

No true scrutiny can be made of Blair's extraordinary insistence, under the guise of humanitarianism – often to the unease and astonishment of his European allies – on intervening so aggressively in the Balkans imbroglio without taking into account the boy Blair's fears in what we have described as the 'house of secrets'; there, as we have emphasised, he was ever frightened that he was being pursued by an invisible disabler intent on mowing down his family, and that if he responded provocatively, he would certainly be the next victim. Then, in the Balkans, at last, he found an opportunity to release his aggression without that fear of fatal retaliation.

History without biography is taxidermy; and few events in my lifetime have more dramatically illustrated that adage than the Balkan conflict. After being denied a theatre for so long, a bloody performance was enacted by a cast all of whom learned their scripts, and have never forgotten them, in their earliest boyhoods. It was upon the Balkan stage that Blair, as one of the principal players, had his catharsis; with Clinton's NATO to shield him, he dared to purge himself of the fears of retribution that haunted his childhood; he released his aggression against a faraway target, well-distanced from the consequences.

The aggressive zeal Blair has brought to his 'humanitarian' intervention has been boundless; when he floated his ploy to send ground troops into Kosovo, the Italian Prime Minister initially demurred and even the German Chancellor pronounced it mad; but Britain's brave premier dismissed and overcame their timorousness. He flew to Washington and lured Clinton to become further involved in a war that gave the President an opportunity both to distract domestic attention from his sexual adventures and, by an over-determined display of bellicosity, to overcome the guilt of his pusillanimous draft-dodging past.

Once upon a time, but in my time, there was an Old Labour prime minister, a major with a good war record, and one not given to extravagant historical gestures, who, in dangerous times, had also flown to America; there he dramatically succeeded in stopping the president from yielding to his frustrated generals urging the atom bomb be dropped upon North Korea. Now we have witnessed a New Labour prime minister, well-adorned in designer clothes – including those suitable for refugee camp visits – but one who, unlike Clement Attlee and my generation, has never worn uniform, inciting an American president to spread, not contain, war.

Responsibility for the Balkan war cannot, however, be said to lie exclusively on the shoulders of Blair, Clinton and, of course, the evil Milosevic. German leaders too, from both ends of the political spectrum, from Christian Democrats and Social Democrats alike, have played a sinister contributory role. It was Kohl who broke ranks with the European Community and gave a premature and fatal recognition to Slovenia and Croatia without initially even asking for guarantees for the protection of the Serb minorities in those states. In the face of avowed opposition of the UN Secretary-General, it was Germany that used its economic muscle to dragoon its EC partners into accepting that position; and spuriously claiming, on the basis of reports by pliant leading German international lawyers, that Germany's interference in the internal affairs of the former Yugoslavia was proper, it enthusiastically gave legitimacy to the break-up of Yugoslavia. No less enthusiastically, responding to the importuning of Blair and Clinton, Germany, now under Social Democratic leadership, eagerly embraced the opportunity to become actively involved in the illegal Kosovo war.

The political leaders of Germany so readily responded because they suffer from the same syndrome as is the constant in Blair's psychic make-up: they too cannot handle their aggression, although in their case that incapacity comes from social rather than individual circumstances.

Chancellor Gerhardt Schröder, Joschka Fischer (Foreign Secretary and leader of the Green Party), and Rudolf Scharping (Minister of Defence) were born in 1944, 1948 and 1947 respectively; all belong to the post-World War II generation; all are men who grew up in the physically hard conditions of the time of the immediate postwar years when large areas of Germany were still under rubble, food supplies were scarce and there were losses to be mourned in almost every family; a scrutiny of their personal biographies reveals that in addition to these grim burdens, all of them suffered within their families or schools severe and sometimes abusive treatment from authoritarian regimes.

The utter helplessness they felt as children was to be echoed and repeated when, as students, they became part of the 'generation '68' and were to find that all their protests against the conservative establishment during their rebellion and during the seventies were to come to naught. The authorities had the whip hand – and the lasting experience these men were fated to endure was of political impotence. They, as politicians, could find no adequate relief for their aggression or any outlet for their need to avenge their humiliations; like sex, aggression, as Blair so notably demonstrates, cannot be extinguished. Fischer extravagantly endeavoured to outlaw his aggression by becoming, for a decade, an absolute pacifist eschewing all violence; but this attempt, like those of his colleagues who were to become the German war Cabinet in the Kosovo war, was a failure; when finally, thirty years after the 1968 events, the much longed for opportunity was there, these men found it irresistible and whooped in triumph at finding that with NATO approval they could, although largely vicariously, participate in the Balkan war.

In an interview about the Rambouillet negotiations, before the war had escalated, the swaggering Fischer boasted: 'I had to decide about the question of war or peace.' Indeed, he did make his lamentable contribution. It was the Germans in particular who arranged the peace negotiations in Rambouillet in such a way that they inevitably ended in deadlock. By using military threats to try and force the signature of the proposed treaty, and by giving an ultimatum, the NATO members themselves created the situation of 'no alternative' which they then used to explain their subsequent bombing campaign. It is impossible then, now that we wish to exculpate modern Germany and its modern democracy from Hitler's evils, not to feel an unease when we see, as we did in 1999, the subterranean forces that can still be triggered off. The Nazi inheritance is not easily jettisoned.

When the German leaders, together with Blair and Clinton, blessed the NATO onslaught on Belgrade, they, by indulging their emotional needs, established a strange symbiotic relationship with Milosevic. Blair, Clinton and the German leaders responded to all the masochistic yearnings of Milosevic. The reclusive and depressive Serbian leader emerged from a family possessed by a death-wish; both his parents, separately and after an interval of some years, committed suicide; upon his psyche is embossed the legend of the heroic Prince Lazar, defeated and killed fighting against the Turks in the battle of Kosovo in the fourteenth century. Milosevic has identified himself with Lazar, who has long assumed Christ-like proportions in Serbia's history and epic poetry; the sick attractions of victory or death, of triumph or martyrdom, are for Milosevic equally seductive. A stately and deadly pavane was danced in which the participants, Blair, Clinton, Milosevic and the German leaders, all followed the steps ordained for them by their earliest environments which, tragically for them and for us, they are never able to transcend.

Any serious scrutiny of the profiles of the German leaders – as of Blair, Clinton and Milosevic – chasteningly tells us the limitations of any historiographer who seeks to diminish the importance of the role of the individual in the determination of events. If, above the din of the Balkans cacophony, we hear and accurately interpret the lessons of the Balkan war, which have been taught to us in a dozen languages in Central and Eastern Europe, we certainly need to be mindful of Disraeli's provocative advice: 'Read no history; nothing but biography for that is life without theory.'

Today, with Milosevic standing trial at The Hague and powerless – except to promote a dangerous myth of martyrdom by committing suicide – Blair would claim justification and vindication and victory for his war of intervention in the same terms as he did when he reported to Parliament in July 1999:

> Between March and June 1999, almost 900,000 Kosovo Albanians were expelled from their homeland, with hundreds of thousands more forced into hiding within Kosovo itself. We could not stand by while ethnic atrocities on this scale were carried out in Europe, and as a humanitarian catastrophe unfolded before our eyes. That is why NATO, with the UK playing a leading part, launched the successful campaign of air strikes against Yugoslavia.
>
> The professionalism and bravery of the armed services has secured all our objectives.
>
> Serb forces have completed their withdrawal.
>
> NATO forces and partners have deployed throughout Kosovo to secure the peace.
>
> The refugees are returning home. Building a more secure future for the whole of the Balkans, based on democracy, prosperity, and respect for human rights, has begun under a UN interim administration.

But this Panglossian perception of the war and its consequences is not shared by those making more realistic appraisals. Simon Jenkins, formerly a *Times* editor and now a columnist for that newspaper, is one who certainly learned the most important lesson to be drawn from Blair's having dragged us, the EU and the United States, into the Balkans conflict. In November 1999 he wrote:

> Humanitarian intervention is a code for political and military meddling in the internal affairs of foreign sovereign states – and damn the consequences . . . What began as humanitarian action in Yugoslavia has so far cost $11 billion in warfare alone. A further $60 billion of cost (according to *The Economist* Intelligence Unit) has been inflicted by the NATO intervention; that does not include the blocking of the Danube. At the end more people are displaced than at the start. If the Balkans is the outcome of 'not standing idly by', God stands for idleness.

But not in Blair's copy of the gospel; he has persistently shown himself to be bent upon compounding the consequences of ill-considered interventionism. By 2001, he was laying claim to being the galvaniser for the creation of a European 'Rapid Reaction Force' (RRF) to which, he pledged, Britain would initially supply 12,500 troops from a pool of about double that amount, as well as 72 aircraft and eighteen surface ships, including an aircraft carrier. This whole concept was befuddled; the mood swings occasioned by Blair's unanchored aggressivity are reflected in the varying roles that he and his ministers wished to assign to this new interventionist force; it was to be used 'to deal with Europe's back-yard', to engage in operations ranging from humanitarian and rescue missions to peace-keeping, and to undertake 'tasks of combat forces in crisis management' and would, too, be available to help 'resolve a crisis between two warring countries or factions'.

Inevitably, the scheme was seen as a predictable successor to all the other failures of tokenism in international affairs, one akin to the empty words of the League of Nations that encouraged the rise of Fascism, and the laggardliness of the United Nations to live up to its charter. When the RRF proposal attracted derision from all quarters, from Thatcher to CND, and from both sides of the Atlantic, Blair, characteristically, took fright about permitting the release of his aggression in the form of RRF. In a flurry, always, as ever, unconsciously fearing retaliatory punishment, he sought to protect himself from his demons by placing checks upon the violences he would permit the RRF to inflict; none would be permitted without consultation with the Americans first or if a proposed action should threaten our reliance upon NATO; more, unanimity in the European Council of Ministers would also be a prerequisite to action. And, as if these checks to swift responses were not enough, from Downing Street came the statement: 'Each country would need to decide whether their own troops should be involved.'

Blair, like a stammerer who uses his disability to inhibit the revengeful oaths that otherwise would be uttered, strives from time to time to clamp down upon his own precariously contained violences. He reverts to form: one step forward, two steps back. The obstacles he attempted to place on the use of force by Europe's 'rapid reaction' army fully reflected the internal struggle of the man, and that unresolved strife resulted, as the *Sunday Times* pronounced, in him attempting to provide 'something that sounds more like Monsieur Hulot's army than a cohesive force with clear objectives'.

We can laugh at French comedians' ataxic behaviour; but it is dismaying to see our Prime Minister so afflicted. The need for a political leadership in Europe which is able to make a cool and effective assessment of our continent's future defence needs has never been greater. By his fumbling role in the proposed RRF Blair, shaped by the fraught exigencies of his childhood, showed himself to be singularly disqualified to meet that challenge. Inevitably, our European partners, weary of Blair's vacillations and of his total submission to Bush's warmongering, are taking steps to ensure that the defence of their countries is not, like Britain's, utterly dependent upon the caprices of the Pentagon. In April 2003 the leaders of France, Germany, Belgium and Luxembourg decided to set up a multinational deployable force which they hope will eventually lead to the formation of a European security and defence union containing as many EU countries as possible.

In the meantime, while these European countries in their defence policy endeavour to disengage from Bush's clumsy and dangerous embrace, Blair, flushed and aglow after the victory in Iraq, is in danger of yielding yet more to the American President's opportunings. Bush, not content to end in May 2003 the Clinton era's ban on research and development of low-yield nuclear weapons for battlefield use, remains fully committed to his disastrous ballistic missile defence project; for that he needs the full facilities at Fylingdales in Yorkshire. To grant him his wish would be, for Britain, an awesome decision. Up to the Iraq war Blair, struggling Laocoön-like with his own aggressivity, hesitated. With Clinton and his special talent to procrastinate no longer available to rescue him from his dilemma, and compromised by his alliance with Bush, the hazards of a dangerous misjudgement are now increased.

It is not extravagant to suggest that it is a decision that can put at risk not only Britain's security but that of the world; it would bring about the end of the anti-ballistic treaty of 1972, signed by the USA and Russia. It inevitably means that if the USA were to feel it was protected by the ballistic missile defence system, Russia and China would feel they had lost their deterrents and were at the mercy of corporate American capitalism; they would feel compelled to restore the balance by increasing their nuclear arsenal. A new nuclear arms race would ensue. The fulfilment or the sabotage of such apocalyptic foreboding depends to a considerable extent upon one man – Blair. Given his incapacity to handle his own aggression, dare we continue to place our destiny in his hands?

A Bible Story

Like Bush, Blair is a great believer that God is on his side and, like every suicide bomber, he believes too in heaven. No matter that the Pope and the Archbishop of Canterbury condemned the Iraq war, his personal communing with the Lord as he meditates during his incessant Bible-reading has left Blair confident that when the day comes for him to appear before God, the Lord's judgement and his own will happily coincide. Even though his decisions led to the deaths of thousands, he has no qualms about this summit meeting: 'I am ready to meet my Maker and answer for those who died as a result of my decisions.' When he joined Bush in unleashing war upon Iraq, he was simply 'doing what was right' – and this God-blessed mantra he ever reasserts.

Cleansed by the prayers that precede every one of his Cabinet meetings and with all his sin thus projected upon the 'axis of evil', Bush has not even a turbulent priest from Canterbury, as has Blair, to temper his Messianic mission. America, a nation of church-goers, with invocations to God being part of the national conversation, has, over the last twenty years, increasingly hearkened to the leaders of the burgeoning Pentecostal movement. The longstanding American churches – Catholic, Presbyterian, Episcopalian and Methodist – have been haemorrhaging members to the Pentecostals, who take scripture as the literal word of God and believe in salvation earned by individual virtue rather than via the mediation of a church. As Will Hutton has commented:

> The Republicans have struck a Faustian pact with the Pentecostal movement; they will concede its arguments that abortion and even stem-cell research are against Biblical text in return for the Church mobilising its members to vote Republican.

This is no cynical misalliance; the Republican high command are as fervent in their faith as any Pentecostal preacher. Today even the most routine meeting of interest groups with the administration is punctuated by calls to pray for guidance from God and the Bible. No distinction is made between religion and politics; America, they claim, is mired in the moral decay of the Clinton era and only by the fervent celebration of patriotism and religion will the character of the nation be rebuilt. American imperialism, following yesterday's British imperialism, goes on the rampage with the sword in one hand and the Bible in the other. Such a display of enthusiasm is not uncongenial to Blair; he has shown that provided the Bible is held up high, he is ready to join the crusade.

In May 2003 when questioned as to what had helped him to get through his recent trials, Blair spoke of his regular religious readings; given that the results in the local and regional council elections had spelled out how, over his Iraq stance, he had estranged British Muslims, unsurprisingly he told of how, in addition to the Bible, he was now turning to the Koran. Expediency and his penchant for the ecumenical dovetailed, leaving him to stress to his American interviewer, David Margolick:

> The remarkable thing about the Koran is that, if any Christian or Jew reads it, everything it talks about is entirely identifiable to us. It contains lavish descriptions of the Old Testament stories.

One of those 'lavish' Old Testament stories is certainly 'identifiable' with Blair. Our impatience with our premier as a simplistic exegete of the Bible should not deter us from attempting a more sophisticated interpretation of the tales that hold Blair in thrall. More so, since at least one of those stories helps us again to elucidate the central personal dilemma which, to our considerable disadvantage, he lacks the capacity to resolve; the constantly smiling man who, his aides say, never shows anger, ever fearing the consequences of the release of his aggression, disavowing conflict and preaching consensus and 'big tent' political theories, is so bottled up that in the end, he inevitably implodes, and the fallout is to be seen among debris covering the slaughtered children of Baghdad.

No tale of a man struggling, as does Blair, with his aggression has a longer lineage than that recounted in Genesis 32. Sometimes overtly, sometimes disguised, sometimes depicted by Renaissance painters or contemporary sculptors, always in every kosher restaurant, the story, slyly or brazenly, is told of the greatest unarmed struggle ever known, of a wrestling match between two well-matched protagonists that lasted a whole night, leaving the victor wounded but in sufficient rude health to establish the State of Israel.

So awesome and explosive is the story, that, unlike the original chronicler, subsequent editors and interpreters of the Bible have created a new title for the tale, 'Jacob and the Angel', in order to temper the combustibility of the original. But there is no angel – and never was; neither in the original Hebrew nor in the King James edition of the Bible does any angel appear. Jacob wrestled with the Man, and so terrifying was that Man that to avoid contemplating the vengefulness of this terminator, he has been metamorphosed by subsequent chroniclers into an angel; thus garbed, it is hoped that the hint that he may be an avenging angel is well-concealed within the drapery that always covers up well brought up angels. The story is thus transmitted in Sunday-schools, *cheders* – and doubtless in the *madrasés* – and, stripped of its homoerotic undertones, continues to reduce this stupendous wrestling match to a boisterous romp which ended in one of the participants suffering a little hurt.

Although attempts have thus been made to sanitise this tale of fierce aggressivity, the sinister Bible story remains. Thousands of years after the first telling of this tribal tale, the story resonates with everyman's continuing predicament, one never resolved by Blair – the Oedipal dilemma of the son who, to achieve his own individuation, must needs overcome his father and yet continue to love him and to be loved by him. For the Man with whom Jacob wrestles, and whom the chronicler is too careful to name, is the father, behind whom looms God, the father of us all.

This then is the story of the ambivalent incestuous love that dare not tell its name. The allegory of Jacob and the Man is a marvellous story of how a son's determination, after decades of acceptance of his exploitation, tardily but effectively released his aggression and overcame his oppressive father-figures; it is a rich illustration of one man's successful negotiation of that fateful rite of passage.

Initially, the chronicler hesitated explicitly to recite this story so seductively redolent with fearful intimations of the ultimate taboo. Jacob's Oedipal struggle is first cunningly displaced from one with his father to one with his oppressive father-in-law, Laban. To gain his beloved Rachel, Jacob was required to work for Laban for seven years; then Laban cheated him and by a stratagem ensured that Leah, his elder daughter, was taken to Jacob's marriage bed; to gain Rachel, therefore, Jacob had to work a further seven years. In all, Jacob's working life – and sexual life – were controlled by his father-in-law for twenty years; then he could suppress his resentments and aggressions no longer and, because he still could not dare a confrontation with Laban, he fled secretly with his wives and sheep to establish his own domain.

But the chronicler knows that thus recounted, the story is only half told and he finally summons up the courage to complete the tale. After sending his entourage ahead, leaving himself all alone, Jacob prepared for his real confrontation, a night-time demand to his progenitor that he should be granted his manumission and no longer submit to patriarchal commands. With the demand not heeded, the awesome power struggle ensued.

Jacob was not to have an easy victory. The castrating Man endeavoured to tear the balls off him but, missing the target, wrenched the hollow of Jacob's thigh, leaving Jacob limping. Every Jewish boy brought up in an observant home knows this detail; for Genesis commands that to ensure we remember the dangerous grappling, the veins of a cow's thigh must never be eaten. Since the costly procedure of removing the sciatic nerve and other tendons and arteries is the prerequisite of observance of that biblical injunction, Orthodox Jews do not eat the hind quarters of a cow; as a boy, filet mignon was denied to me in my mother's house and as every gourmet knows, no good steak and chips is ever available at a kosher restaurant.

These are whimsical consequences of the myth; there are more sombre sequelae. When the dawn broke and the exhausted Man conceded defeat, the occasion was acknowledged by Jacob contemptuously repudiating the name given to him by his father: henceforth he was to be Israel, blessed with inheritance of lands promised by God to his grandfather Abraham. Nowadays in the Middle Eastern Jewish state bearing Israel's name, rabid right-wing Jewish settlers, backed by American Pentecostals, draw on the myth to 'prove' their title to land on the West Bank in occupied Palestine.

Withal, the myth has, however, grander and nobler themes. The Jewish biblical myths are never entirely fanciful and are invariably didactic; the telling of this wrestling match is a moral exhortation. It addresses the problem with which, as part of our maturation from dependency to adulthood, all must wrestle: how to dare to give up enjoying the shelter and security that masochistic submission affords, to break the chains of our bondage and, abandoning passivity, turn around our masochism into well-directed aggression, in the therapeutic rite of passage that destiny demands of mankind.

Peniel, the name in Hebrew of the place where the significant struggle occurred, tells us that Jacob stood up to face the Man direct and give his forceful but measured response in such a fashion that when he became Israel, his own man, he still retained the affection of the Man who then bountifully blessed him. The happy resolution of a man coming to terms with his own aggression was never better told. One night, more than two millennia later, far from Peniel, high in the mountains of the Pyrenees, the irresolute British Prime Minister was similarly to be engaged in a wrestling match with the Man; but his was a fight that was to get disastrously out of control.

In August 2002 Blair, putting aside the brewing Iraq crisis, went, as in previous years, for a day's hike with a friend in the Pyrenees. Before the day was over, his friend had persuaded him to stay overnight in a chalet-hotel in the mountains; it was to prove a fateful night for Blair and for Britain. His friend was later to tell the political editor of the *Financial Times* that when Blair came down to breakfast he was in a surly mood, leaving his coffee untouched and anxious to return immediately to London:

> I asked Tony if he was OK and he apologised for being a bit grumpy. He said he'd been up all night in his room in the hotel because he couldn't get to sleep. And then he said 'I've made some big decisions.'

Indeed he had; come what may after this night of turmoil nothing, nothing at all, would thereafter stop Blair joining Bush in waging war on Iraq.

After his Pyrenean encounter, for Blair there was no alternative; now he was a man possessed, intoxicated, favouring the newly found delights of abandonment to his fearless aggressivity. No one would be allowed to thwart his desire to find consummation in war; Cabinet ministers resigned, a large-scale rebellion of Labour MPs was precipitated, a million marched in dissent, Germany and France refused to permit a United Nations endorsement of an illegal war; but such attempts to restrain Blair could be of no avail. On the French mountain the Christian had forsworn the pacific Christ and had given his allegiance to Thanatos, God of Destruction. Under no circumstances was Blix, the UN inspector in Iraq, to be given more time to seek out weapons of mass destruction lest he concluded that none existed.

The existence of those weapons was the crucial pretext for Britain going to war. The pretext that Iraq was approaching nuclear capability, that it possessed biological and chemical weapons which were, Blair claimed, able to be hurled out of Iraq in 45 minutes, was camouflage masking the decision that Blair had already made. As Hugo Young, in a discerning *Guardian* article in June 2003 unequivocally stated: 'WMD or not, Blair had already made up his mind.' Young, scrupulously adumbrating the facts, insisted that Blair had already decided to go to war by August 2002 – the month of Blair's mountain trip. A year later, in August 2003, at Lord Hutton's inquiry, Blair was to reluctantly concede that it was immediately after his mountain break that he had a phone conversation with Bush, during which they agreed they had to get on 'with confronting the problem of Saddam'. 'President Bush and I . . . decided we really had to confront the issue, devise our strategy, and get on with it,' said Blair. The die was cast. The entire performance given by Blair during the subsequent autumn and winter, when he played the part of a cool restrainer holding back a precipitate Bush, was little more than a charade; his momentous mountain decision had been irreversibly taken and the main effect of the delay was to allow time to assemble a United States and UK army for attack.

The fear of retaliation of the terminator which, as has been repetitiously stressed throughout this work, has so often inhibited Blair from releasing his aggression was, in 2002, temporarily diminished; his Balkan war intervention and his success in contributing to the creation of an alliance of all countries against the Taliban had not provoked any punishment from the disabling ghost which, from his childhood onwards, Blair has so feared. And thus emboldened by that sleepless night on the mountains, overcoming his pusillanimity and, no doubt, already half-compromised by pledges given to Bush, he released the floodgates damming his aggression. When, but a few weeks later at Camp David together with Bush he began beating the war-drums, he told of his 'preoccupation' with a rogue state acquiring weapons of mass destruction and called on 'the entire civilised orderly international community' to muster; he was not inviting other views but giving public note of a personal and private irreversible decision already taken.

There were, of course, as many thought, other ways than war to bring down the evil dictator Saddam Hussein. A few days after an unprecedented march of one million protesters challenging Blair's belligerency, I wrote to *The Times*:

> If age and a recent stroke had not prevented me I would have joined the anti-war march carrying my banner 'No War on Iraq. Assassinate Saddam'. That is the answer I give to those who ask: 'What is the alternative to war now?'
>
> We should be encouraging the US to learn from the mistakes it made in its bungled attempts to assassinate Castro and Gaddafi, and urge it to lead a successful assassination of Saddam. Instead of mealy-mouthed talk of regime change it should act on what it really means.
>
> The ambivalence of the Allies to the use of assassination was unhelpful to the German generals attempting to kill Hitler in 1944; if they had succeeded, the lives of millions who were slain in the closing stages of the war would have been saved. Instead of

precipitating a war against all the people of Iraq our
combined intelligence services should be directed to
achieve one death, that of the Iraqi dictator – and
millions again could be saved.

Only the rules of the political leadership club inhibit its
use; deadly weaponry is permitted but assassination,
inviting retaliatory action, is out. And the morality of all
this? Not to worry. Our PM, now preaching the morality
of a war that could kill hundreds of thousands, should
have no difficulty in providing us with the moral
justification for the murder of one evil man.

There can be little doubt that, with patience, what I then
advocated could have been effected. An alliance of the US
Intelligence Services, possessed of unlimited funds for bribery,
which brought about the assassination of Allende; the British
Secret Service, accused of assassinating inconvenient defence
lawyers in Northern Ireland; the Russian Secret Service which
has, ever since Stalin arranged Trotsky's murder, continued its
killing-off of political opponents, and the Israeli Mossad, who
assassinate Hamas terrorists almost daily, most certainly had
the potential resource to eliminate Hussein. When, some weeks
after the war broke out, the coalition forces belatedly did
attempt to assassinate Saddam Hussein, it was too late; the
alerted bird had flown.

To persuade a sceptical Commons and public that no
decision to go to war had yet been taken, and that only the
growing evidence of Saddam's threat to national security was
driving a reluctant, peace-loving Blair to such a distasteful step,
the lying propaganda campaign, as described by Hugo Young,
was launched:

More blatant was Downing Street's serial exploitation of
MI6 and GCHQ material in a way quite disrespectful
of the health warnings that invariably accompany Intelli-

gence reports to ministers. They became raw facts for manipulation by a government machine that has spent six years treating all facts – speeches, statistics, meetings, journeys, policy commitments – as the beginning of a propaganda spate.

To contain the disquiet which a growing awareness of these deceits has occasioned, public or semi-public inquiries were set up by a House of Commons select committee, the Joint Intelligence Committee and Lord Hutton's judicial review; their inquisitions and findings can be of little avail, and could be a distraction. To understand how Britain was drawn into the fraudulent war, the real scrutiny that is required is of Blair's tortured psyche.

When Clare Short, having resigned from her Cabinet post, announced in June 2003 that the prime minister 'duped us all along' and that she had 'a growing conviction that Blair committed us to war in September 2002, if not before', she expressed her bewilderment: 'The enormous question that hangs over all this is: Why did Blair do it?' Like many others, she is seeking a rationale in some external circumstance to which she is not privy in order to explicate what otherwise can only be seen as manifest folly; but there is no such circumstance, no smoking bomb which when discovered will reveal all; the only smoking bomb is Blair himself. Blair, like his friend Clinton, is a man suffering from incontinence; Clinton indiscriminately releases his sexuality, Blair loses control of the flow of his aggression.

Bush's war was driven by less masked motivation. The appalling 9/11 onslaught on the phallic twin towers had been experienced in the USA as a castration; with Osama bin Laden vanishing into thin air, the deserved retribution remained unexacted, the wound remained unhealed; the crushing of the Taliban was seen as an inadequate punishment for so heinous an offence. A catharsis, releasing the USA from its continuing fury, was an imperative, the fantasy of a link between al-Qaeda and Saddam Hussein had to be imagined. The thirst for revenge could only be assuaged by the bombing of Baghdad. With the full support of the American people, Bush, responding to his nation's emotional needs, unleashed the war. No such an apologia can be presented on behalf of Blair; when he unnecessarily took Britain into the unpopular war he was responding to no one's emotional needs except his own.

The consequences of these incontinent spasms cannot be underestimated. By ignoring all Britain's obligations under the United Nations Charter, by by-passing the United Nations Security Council, by cocking a snook at international law and risking the heritage of our strategic alliances within NATO, Blair gave Britain's approval to a new and dangerous go-anywhere doctrine of unilateral pre-emptive war-making. In my lifetime, not since Neville Chamberlain led a Hitler-appeasing government have we had a Prime Minister who, by condoning anarchic international lawlessness, so put at risk our own national security.

We do not place a drug addict to manage a pharmaceutical company or put an alcoholic in charge of a brewery; arsonists too should be kept away from fuse-boxes. In a nuclear age, we want near the button no one whose trembling hands may be jerked by a sudden involuntary seizure. Millions deceived into relying on this PM's judgement, deeming it sober and rational, no longer trust him; the electoral consequences of that mistrust bring nearer the day when we shall all sleep more soundly in our beds.

The Thrills of a Rum Entourage

Chaucer, in 'The Parson's Tale', warns us:

> It is certain that envy is the worst sin that is; for all other
> sins are sins only against one virtue, whereas envy is
> against all virtue and against all goodness.

Envy, above all else, spurs on a craving for priority, for power
and prestige. Chaucer, in placing it first of the seven deadly
sins, knew how destructive and all-pervading it can be. He
knew that it should not be regarded as a mere peccadillo. But
this is the sin that is endemic in the fiercely and increasingly
competitive Commons; and nowhere in Westminster does the
green-eyed god stalk more shamelessly than among the élite of
the New Labour and Tory Parties. From these addicts, possessed with a compulsive craving for priority, in an endeavour
to refute their guilt, comes the lying claim that their ambition to
reach the top is not a sin but a virtue, bringing manifold benefits
to our society.

Competitiveness in the House of Commons has always been
extraordinarily intense; but now, with the growing profes-
sionalisation of British politics, rivalries between those seeking
advancement and acknowledgement have flared up as never

before. The capacity to suppress the hostile wishes felt against
each other by contenders as they work together to obtain or
retain power for their party is diminishing; each Member, no
longer regarding his political activities as only a part of his life,
invests all his narcissism in his personal political success. For
too many MPs all their self-worth is measured only by the
acclamations and the notice their febrile political activities
bring.

The phenomenon of such rivalries is not new; its present
vehemence is. The Conservative Party is prostrate, still
exhausted by the public brawling that took place between the
leadership and Clarke, Heseltine and Patten. Few would accept
that the differences which aroused such passions under William
Hague's leadership arose simply from varying emphases on
European policy. The Conservatives have displayed internecine savagery in the past, as in Macmillan's 'Night of the
Long Knives', but the more recent hostilities were fought out in
open daylight. Their attacks on one another ceased to be
encoded and became overt. The Tories, who in the past so often
could mask their intra-party hostilities, are certainly no longer
in a position to persuade the public that intra-party hostilities
are a monopoly of a loutish Labour Party.

The psychological truth is that in Parliament, in all parties,
there operate compulsive drives that prompt these oscillations
between brotherhood and fratricide. The behaviour of the
present Cabinet is occasioned in large measure by the selfsame
mechanism that operates at the end of Labour Party conferences when men band together, holding hands, singing
'Auld Lang Syne', after they have for days been savaging each
other to their political depths. And it is the mechanism that has
been operating to deadly effect in the notorious feuding
between Blair and Brown which has destabilised the whole
party hierarchy, dividing it into Blairites and Brownites. The
distinguished veteran journalist Ian Aitken, one not given to
psychologising, ventilated the frustration and bewilderment of

so many party activists as long ago as November 1999 when he wrote of:

> the infantile feud between Brownites and the Blairites. What in God's name is this long-running vendetta actually about? If there are policy issues at stake, we should be told what they are, so that an informed and sensible debate can take place around them. But, on the contrary, the entire guerrilla war has been conducted in almost exclusively personal terms.

It has been conducted in those terms because it is personal. Aitken is right to describe the feud as 'infantile', perhaps more than he appreciates. The origin of this feud is to be found in the cradle, not in any political issue. To understand such intense rivalries, like those prevailing within Blair's entourage, one needs to note what Edward Glover, doyen of the last generation of British psychoanalysts, has always emphasised: that early sibling rivalry, giving rise to intense unconscious hostility, can later lead to a positive homosexual attachment to brother substitutes. Early childhood impulses of jealousy derived from competition against rivals, usually with older brothers for a mother's love, lead to hostile and aggressive attitudes towards those brothers which can reach the pitch of actual death wishes; but these dangerous impulses cannot maintain themselves. Under the influence of upbringing, with the awareness of his continued powerlessness, the little boy's impulses yield to repression and undergo a transformation, so that the rivalries of the earlier period become the first homosexual love object. The process, as Freud has explained, is:

> a complete contrast to the development of persecutory paranoia, in which the person who has before been loved becomes the hated persecutor, whereas here the hated rivals are transformed into love objects. It represents too

an exaggeration of the process which, according to my view, leads to the birth of social instincts in the individual. In both processes there is first the presence of jealous and hostile influences which cannot achieve satisfaction; and both the affectionate and social feelings of identification arise as reactive formations against the repressive aggressive impulses.

From time to time, however, and at no time more than in the present House of Commons, the repressed aggressive impulses of which Freud writes become so violent that the feelings of identification created with other members of the same party are not powerful enough to contain them. Living as I did for decades in a House plagued always with intrigue and rumour, I was ever aware of the homosexual rivalries that expressed themselves not in overt homosexual conduct but in rationalisations of political policy. These homosexual elements can be distastefully observed in both the Conservative and New Labour Parties.

In the Conservative Party, the old Tory loyalties – to the party and to each other – began collapsing in the nineties; under cover of different views, such as those on ERM, battles ensued between rival contenders. In a club like the Commons, male bonding has always played a particularly significant part; misogyny and paucity of women members within the Conservative Party used to mean that group identification could hold in check the repressed aggressive wishes. Now, however, Tory MPs are impaled on their own ideology. Their mocking of 'society', deliberate weakening of the group, and their apotheosising of individualism has led to the slackening of party ties – and homosexual rivalries have escaped into the public arena. Rivalries of this order are to be clearly distinguished from jealousies that may arise from actual physical sexual relationships; but they are rivalries that can be powerful and destructive.

And, no less than in the Conservative Party, but without the protagonists even wearing the fig-leaf of ideological or political difference, rivalries of a similar nature have been acted out within Blair's entourage; there is to be found a heady brew, spiked with more than mere malice. The excessive warmth and anxieties, and the permutations in their emotional patterns of the immature quartet – Blair, Brown, Mandelson and Alistair Campbell – as they have quarrelled and reconciled, have been of a similar order to those found in the charged hothouse atmosphere of a sixth-form boarding-school where adolescent boys, still wrestling with their sexuality, squabble and make up, forever forming and re-forming cliques as they endeavour to displace their repressed steaming passions on to fault-finding or idealisation of their peers. That not dissimilar immature responses have prevailed in a circle governed by a leadership with marked androgynous qualities was inevitable.

Peter Mandelson

To identify the cause of the tensions within the Blair circle simply as Brown's thwarted ambition, or Mandelson's 'betrayal' when he switched his allegiance in the leadership contest from Brown to Blair, would be proffering too simplistic a diagnosis; it would be attributing symptoms to causes. It is understandable, but not necessarily correct, to say that when quarrels occur between politicians who have long and deep friendships and who share a common ideology, the cause of the break is 'ambition'. We have to dig deeper. At the least, a glance is required at the individual psychological make-up of the three protagonists who, with Blair, have misgoverned us for six years; above all, we need to focus on Mandelson, the man to whom Blair wrote in December 1998 upon his first ministerial resignation: 'It is no exaggeration to say that without your support and advice we would never have built New Labour.'

By January 2001, on Mandelson's second resignation, the Prime Minister could have added that without his reckless risk-taking, the 'New Labour Project' could still have, in the 2001 election, been presented as intact; but what Mandelson built, he destroyed. He had no alternative; 'each man kills the thing he loves' is the injunction Mandelson is doomed to obey.

Behind the terraced house in suburban Cardiff where I spent my earliest childhood was my playground, a field flanked by a high boundary wall behind which lay an apple orchard. Apples were always available to me at home, but the lure of that orchard's fruit was as compulsive as Adam's in Eden; the thrill of mounting that wall, despite the grazing of my knees, frequent falls and oftimes bleeding hands, was worth all the risks. Stolen fruit is sweetest; no allure exceeds that of the prohibited. And so often, in my political and professional life, have I seen the selfsame perverse dynamic at work. The sulks of some homo-sexuals who resented my ending the criminality of their conduct, taking away the thrill of their defiance of the law, the clients whose divorces were occasioned not by their passions but by the thrills of their clandestine adulteries, the confidence tricksters whom I defended who enjoyed the thrills of their deceptions far more than their ill-gotten gains, all were phenomena telling me of the force and the ubiquity of man's urge to revel in the thrill of risk-taking. Governed, that urge can literally take us to the moon, stimulate the adventure of man's evolutionary ascent; but ungoverned, as a way of life, it can be antisocial and self-destructive; and nowhere is this more clearly delineated than in the politician fated to be denied a capacity to resist its temptations.

The moral of Peter Mandelson's resignation in January 2001, appears from a comment made by his former aide and confidant Benjamin Wegg-Prosser:

He wore his appetite for risk-taking as a badge of honour
– 'that's how I got where I am' he would say when asked
why he seemed so willing to play with fire . . . Peter is a
born gambler.

Only the man of androgynous qualities could have yielded, as
Blair has, to Mandelson's seductions and be blinded to the
hazards of a dependency relationship with a man who must
needs gain his thrills in the political process; with infatuation
comes overvaluation, and Blair has endowed Mandelson with
qualities he conspicuously lacks and designated him to be his
most trusted adviser with a finger on the pulse of the nation and
the party, the safe pair of hands always to be relied upon in the
event of a serious crisis or political fire that must be extinguished. It is a role for which Mandelson is totally unsuited;
conflagrations inevitably follow if an arsonist is appointed as
a fire-fighter.

The quest for thrills, the courting of dangers, are certainly not
confined to the Mandelsons of this world. Within all of us there
is an unquenchable thirst for thrills – either to identify them and
so avoid them, or to find and revel in them. The fundamental
element of all our thrills is to be found in a mixture of fear,
pleasure and confident hope in the face of external danger. The
thrills are gained by way of unconscious fear, an apprehension
of danger, of a voluntary exposure to the hazard, and a confident – often overconfident – belief that the aroused fear can
be tolerated and mastered; that the danger will pass and,
unharmed, safety will be regained. So we gain our thrills in
multifarious manner; we find them in high speeds: in skiing,
motor-racing, sailing, flying; we expose ourselves to risky
situations: rock-climbing, gliding, taming wild animals,
travelling into unknown lands; or we turn to unfamiliar or
completely new forms of satisfaction: searching for the
pristine, the virgin peak, the virginal routes to that peak or,
indeed, the young virgin; or we search for a new sexual partner,

strange to us, belonging to another race, colour or creed; and for
some the thrill is found in the frisson of the forbidden love, the
love that dare not speak its name.

But for Mandelson the off-piste private thrills are inadequate.
His public life is where he must find his agonies and ecstasies.
His painstaking biographer, Paul Routledge, has concluded:
'Peter Mandelson lives on the edge . . . and is magnetised by
danger'. Indeed, in an unguarded moment, Mandelson once
confessed: 'I don't like conformity. I like people who are
different, exotic or dangerous'. Like a moth to the flame, he
flutters dangerously around wealth, power and prestige; he
cannot desist until he is singed, for indeed, his true and unconscious need, as his frenetic activity betrays, is the fulfilment of a
masochistic wish to be punished and left bereft. Unconsciously,
Mandelson always encompasses his own political tumbles and,
in so doing, presents us with the same symptoms as those of a
chronic gambler that every bookmaker, enjoying his prey, spots
in the punter who is playing to lose, not to win.

For some years before I went into the House, I was
increasingly professionally involved with one of Britain's
largest bookmakers and football pools promoters. The considerable clinical material to which I then gained access
validated so many of the hypotheses in psychoanalytical
literature on punters' risk-taking and gambling; and, no less,
those psychoanalytical theories explained to me that highly
intelligent men with whom I worked – such as Reggie
Maudling and Edward du Cann, both of whom nearly became
prime minister before ensuring tawdry risk-taking brought
about their fall – were victims of their temperaments.
Mandelson, in my judgement, falls into the same category of
losers as did those potential leaders of the Conservative Party
and their fate, like his, was determined by inner compulsions
outside their conscious control.

The phenomenon of risk-taking that aims at loss – whether it
is taking place in the betting-shop, at the card-table, or on the

floor of the House of Commons, or in Downing Street – is not inexplicable. It was explored in some revealing and startling asides within Freud's essay *Dostoyevsky and Parricide*. Freud found the causality of Dostoyevsky's compulsive gambling habits in a particular variation of the Oedipus complex; it was a variation which probably plays a part in all our lives but it was one which, because of Dostoyevsky's particular experiences as an infant, had a shattering impact on his adult life. Freud emphasised how when the child is in his Oedipal phase – in intense rivalry with his father and resenting the father's posses-sion of the mother – he not only has parricidal wishes against his 'rival' but simultaneously has the desire to be the father's love-object. This bisexuality, prompting the boy's wish both to become his mother's lover and to be taken by his father to displace the wife, can, in adverse external circumstances, bring about intolerable dilemmas which often reach into adulthood.

The boy fears that his wish to slay the father may bring him the retaliation of castration; at the same time he fears submission as a feminine love-object will bring about the same result. The ideal resolution of these dilemmas may never be possible, but most of us, from fear of castration, in the interests of preserving our masculinity, give up the wish to possess our mother and to slay our father, and confine both impulses – hatred of the father and being in love with the father – to the unconscious. There, albeit imperfectly, they remain repressed but still prompting in all of us a feeling of guilt and a need for expiation. Freud finds, however, that in those whose bisexual disposition has caused them especially to fear the consequences of their feminine attitudes, a pathogenic intensification of their feelings of guilt arises. In adulthood such boys are prone to attempt to relieve their guilt by placing themselves at the mercy of fate and demanding that it provides a means of resolving their impossible dilemmas.

For, in the Freudian view, gambling is in essence provo-cation of fate, forcing it to take decisions for or against the individual. With every throw of the dice, with every turn of the card, with every spin of the wheel, the questions being asked over and over again reflect the earlier Oedipal dilemmas: am I omnipotent, able by my secret wishes to kill my father; and have I, if he is in fact dead, killed him? And simultaneously – since formal logic is not part of the unconscious – am I the beloved of my father? He loves me, he loves me not. If the gambler wins, he receives affirmative answers to all his questions. He is the killer *and* the beloved. But in either case he must pay the price of emasculation, a totally unacceptable and terrifying conclusion. So, to remain intact, the compulsive gambler never desists; he is determined to continue until he loses in order to survive. Only by losing does he gain relief from his guilt as killer and lover, for then he obtains the punishment he deserves for his parricidal and incestuous wishes.

During the years that I observed my bookmaker client supplying these masochistic needs to thousands of customers, it was clear that although the punters, to maintain their psychic equilibrium, were determined to lose their money, the thrills that they had en route were sustaining them. Those joyless thrills were paralleled by Freud to masturbation. Indeed, Dostoyevsky himself described the tremulous excitement that losing afforded him and pointed out that the punishment of total loss at the end of a losing run led to orgasm. Thus the psychic masochist pursues his lonely path, producing pleasure out of displeasure. It is a solitary journey; onanism turns its back on mature human relationships. Whether the punter lays his bets at a crowded racecourse or in the packed gambling-room of a luxuriously appointed London casino, he is in truth alone. There is no more lonely and sadder place than the silent gambling-room of a fashionable casino; to enter one is to enter a lavish mausoleum. The gambler enters, and leaves it, alone; the compulsive risk-taker in politics too is ever the solitary; when he loses, as Mandelson has found, he has few friends to come to his aid.

The most distinguishing feature of the chronic risk-taker is his total denial of responsibility for the débâcle he has occasioned; the card-player blames the cards, the punter the horse. A sustained acknowledgement of his own guilt cannot be tolerated; to do so would mean wrestling with the demons that possess him, to dare to recall the incestuous taboos that in childhood fantasies he has broken. This is the behavioural pattern to be observed in Peter Mandelson in his 'passports for money' imbroglio. When he was summoned to Downing Street on 24 January 2001 to explain his conduct in the affair, he acknowledged his guilt; by Sunday, 28 January, he was repudiating the admission that had compelled his immediate resignation: 'I came briefly to be persuaded that my recollection was entirely wrong, that I had erred, and that I should resign.' I do not believe Mandelson was lying about his failed recollection: his amnesia was determined by unconscious factors.

Mandelson is a slippery politician, not a criminal; but the admission and confession, followed by their speedy denial and repudiation, were manifestations of the same affliction carried by the most overt of risk-takers, the recidivist burglars and thieves that daily, in the early years of my law practice, I was defending. Few of these men, professional criminals, really wanted to be acquitted. If I succeeded in obtaining an acquittal, they were resentful; if, after a spirited defence, they were sentenced, they readily expressed their gratitude to me; neurotically burdened by their childhood 'crimes', which in fantasy they had committed, punishment temporarily relieved them of their burden, for now they had received their deserts; and to be certain that they would not be cheated out of them, they so often readily responded to their arrest by giving a confession. But having thus, by their own admission, lightened their load, they would then require their solicitor to plead not guilty and claim that only by inducement or coercion had the confession been wrested from them; they wanted to eat their cake and keep it. They wanted at an unconscious level to receive their punishment; consciously they could not tolerate an admission which acknowledged they had yielded to their shameful masochism. This pattern of confession followed by repudiation is the hallmark of so many of our old lags; and thus in prison they keep their heads high, claiming the court had unjustly convicted them.

In the same mode Mandelson railed against the sentence meted out by Blair's court in January 2001: 'Downing Street sentenced me to commit political suicide without a fair trial,' he whined, three days after the condemnatory adjudication. No acknowledgement could come from him that he was his own executioner; that would have brought him insights into his own condition and that would be unbearable. He can live on only in denial, even as my sentenced clients lived on during their imprisonment. Lawful and involuntary though it may be, and out of conscious control, Mandelson's political conduct is, however, in my book more heinous than that of the brigands that I once defended. They stole property; he, in conspiracy with Blair, set out to steal the soul of my party. In that quest he is destroying himself; it remains an open question as to whether, in the meantime, he has also irreparably destroyed the party I love.

Gordon Brown

Peter Mandelson is the sort of homosexual who gives homo-sexuality a bad name. Except to incorrigible homophobes, the benefits that homosexuals with their special sensibilities often bestow upon society are manifest; but the disturbed homo-sexual who is at odds with his sexual orientation can be bitterly destructive, and negative traits can sometimes find expression in a rare talent for mischief. When deployed as raillery, this can be used with effect to mock pretentiousness, but its iconoclasm can sometimes be far from fun; it can be repellent. In May 2003, Mandelson gave a lunch-time talk to a private club of women correspondents, at which he excelled even himself as a mischief-maker.

Well knowing that his remarks would inevitably be leaked, Mandelson told his listeners that Tony Blair had been 'out-manoeuvred' by Gordon Brown over the euro and had allowed Brown to construct a Treasury veto over entry into the single currency with his five economic tests. The Chancellor:

> would never have got his hands on the euro policy if the prime minister had been a more obsessive politician. Gordon Brown is a politician right down to his finger-tips, twenty-four hours a day, seven days a week. Tony Blair is not. If he was as obsessed with politics as Gordon Brown he would not have let himself be out-manoeuvred in the way that he potentially has.

Opportunistically, Michael Howard, the Shadow Chancellor, immediately pronounced:

> Peter Mandelson's comments that Blair has been out-manoeuvred by his own Chancellor shows quite how vicious and personal the in-fighting in Labour has become. Britain's national economic interest is coming a poor second to Labour's bitter and personalised faction fighting.

At the very time that Mandelson was poisonously spelling out the personal rivalries of the two men which had invaded the issue of Britain's entry into the euro, Brown, ironically, was endeavouring to convince two sceptical and sophisticated *Times* journalists how irrelevant and specious was the speculation, and how effective was his working relationship

with Blair. In his sparse Treasury office to which they had been
invited, he deluged them with more facts and statistics to justify
his soon-to-be-announced euro decision of 'Yes, but not yet.'
The journalists, not to be sidetracked by such obfuscation,
sounded out Brown about reports of the issue causing strains
between him and Blair. The Chancellor was dismissive and, in
the fashion of his scolding preacher father with whom he ever
identifies, he didactically reprimanded them:

> I think that the real story of decision-making in politics is
> about ideas and ideals, and it is about a policy that reflects
> the concerns of people. The central question of Britain and
> Europe's future in the world cannot be reduced to
> personality issues without trivialising what are great and
> major questions about our future.

Brown evidently sensed that such a high-faluting description of
the decision-making process operating within the strife-ridden
and ragged Labour Cabinet was leaving his reluctant pupils,
both hard-boiled political correspondents, distinctly less than
impressed. So, *de haut en bas*, he patronisingly asserted his
authority and superior qualifications: 'I studied history,' he
immodestly, albeit truthfully, boasted. Then, insisting on
turning the interview into a seminar, he, revealingly, fiercely
attacked the 'Namier school of history' and led the attendant
journalists away from the Blair–Brown rivalries on a detour
into eighteenth-century political history.

The excursion may have bemused his interviewers, probably
in short trousers when the Polish-born Jew, Sir Lewis Namier,
died. Namier for me has always been one of the most beguiling
of English historians and clearly Brown has read his works –
for, unlike Blair, he is no flibbertigibbet pretentiously laying
claim to be a reader of works at which he has in fact barely
glanced. Unsurprisingly, Brown continues to find Namier
disturbingly challenging, for it was Namier who insisted on the

overriding importance of personality in the determination of politics. By microscopic biographical examination of the members of several parliaments, Namier determined that politics in the mid-eighteenth century was controlled by a series of small and fluid groups and that unconscious self-interest was as important as great issues in dictating political allegiance. His methodology, which came to be called 'Namierism', was adopted by other historians and led to much re-evaluation of English history. Namier's interpretation of history stressed that:

> Unconscious promptings combine with rational thought and in every action there are inscrutable components. Undoubtedly one of the most important lines of advance for history, and especially for biography, will be a thorough knowledge of modern psychology.

It was with the declared principles of the 1688 'Glorious Revolution' in mind, but with a comment that is pertinent to the Chancellor's efforts to persuade us that we trivialise great issues by dwelling on personality conflicts, that Namier wrote:

> One inevitable result of heightened psychological aware-ness is, however, a change of attitude towards so-called political ideas. To treat them as the offspring of pure reason would be to assign them a parentage about as mythological as that of Paris Athene. What matters most is the underlying emotions, the music to which ideas are a mere libretto, often of a very inferior quality; and once the emotions have ebbed, the ideas . . . become doctrine or . . . clichés.

Such notions are, of course, an affront to Brown for they tell us how paper-thin is the protective armour of the practising politician when he assumes the affectation of undiluted commitment to principle and community, and dismisses the *ad hominem* arguments as irrelevancies in no way invalidating his manifesto.

The psychiatrist Carl Jung, in his work on typology, has claimed that there are some men, propelled by specific temperament, who are forever intellectualising, overvaluing thought processes, seeking for intellectual solutions for what are properly emotional problems; their own thought processes can become highly libidinised and their predominant mode of self-expression is not in relation to other people but is in the world of thoughts; ideas tend to become substitutes for feelings, and intellectual values replace emotional values. The basic psychological functions we exercise, Jung has explicated, are thinking, feeling, sensation and intuition; with such men the undue predominance of one such function, thinking, can lead to the impoverishment of other functions which, drained of libidinal energy, wilt.

Certainly not a few of the characteristics Jung has attributed to this type apply, unfortunately, to Brown. His relegation of the significance of irrational, emotional factors which Namier insists have played so large a part in historic political decisions, is a mere epiphenomenon – an expression of the imbalance of Brown's temperament; his deprecations in no way tell us of the reality of the past or present operation of our political process.

Reflecting his temperamental imbalance, valiantly and over-determinedly, he seeks the impossible – the expurgation of emotion and biography from his decision-making; he buries the Cabinet, the Commons and his darker self under an avalanche of statistics, so that atop he can proclaim the total logic and rationality of the course upon which he is embarking; like history, political science without biography is taxidermy and too often, although not always, his discourse is lifeless and his listeners, out of exhaustion not conviction, yield to his per-suasions. His affiliation to the famed Prudence, symbol of his economic policies, was presented to us as an occasion for celebration in which all sensible and rational men could join, and where only the profligates would sulk; that 'rational' unnecessary decision of placing a ceiling on state spending, obsessively carried through with its three-year stranglehold on expenditure, led to an exacerbation of the parlous condition of our underfunded public services which no belated splurge will easily repair.

In my book *Private Member* I described in some detail occasions when I insisted on building the illogical into the bills I was introducing, a practice that brought me into conflict with weighty lawyers and legislators; that I often won resultant arguments was because I had the forces of the irrational on my side and they had mere logic as their shield. Sometimes the props of logic must be thrown aside and we need to stride boldly towards the vision of super-reality that only feeling not ratiocination can provide; but feeling is a quality in which Brown is deficient, for it has been drained to provide sustenance for his formidable intellect.

This jagged sensibility has, in his private life, inevitably caused difficulties which are honestly acknowledged in the meticulous biography by Paul Routledge with which Brown co-operated. There we see how repeatedly during his long bachelorhood his personal relationships with his girlfriends foundered; his emotional, as distinct from his intellectual, involvement was at that time too attenuated to meet the needs of his warm-blooded women. Gordon Brown preferred the committee room to the bedroom. Princess Margarita, daughter of the then-exiled King of Romania, with whom Brown had a five-year association, subsequently frankly told of the dénouement: 'It was a very solid and romantic story. I never stopped loving him, but one day it didn't seem right any more. It was politics, politics, politics, and I needed nurturing.'

It is in many respects lamentable that Gordon Brown, essentially a private man, was forced to co-operate in emblazoning abroad the intimate details of his personal

relationships with past girlfriends. Politicians, having chosen
to live on a public stage, cannot claim the same rights of
privacy to which the private citizen is entitled; a scrutiny of the
prejudices and motivations that may invalidate or distort
policies which they commend to us is legitimate and, indeed,
as I have often insisted, absolutely necessary; but the politician
today, unlike yesteryear, no longer has any protection afforded
by the canons of taste and etiquette which once laid down
boundaries at which enquiry into their private lives was
required to halt. Nowadays prurient curiosity, undirected and
destructive voyeurism, with no purpose except obscene
titillation, have burst through the protective barriers that were
once in place and mercenary press lords, finding there is
money in filth, have created a popular press awash in scum
and trivia.

Gordon Brown certainly became a victim of the prevailing
foetid media salaciousness; innuendoes proliferated and
culminated in a notorious 1996 radio interview in a *Desert
Island Discs* programme when the publicity-seeking interviewer, for no reason except to preen herself on her prowess
and derring-do as interrogator, directly challenged him on
his sexual orientation. It was a spectacle that demeaned her,
not Brown. To add to the smears, the press reported a
widely circulated comment, believed by many to have
emanated from Alistair Campbell, that Brown was 'psychologically flawed'. After such incidents, it is not surprising
that Brown put no brake on his biographer listing all his
girlfriends from the time of his adolescence; the harridans and
scavengers of a defiled society had compelled him to prove his
heterosexuality.

The phenomenon of a reluctant man being forced by societal
pressures into exaggerated displays of his heterosexuality
engaged the attention of Freud's closest interlocutor, the daring
Sandor Ferenczi, who, as long ago as 1911, in a character-

istically shocking essay, told of the consequences to the community and the individual of society's insistence upon making men what he called 'compulsively heterosexual'.

Ferenczi's clinical findings have singular relevance to Brown's predicament; drawing upon those findings may help us to gain an understanding of some of the palpable strengths and many weaknesses of this obsessive political animal. Any attempt, however tentative, to unravel the tangled skein of the psyche of this complex man, is no prurient or academic exercise; it is a political necessity, an invigilation of a leader who when Blair crumbles, as is inevitable, will, unless events at present unimaginable occur, be the prime minister determining Britain's future.

Ferenczi neatly illustrated his view that modern man is in flight from the homosexual component of his nature by recalling an epigram of Lessing:

> The unjust mob falsely imputed love of boys to the
> Righteous Turan.
> To chastise the lies what else could he do but –
> Sleep with his sister

It was the grievous loss of male friendships that in other times received societal approval, and their replacement by 'resistance and rivalry', which Ferenczi found precipitated the obsessional neurosis of some of his patients. Stating that the contemporary sublimations of homosexual components are inadequate, and never one to understate his case, Ferenczi declared:

> A part of the unsatisfied homoeroticism remains 'free-floating', and demands to be appeased . . . this quantity of libido has to undergo a displacement, namely, on to feelings for and relationships with the opposite sex. I quite seriously believe that the men of today are one and all compulsively heterosexual as a result of this affective

displacement; in order to free themselves from men, they
become the slaves of women.

Even if some may discount Ferenczi's extravagances, the
physician's diagnosis – that the aetiology of his patients'
obsessional neurosis lay in their incapacity to metabolise their
homosexual compulsions – surely cannot be denied; their
compulsive obsessional rituals were in place to contain and
hold down their homosexual feelings which threatened to over-
whelm them. Vainly endeavouring to deal with homosexual
feelings by caging them within a neurosis maims the personality; but we should not patronise those suffering from such
a disability. All of us, men and women, have homosexual
components within our make-up, but however we deal with
them – whether, as in homophobia, we fearfully and vainly
endeavour to repudiate their presence; whether we sublimate
them in a bonding to advance a political or religious cause;
whether we deploy them within a heterosexual relationship to
enrich our identification and empathy with our partner; whether
they find expression in overt sexual conduct – what is
irrevocable is their continuing presence; they cannot be
cancelled out. And the psychoanalyst Edward Glover, who
incited me to end the criminality of adult homosexual conduct,
always reminded us that Freud had emphasised that hate
constitutes one of the aetiological factors in homosexuality. As
Glover expressed it:

> Earlier jealousy and rivalry can be resolved or countered
> or kept in successful repression by what we might call a
> reaction-formation of homosexual attachment.

With jealousies and rivalries forever simmering beneath these
homosexual elements, there are those who, because they find
those elements too compulsive and untamed to be dealt with by
any other means, turn to a 'reaction-formation of homosexual

attachment' which may or may not take an overt form. It is, however, a reaction-formation which is fraught with hazards, for even if slightly punctured, the jealousies and rivalries beneath burst forth – often with terrifying force.

The disputatious senior common rooms of Oxbridge colleges, as I have noted when invited to High Table, are littered with the intellectual debris of exploded homosexual attachments. The syndrome, notoriously displayed in those quarrelsome academic circles, has been no less on show in Blair's inner circle and it is witnessed, in its most exotic form, in the prevailing bitterness between Blair and Brown, the pair once described as 'twins' and 'blood brothers' who entered Parliament on the same day and, during the years while I was in the House, shared an office in the Commons, living in each other's pockets. As the *Observer*'s Andrew Rawnsley noted in March 2000: 'Blair's favoured way of describing the closeness of his relationship with Gordon Brown is as a "marriage".'

I doubt if, since 1994, Brown would so describe it. It was in that year that the explosion between Blair and Brown took place at Granita, a restaurant in Islington, at the height of the Labour leadership contest in 1994. The event and consequence were accurately recorded by the *Express* correspondent Peter Oborne:

> Gordon Brown reluctantly agreed to stand down but insisted on conditions which Blair, guilt-stricken at the turn events had taken, was weak enough to concede. Brown demanded complete control over the economy and sweeping powers of other areas of policy as well. In effect, he demanded, and got, something approaching a dual premiership.

Gordon Brown is a tough operator, schooled in the machine politics of Scotland; he was to emerge as a so-called moderniser, champion of one-member-one-vote and of internal

party democracy, but his past belies his later pretensions; he
became the Labour candidate for the safe seat of Dunfermline
East by conducting a ruthless and cunning campaign of
wheeler-dealing with the unions, communists and local party
bosses which showed he was well-versed in the politics of
Labour's highways and byways. Such a man was not to be
duped by Blair and, as a document leaked in June 2003 was to
show, he insisted on and obtained as a condition of supporting
Blair a written six-paragraph 'contract' guaranteeing the
fulfilment of all his demands.

Robert Harris, an able and discerning writer, sensing the
combustibility of the pact which had been struck between the
two men, has insightfully commented:

A novelist would be hard put to invent a potentially more
explosive mixture than that offered by Labour's Big Four.

Homing in on the particular relationship between Blair and
Brown, he postulated that these men, once 'close as brothers',
had a relationship possessing a potential for dramatic tension
that was almost limitless; and that Brown's unhealed wound
'runs across the political landscape like a San Andreas fault'.

Harris rightly drew attention to the precedent of the ruptured
relationship of Roy Jenkins and Tony Crosland, very close
friends for thirty years until, to Crosland's undisguised dismay,
Jenkins in 1967 obtained the chancellorship which Crosland
coveted. 'It would be idle to pretend,' wrote Jenkins in his
memoirs, 'that these events . . . did not leave a scar on Crosland
which had the effect of crucially damaging the cohesion of the
Labour Right over the next eight or nine years.' Harris
eloquently concluded, observing the potential for tumult in the
Blair–Brown relationship and the severe political consequences of the Jenkins–Crosland estrangement, that: 'The
intangible elusive indefinable action of one human personality
upon another is what will make history.'

But Harris's 'intangible' and 'elusive' element – although buried in the unconscious – is by no means indefinable. The psychodynamics that Freud delineated most certainly operated in the Jenkins and Crosland quarrel. I had ample opportunity to observe the interplay in that quarrel for even before I had entered the Commons, Crosland (who was a stimulating guest for me but not for my wife – since he was almost invariably petulant with women until he was to encounter the transatlantic freshness and vigour of the novelist Susan Barnes) would stay with us at our Welsh home. And the selfsame psychodynamics that Freud and Glover have delineated certainly operated in that quarrel – as they do in today's Blair–Brown feud.

In this feud, however, there are other provocations at work. Blair and Brown are second sons, as is Mandelson. Fated by their place within the family constellation, as adults, the three men have brazenly acted out the unassuaged rivalries of their childhood; the struggle for priority, the contest with the older brother, ever competing for love and attention, continue unmortified. Fraternal affection is displaced by envy and resentment as, successively, one or the other is identified as the older brother surrogate. Thus, before 2001 was out, Brown and Mandelson were not on speaking terms and Mandelson, denied the affection of the Chancellor of the Exchequer, his former close associate, was soon found to be seeking hollow compensation in the acquisition of large houses too big for his pocket, in adulatory parties paid for by someone else, and being bedazzled by the manipulative Hindujah millionaires – a living-out of vulgar fantasies that led to his downfall.

If the envy, often raw and unforgiving, displayed in this circle was confined to the private enclosure, one could leave it to these essentially emotionally immature men to get on with their unseemly quarrelling; unhappily it can overspill into public policy. Fearing his intellectual domination and political sophistication, Blair, Mandelson and Campbell continuously attempt to confine Brown within their hothouse. In that polluted atmosphere, lacking space and oxygen, he does not thrive; and it is not the man but his rivalrous disposition and envious traits that too often flourish. Then we find his inflamed responses to the provocations of his inferior and envious colleagues are not limited to private duelling; in self-justification of his smouldering anger, underneath the rubric of 'enterprise', he exaggerates the economic benefits of competition; his weakness becomes a public virtue.

Sometimes this displacement of his own competitiveness from the private sphere to the public arena is so ill-disguised as to be droll. In his 1999 autumn pre-Budget statement, one meant to be about State finances, he cited competitiveness ten times – its virtues and the need to enforce it, have much more of it, and to promote yet more entrants to its world. To Brown, reflecting his own psychological needs, competitiveness is the doctrinal absolute of the enterprise society and, with the rigour and obsessionalism of a true son of a Scottish manse, he enshrined his faith in the 2001 New Labour election manifesto, over which he had complete control; there, his emphases on the benefits that would flow from giving aid to small businesses led some to comment resentfully that Brown now believed that, with competition as the spur, we could become a nation of entrepreneurs and experience all the blessings he had once believed were only in the gift of a socialist commonwealth.

However, this understandable but simplistic interpretation is a misreading of the man and of his policies. Brown does not ruminate; that would put him dangerously in touch with his feelings; what he does is to think aloud. During the period from 2001 to 2003 he has given three elaborate public lectures; in each lecture, endeavouring to persuade sceptics unconvinced that he has found a wondrous new route taking us away from what he describes as 'the old sterile and debilitating conflict of the past', he presents a list – there is always a list – of the long-term radical reforms needed on the one hand to enhance the efficiency of the market and stimulate productivity and, on the

THE THRILLS OF A RUM ENTOURAGE   283

other, to improve our public services; only, he claims, by defining the boundaries, by fine-drawing of the lines between the private and public sector and identifying where they can, and cannot, intermingle, can we have a tidy harmonious world in place of the one which is now in such disarray. This cataloguing, this attempt to impose a pattern excluding the contingent in a world replete with the exigent, is obsessive. This ritual of list-making may help Brown to contain forbidden and buried impulses; it in no way establishes the validity and practicability of the contents of his lists. Few would demur if in the real conflict-ridden world of men and women of flesh and blood there was a realistic possibility, as he suggests, of a firm and warm handshake between 'on the one hand' and 'on the other hand' which sealed a relationship giving us the fulfilment of Brown's objectives; but it would require a thaumaturgist, not a politician, to transform such a possibility into reality.

When the comedian Rory Bremner, hilariously mimicking Brown, growls: 'What the people of this country want is lists; long lists, short lists, depressing statistics, disturbing industry results and gloomy surveys,' he is unwittingly drawing attention not to an innocuous quirk but to a distress signal. These lists are symptoms of the same disorder as the pronounced facial tics and lugubrious grimaces that he so often displays. They are all part of the defence reaction which Ferenczi has taught us is deployed by those who, finding the challenge unendurable, endeavour to ward off the illicit physical stimuli assailing them. The lists and the body language advertise the drama being enacted in Brown's interior life; but to that theatre he will give no admission tickets. In 1998 an able *Guardian* interviewer, after a long session with Brown, wrote:

> But the galling thing for Brown is that what people want to know about him is all personal, and personal things are what he hates to talk about. Politics, yes, till the mountains

fall into the sea. But not personal . . . It's just that he finds any personal inquiry excruciating.

After asking about Sarah Macaulay, the woman who was to become Brown's wife, and being denied a coherent answer, the interviewer concluded: 'Stones sweat more comfortably.'

Brown indeed sentences himself to a cruel strangulation of affect; we are witnessing a courageous and able politician – and no one can gainsay that he earns such compliments – prepared to meet and confront anyone except himself. At all costs, no time is to be made available for such a rendezvous; his long working hours are legendary, permitting no hiatus; in the extraordinarily rapid and breathless delivery of his speeches, no interstices are to be found; always, strenuously, he attempts to block any possible entry by the intruding dangerous self with whom he has yet to come to terms. He is attempting the impossible; a total dichotomy between the public and the private man.

But feelings thus repressed or repudiated can still remain insistent, and the creation of elaborate defence mechanisms is needed to keep them at bay. Even as many an obsessional neurotic uses his rituals in a vain effort to exorcise the homosexual components of his nature which he finds threatening, so political policies can be ritualised for a similar purpose – the keeping of the prohibited under control. Once a policy has been categorised, once it has been defined, placed within a strict configuration, once the steps for its implementation have been numbered, any interference is deemed to be dangerous meddling; like a Catholic with his beads, the *Ave Maria*s must be recited in a pre-determined order and it becomes sacrilege to deviate. With Brown we see the process at work when he savages anyone, like the former Health Minister Alan Milburn, who dared, by way of espousing foundation hospitals, to blur the lines between private medicine, which Brown abhors, and the NHS; and, far less happily, despite the disaster of rail privatisation, he thwarted all efforts to place the London

Underground system wholly under public ownership once the Tube had been itemised under the category of Private Finance Initiative (PFI) and, obsessively, insisted that there it remain.

The psychiatrist Anthony Storr, despairing of finding 'normal' leading politicians, once sought to persuade me that it is not the fact that politicians have a psycho-pathology which is important, but that what is important is the creative use they may make of that pathology; there are some occasions when Storr's view seems persuasive, as when Brown obsessively lays down the demarcation lines between private medicine and the NHS – for then we sing 'Hallelujah!' knowing that our hopes for it are indeed safe in his hands; but Storr's view is far too complacent. When we have seen the consequences of Hitler, Stalin and Mao, all of whose personal problems – acted out in times of socially resonating conditions – became so catastrophically enmeshed, through symbolic resonance, with the public domain. Storr's view is indeed too optimistic.

The pathogens carried by our politicians are certainly not as deadly as those of the savage dictators; nevertheless, a milder pathogen carried by a man with decision-making powers of a chancellor of the exchequer can seriously infect the body politic. The evident difficulties that Brown has in tolerating the homosexual components seriated within his psyche, as in all ours, and the extraordinary dishevelled living conditions of his bachelor days, all indicate the site of the pathogen which he carries and which can have unfortunate public consequences; that site lies in the anal erotogenic zone.

Freud and his followers have instructed us that approximately between the ages of two and four we pass through a phase in our development in which the anus, defecation and our faeces are the major source of sexual pleasure; during that phase mastery of the body, particularly of the sphincter, and the socialisation of the excretory impulses are the major preoccupations of the infant. While none of us totally relinquish the pleasure, pains and frustrations experienced during this

phase of our lives, there are some whose nostalgia for the lost
infantile delights is so overwhelming that in adulthood, in their
behavioural patterns, unconsciously they persistently re-enact
the joys and tribulations of that early interlude. Those who
remain so attached to, or fixated on, that phase have long since
been labelled as 'anal character types', still sitting on their
potties, and either displaying the evocative traits in their
obstinacy, parsimony, obsessive orderliness or, contrariwise
and sometimes simultaneously, in traits which act as reaction-
formations, in excessive pliancy, in revelling in dirt and
untidiness, and in bouts of ill-considered generosity – all
analogical symptoms of the retentions/expulsions of the
shitting habits of their yesteryears. Uneasily we find too many
of these traits displayed, sometimes exotically, by our
Chancellor of the Exchequer.

During his undergraduate days his flat, even by student
standards, was deemed to be 'filthy'. One contemporary
recalls: 'it was disgusting . . . chaotic'; later in his life, another
flat in which he continued to live after he became an MP, was
described as being 'if never quite so dirty . . . equally untidy'.
In more recent days aides have been bemused by the jumble of
mixed-up official papers and dirty shirts which he carries in the
same bag to overnight conferences, a quirk that recalls his old
habits when, as prospective parliamentary candidate, he was
forever carrying around plastic bags stuffed with newspaper
cuttings and statistical papers:

> Faced with an awkward question, he would fish about in
> the pile of documents and triumphantly pull out facts and
> figures to prove his point . . . Fellow-workers in the Party
> shook their heads in disbelief at the general air of
> disorganisation that surrounded him.

There are occasions when his behaviour provides an exquisite
corroborative case history of the sensuous gains an anal-

retentive personality may, by delaying his evacuation, wrest from his sphincter control. His biographer has told how the PhD thesis on which Brown had been toiling intermittently for the best part of a decade was brought to a conclusion:

> He only just made it. The 532-page tome . . . was delivered at the last possible moment after Brown telephoned his flatmate in Marchmond Road from Edinburgh airport, where he was on his way to Spain to prepare Scottish Television coverage of the 1982 World Cup football tournament. Could someone get his thesis down to the binders? It was delivered with five minutes to spare.

Such idiosyncratic behaviour should alert us; his intellectual prowess, his gravitas, the respect he commands from so many of his parliamentary colleagues and from a large section of the public, should not, in a dependency-yearning for leadership and a commendable eagerness to displace Blair, cause us to overlook the man's deficiencies. There are questions to be asked, not least the one querying the rationale of his tight control of the nation's finances for some years followed by an almost unprecedented splurge. Claims of valid objective reasons can be advanced for such policy-making; but there is a babe in Everyman, and the stubborn infant first refusing to give up his faeces and then enjoying defecating in a great splurge is a disquieting analogue when related to Brown's financial policy. No one has better understood than the great economist John Maynard Keynes, who had immersed himself in Freud's work in 1925, the connection between anality and financial policy-making, and no one more adeptly defended the view that the link between the infant's stools and money was clinically well established. But Brown, although sometimes making large claims, is no Keynes and we should be aware of his lack of insight into his own motivations. We should ask whether his apotheosis of prudence was a Calvinistic effort to cloak and morally justify the anal delights of tightening and loosening the sphincter.

Drawing attention in this manner to Brown's frailties does not, however, necessarily invalidate his right to usurp Blair. As prime minister he would no longer be encumbered by Mandelson and Campbell and, indeed, Blair; in Downing Street fresh air would dispel the fetid atmosphere in which competitive rivalries presently incubate and are injected into policy-making. More, his marriage and the blessings of parenthood which he well deserves, together with the realisation of his ambition to be PM, could result in the emergence of a man less angry, more relaxed and confident; with private emotions thus less clamorous and threatening, he is likely to have less need to impose the rigid obsessional policy-making which in the past has helped him to keep his world in place. If it is contended, as it well may be, that such a scenario is over-optimistic and psychologically improbable, the riposte must be that it depends as much upon the Parliamentary Labour Party as upon Brown. Under Blair, some of its members are at last learning how to rebel. If they have the integrity to resist the blandishments of patronage and recognise the need for constant invigilation by the legislature of the executive, they, and the nation, will be able to use Brown's considerable talents without becoming victims of the foibles of his temperament. When and if Brown enters No. 10 Downing Street, that is a possible though not certain outcome.

Alistair Campbell

Alistair Campbell, Blair's hyperactive director of communications, the fourth man of the ataxic quartet that fell apart in January 2001, was designated to be the back-seat driver of the 2001 election campaign, to peddle Brown's dross; his sales talk was to ensure the electors, without askance, accepted the pre-election bribes Brown was to shower upon them without realising the sop was but a return of taxes already levied upon them. Campbell's CV showed that he was well equipped to perform the necessary political confidence trick.

Following upon his appearance as a witness in a High Court action, the *Sunday Times*, on 5 May 1996, published a profile of the man which has never been challenged; it tells of a personal history and temperament guaranteed to exacerbate, not still, the turbulences which distinguished the quartet. The *Sunday Times* recounted:

> The bagpipe-playing former boozer who began his writing career composing soft porn, and once thumped a journalistic colleague in defence of Robert Maxwell's honour, was last week described by a High Court judge as 'not a witness in whom I could feel 100 per cent confidence'.

And the judge's other admonition, 'less than completely open and frank', added to the disquiet occasioned by Campbell's CV. After he left Cambridge, where, the *Sunday Times* tells us, he 'specialised in drinking and football' and went in his third year at university to teach in Nice, he made his debut in soft pornography:

> Then 22, he wrote an article for Forum magazine under the headline 'The Riviera Gigolo', recounting the sexual exploits of, well, a Cambridge modern language student teaching in Nice. Other articles followed, one on the pleasures of busking with 'incredibly phallic' bagpipes which turned women on, and another urging sexual athletes to give up smoking; 'the smoker, unfit as he is, is unlikely to be able to keep the bedsprings bouncing all night'.

With such qualifications he went on to work as a journalist on the tabloids, recording how much drink he consumed in a not untypical day: '15 pints of beer, half a bottle of Scotch, 4 bottles of wine with David Mellor at lunch . . .' Unsurprisingly, he suffered a nervous breakdown and, to survive, renounced alcohol, resumed his career, worked singularly unambivalently for Maxwell and was then head-hunted by Blair.

Blair thought so much of Campbell's talents that he sought him out personally in France on holiday in 1994 to persuade him to work for him. He was soon displaying his wiles to his master by masterminding at the 1994 Labour conference the ditching of Clause Four by not distributing in advance the pages of Blair's speech which contained that contentious proposal, and thus opponents were caught off balance; he continued to bring the same skills and lack of political scruples to his organisation of New Labour's election campaigns and government information services.

Almost all the conventions and regulations that in the past governed the Government Information Service (GIS) were swept aside; the service created to give the public genuine information became, under Campbell, an outrageously partisan channel for government propaganda; the subtleties inhibiting civil servants from being other than the dispassionate, information officers they were appointed to be, were mocked and set aside; the age of the unabashed spin doctor was inaugurated.

The spin doctors under Campbell have had some presentational successes but in the end, after their repeated bungled efforts to mask the government's scandals, they have discredited themselves and left an unbelieving public, unable to distinguish between fact and fiction, dangerously cynical of all politics and politicians. No single individual associated with the Labour government has contributed more to the creation of this mood than Campbell.

Six months after the election of Labour in 1997, Campbell, always ready to aggressively defend the indefensible, tried in vain to cloud the sickening spectacle of Blair, in return for a £2 million donation to party funds by Bernie Ecclestone, agreeing to continue peddling cancer at Silverstone despite Labour having given, in the May 1997 election, an unequivocal pledge to bar tobacco advertising.

In the second Labour government Campbell, unabashed, continued to spin. One of the most blatant of his attempts to mislead the press and public was seen in his handling of the Mittal affair, which he had foolishly first encouraged Blair to dismiss as 'Garbagegate'. The facts were that an Indian steel billionaire, Lakshmi Mittal, with a home in London, gave £125,000 to the Labour Party just before the 2001 General Election. Two months later Blair sent a favourable letter about Mittal's company to the President of Romania, where Mittal was trying to buy a huge steel-works, even though his company was registered in a Caribbean tax haven and employed only ninety people in the UK. Meantime, the Department of International Development backed a loan of £70 million from the European Bank of Reconstruction & Development to support the privatisation of Romania's steel-works which would, of course, help Mittal's purchase. As the press closed in on the matter, Campbell changed the government's story on Mittal several times; in a mishmash of confusing dates and half-truths he claimed that Mittal's donation came after the election, that the Romanian deal had already been completed when Blair signed his letter, that Mittal's company was British, and that the letter that Blair signed had not been changed to remove a reference to Mittal being his 'friend'. Not surprisingly, the headlines in the *Sunday Times* and other newspapers, as the real facts were discovered, were 'Lies, damned lies and Labour spin'.

With characteristic insouciance, Campbell was again, before long, up to his usual tricks and attempted to muddy the waters when the story emerged of Paul Drayson's, the chief executive of PowderJect Pharmaceuticals, two £50,000 donations to the

Labour Party coinciding with the company's being awarded contracts by the Health Department totalling £49 million – one of which, for smallpox vaccine, was valued at £32 million. No wonder that Bill Morris, before his retirement as general secretary of the Transport & General Workers Union, in April 2002 voiced his concerns: 'It seems to a lot of people,' he said, 'that the party is more or less abandoning its roots and the party is almost up for sale to the highest bidder.' Engendered by Campbell's antics, that is a belief shared by many, and is strengthened by the fact that Lord Sainsbury, himself a government minister, has given upwards of £8.5 million to the Labour Party.

The fantasies Campbell spun as a pornographer had indeed an innocence which is wholly lacking in the tales he continued to spin in the service of Tony Blair. When, in 2003, the dossiers provided by the Joint Intelligence Committee on Iraq relating to weapons of mass destruction were initially found to be too inconclusive and bland, Campbell, although strenuously denying he was responsible for the later insertion of the notorious claim that Iraq could deploy chemical or biological weapons within 45 minutes, was nevertheless certainly privy to the unequivocal and express misgiving of Jonathan Powell, Downing Street's Chief of Staff, that such an unfounded claim should be made; despite being thus warned, in no way did Campbell restrain Blair from using that alarmist claim when he launched the final document and, later, misled the Commons. More, by cunning sleight of hand, he turned press and public attention away from the House of Commons Select Committee on Foreign Affairs' appointed task, that of investigating the murky origins of the Iraqi war, to his own private war against the BBC, which, under his orders, Blair intemperately supported, by accusing it, in its reporting, of bias and lack of objectivity; it was one spin too far.

In the cross-fire of his war an innocent David Kelly, the scrupulous United Nations weapons inspector, was murdered.

Although Kelly cut his own wrist and bled to death, a coroner's verdict of suicide is bound to be unacceptable to an outraged public – seeing blood on the hands of those involved in the ignoble imbroglio. In a vain attempt to contain public indignation, Blair, prompted by Campbell, appointed Lord Hutton's inquiry into the events; at that inquiry, entrapped in the coils of his own making, we heard the last gasps of Campbell's political life: exhausted, he quit his post.

Now he is free to return to the gutter press from which he emerged and, untrammelled, to peddle at high prices the daily shorthand diaries which he has maintained; he will be able to regale us with tales of how, as any dominatrix, he lashed Britain's Prime Minister into willing submission.

Such tales would have an authenticity that his pornographic stories lacked. In July 2003 Robert Harris vividly told us of the morbid relationship between the two men:

> Mr Campbell exercises an extraordinary psychological dominance over the prime minister. It seems that he can get away with anything. He has called him 'a prat' in front of one witness and has told him to 'get a f . . . move on' when he believes a meeting has gone on too long, and instructed him to drop what he is doing and concentrate on something else 'because it can't f . . . wait'. Watching him once on a mobile phone to Blair, striding up and down and wagging his finger, I felt I was hallucinating; surely here was the prime minister issuing orders to an official rather than the other way round?

Blair will, ere long, pay a heavy price for the masochistic pleasures Campbell afforded him. In his self-indulgence and dependence on Campbell to defend his own reputation, Blair has dug his own grave. With Campbell's spin replacing conviction, the ruthless manipulation of the message and the media untrammelled by civil service ethics and constitutional restraint, the polls repeatedly reveal that New Labour is now regarded as more sleazy than the Tories; it is indeed a dismal judgement on six years of New Labour government.

Peter Thomson

In the 1997 election campaign, unlike the later ones, there was a fifth man hovering around the quartet. Now we hear little of him; he has disappeared into the shadows – but his influence remains. To support him in the 1997 election, Blair called back to London from Australia his old Oxford mentor Peter Thomson, a disciple of Macmurray, who brought 'glad tidings'. But he was always unlikely to dispel the fetid atmosphere of Blair's quartet for, as Thomson explained in June 1996, he brought with him his favourite quote from that Scottish moral philosopher: 'All meaningful action is for the sake of friendship.' 'But I want no role,' he explained, when Blair found for him the vicarage of St Luke's, Holloway, 'other than friendship.' Doubtless he found responses to his message at self-styled post-evangelical St Luke's, a happy-clappy, pew-less, uncluttered world filled by trendy young Christians much addicted to histrionic audience participation in services that can start with a man dragging a full-sized cross across the floor and then continue in a demotic style of worship which would cause traditional Anglicans to choke on their vespers. But because the message was fatally flawed, far from finding resonances within Blair's circle, it excited further rivalry and heightened the tensions.

It has been seen, when exploring Macmurray's Boy Scout proselytising themes, that his constant affirmations 'that the noblest form of human existence is friendship', and that, in friendship as in community, antagonism and estrangement lead only to 'despair', contain a massive denial of the ambivalences that must pervade any genuine flesh-and-blood relationship; that to seek to outlaw the inherent aggressiveness within sexuality is a vain quest, and can lead only to distortions of the human spirit which can have lamentable personal and social consequences.

For the restless Thomson, the one-time 'mature' theological student, one-time Australian television newsreader, one-time estate agent, twice thrown out of his parishes, one-time headmaster of an Australian public school and one-time farmer was never likely to bring stability to the quartet. But, more seriously, the doctrine this cove emphasised, far from directing attention to the causes of the inner circle's disharmony, the androgynous and homoerotic elements with which it is excessively infused, totally denied their existence. Thomson's appointment under the patronage of Blair was a short-lived and part-time addition to the quartet, and it most certainly did not result in the exposure of the immature foursome to a maturational process. Preaching sweetness, light and 'pure' friendship ensures – since sex and aggression when repudiated will always hit back and wage incessant guerrilla war – that discords swell into a deafening cacophony.

With Campbell and Mandelson publicly questioning each other's sanity, it was that cacophony that Blair and his rum entourage condemned us to endure as an overture to the 2001 election. Turned off by the discord, many were left feeling their only option was to register their disgust with the unseemly hooligan brawling presented by Blair and his politically adolescent circle by refusing to register their vote; it was a sorry time for our parliamentary democracy.

Disappointment and Hope

In June 1996 Blair put his name to a contribution in *Prospect*. There, provocatively, in manic mood, and speaking of his New Labour Party, he triumphantly announced: 'We have cleared out the deadwood of outdated ideology, policy and organisation.' The referents no doubt included veterans like myself; but although he may be only a little premature in announcing my funeral, he fortunately gravely errs in believing that there is no life left for Old Labour.

He was mistaking silence for acquiescence, exploiting the loyalties of the traditional core of the Labour Party, and relying on their allegiance not to break ranks even as he outrageously repudiated all their essential values. He was relying too on their defeatism. The exclusion of the party from government for so many years, the hopes raised and then dashed, left traditional supporters lacking confidence. Deliberately raising the 'anxiety level' within the party by warning dissidents that express criticism meant electoral failure, he created a political mood where criticism was quenched lest it helped the Tories to retain power.

For me, such apprehensions recalled those of 1945 when so many of the political 'sophisticates' on the left, believing it was incredible that Churchill could be dislodged by the Labour Party alone, were urging caution and alliances; indeed, the Communist Party, then a relevant force in British politics, called for a government of national unity to be created. That timidity was not shared by those of us in the ranks in the Forces, and I still retain yellowing sheaves of articles which I as a young man wrote mocking those who, after the wilderness years of the 1930s, could not believe in the prospect of an overwhelming Labour victory. There are rare moments in British politics when elections can yield far more than a mere alternation of office-holders: 1945 was such a moment. It was briskly used; the Welfare State was created. In 1997, the opportunity was available to emulate the Attlee Government; it was spurned.

There is a tide in the affairs of men which must be taken at the flood, and on such a sea we were, in 1997, afloat. We were living under a totally discredited, decrepit and demoralised regime; estrangements within the Tory Party were chronic, and no political cosmetics could heal them. Amidst the clamour of Tory self-destruction, there was no need for Old Labour to talk in whispers, but Blair and his spin doctors sought to persuade us otherwise.

Those spin doctors were trenchantly attacked in 1996 by Joy Johnson, the Labour Party's one-time media director, who quit her post rather than endure their antics. She deplored their 'language of exclusivity'; they spoke, she said, a ghetto language, a tongue confined to a small Westminster enclave; thus:

the lobby [is] feeding off the politicians and the politicians feeding off the lobby – traipsing between Number Four Millbank, the broadcasting centre for BBC, Sky TV and ITN and the House of Commons. Our political post has become a story of sophisticated games with rules only understood by the few.

We of Old Labour need neither to unravel those rules, nor to abide by them, nor to demean ourselves by using their debased marketing vocabulary.

If Britain's decline is to be fully arrested, its infrastructure properly developed and refurbished, its social, education and health services adequately funded, the poverty and home-lessness to be alleviated, then Labour needs to use its traditional language and to direct it against its traditional enemies. Never was it more relevant than now to assail finance capitalism. The City and the bankers, in their greed for ever more obscene profits, in their notorious short-termism, are still frustrating the development of British technology and sabotaging the growth of manufacturing industries upon whose wealth-creation so much depends if we are to fulfil our aspirations to have a happier and more just society.

But the institutions, if permitted, will continue to seek speedy dividends and eschew involvement in, and respon-sibility for, long-term investment in industries; the bankers will not easily come out of their anonymous centralised citadels to journey to the smaller manufacturers in the regions. The culture of the takeover bid, of defensive asset-stripping, of the slashing of research funding, will, unless seriously challenged, continue to envelop the Square Mile. The City's walls, protecting the malpractices, are high and thick; and Blair's is a muted trumpet, to which they will not fall; strong legislative battering-rams and tough fiscal policies are needed before those walls crumble.

In 1996 even orthodox economists were advocating increased taxation. In July Anatole Kaletsky, writing in *The Times*, recommended that the response to the expected 1997 consumer boom be tough fiscal policies; Blair, therefore, had economic as well as equitable justifications for increasing taxes on those well able to bear them. But that required a confrontational stance vetoed by Blair's temperament. In the General Election campaign of 1997, without fear of effective backlash, there was no need, in order to obtain electoral victory, to expunge from its manifesto Labour's traditional language directed at its traditional enemy. The electorate, despairing of the Tories, was at that time ready to approve an assault on the obscene excesses of financial capitalism and was no less ready to be led, as their fathers had been in 1945, to accept sacrifices that could arrest Britain's decline, develop and refurbish its infrastructure, ensure adequately funded social-cum-education-cum-health services, and alleviate existing poverty and homelessness; the electors were ready to respond to a manifesto advocating an attack on inimical vested interests.

But this would have been a manifesto advocating the policies of confrontation, a stance totally alien to Blair's temperament and emotional needs. Aware of the potential pressures for a far more courageous programme than would be awakened by his timorous approach, Blair and his entourage acted defensively by devising a ballot of all members to approve the 1997 party manifesto which had been provisionally set out in *The Road to the Manifesto*; they had to approve it as a package; no amendment or addition allowed. More skilful spin doctors would have avoided bestowing such a title, one telling of highways, on the document, for to Old Labour it immediately recalled the famous gibe of Nye Bevan against those who, over forty years before, sought to move the Labour Party to the centre: 'We know what happens to people who stay in the middle of the road. They get run down.'

Few party manifestoes are very important. There was one notable exception. In 1848, in London, at the request of a handful of émigré political refugees, tailors and print-workers, the 29-year-old Marx and 28-year-old Engels composed *The Communist Manifesto*, that extraordinary compound of the universal and particular which, for good and bad, was over the decades to become the accepted creed for millions of mankind. Marx's document was of similar length to Blair's 1997 manifesto; and it moved the earth. Blair's caused not the slightest tremor in a single City bank; he, to trap party members into irrevocable commitment, elevated its importance, so that every sentence in the flaccid document could be regarded as a sacred text binding Labour Party members who, to retain or gain

membership, were called upon to declare themselves devotees of
this insipid holy writ. Meantime, to ensure non-believers within
the older membership were swamped, Blair, in well-advertised
recruitment drives, built up his new personal electorate.

In practice, of course, governance, after elections, is almost
always shaped by the exigent, not by the proclaimed priorities
within vote-baited manifestoes; as Harold Macmillan told us,
the real determinants are 'events, events'. That 1997 manifesto
left action by the Labour government open to be determined by
events; a manifesto remembered, if at all, by what was left out,
rather than its ambiguous promises; a manifesto not wordless,
but one deficient in verbs – for verbs import action, specific
deeds, and these are largely eschewed.

Writing in the *Guardian*, Simon Hoggart, far too
experienced a political observer to be bemused by Blair, in
penetrating parody described his reaction as he listened to the
leader's presentation of *The Road to the Manifesto*:

As so often in a Blair speech, as it progressed, it began to
shed verbs. Sentences were reduced to a cluster. Nouns
and pronouns. Sentences, verbless.

'Fairness at work. Practical proposals. In crime, tough
on crime, tough on the causes of crime. In Europe, leadership not isolation . . .'

'In every area policy is New Labour.' (Sorry, that does
contain a verb, but sounds as if it doesn't.) 'Smaller
classes. Shorter waiting lists. A turning point in British
politics. New Labour. New Life for Britain.'

For too long, the party's energy wasted. On verbs. For
the British people, now, no more verbs. Tough on verbs,
tough on the causes of verbs. New Labour. New nouns,
adjectives. Real words. Words for a new Britain.

There is a purpose to this. Verbless sentences sound as
if they are firm promises. The mind supplies the missing
phrases: 'we shall provide . . . we will legislate for . . .'

Yet nothing concrete has been proposed. Like so much of the manifesto, each verbless phrase offers a fine aspiration, worthy in every way, utterly estimable, and entirely vague.

But vague as it was, certain directions were only too clear. Barbara Castle, a great fighter, loathing the prevarication and ageism enveloping the document as expressed in its policy U-turn reversing Labour's plan for basic state pensions to rise in line with earnings, defiantly said that this unalterable manifesto was making the vote upon its contents 'a loyalty test – like an election in a one-party state'. And that is precisely what it was. When asked whether the whole stratagem of manifesto and ballot was another example of centralising power in his own hands, Blair arrogantly replied:

With a modern political party you have to have effective ways of decision-making. My attitude has always been: if you don't like the leader, get rid of the leader and get someone else in to do the job.

Consensus, his false consensus, was to be inviolable; plurality could not be tolerated.

When, in the summer of 1996 Blair, in a series of private meetings wooed Labour MPs in an endeavour to avoid contentiousness in the annual elections to the shadow Cabinet, some present played a little game. They counted the number of times Blair in his presentations used the first person singular and how many times the first person plural; there was no score for 'we' – but the 'I's proliferated. With favourable opinion polls continuing to inflame Blair's narcissism it increasingly emerged, publicly and unmortified. His MP audiences, noting these personality traits and tardily becoming wary, resisted his blandishments. In the subsequent ballot eighty MPs refused to vote for his shadow chancellor and home secretary, and to

make their resentments no less explicit placed the most
prominent woman dissident high in the poll. Blair's response
was dictated by his emotional needs not those of his party. He
demoted those not prepared to submit unconditionally to his
ukase, and let it be known his Whips were to prepare tougher
disciplinary measures against those MPs who dared to demur.
Blair's only concession to those resentful of the timidity of his
programme was to preach patience, explaining it would take
time and continuous Labour governments to bring about the
needed changes. This was the counsel of the pusillanimous; it
was not patience that was required, but impatience. Any halfwit
can work according to the doctrine that politics is the art of the
possible; all my legislative experience tells me that politics
worth the candle is the art of the impossible.

Blair threw that option away when he arrived in Downing
Street in 1997. Although he had at his disposal a huge majority,
the power of patronage, and a legacy of the excessive power
that a legislature, from Thatcher onwards, had yielded to the
executive, he nevertheless acted as if his purpose was little
more than 'good management' of the country; in both of his
governments, always a becalmed consensus has been sought,
not any fundamental change that could cause problems. It is
because Blair's consensus and timorous policies essentially
accommodate defeatism that he has treated as relics those
within the Labour Party who use their radical socialist
traditions to challenge his assumptions.

Nevertheless, despite his endeavours, Blair has not quite
succeeded in firmly pinning the label of anachronism upon
British socialism; but he has inflicted self-doubt on some
within the Labour movement who, to gain power and position,
have acted as if there were no alternative but to accept post-
Thatcherite pollution as a permanent feature of our political
environment. There is no such inevitability. I have too often
seen politicians use that type of historicism as an excuse for
inaction and I have always admired Leon Trotsky's scorn of:

the pusillanimity of an historic fatalism which in all questions, whether concrete or private, passively seeks a solution in general laws and leaves out of the count the mainspring of all human decisions – the living and acting individual

It remains open to us, young and old, who find Blair's imprint upon the Labour Party unacceptable to prove that his dismissal of Old Labour as 'deadwood' is the most colossal arboreal misjudgement in contemporary politics. If, like Blair, there are those in political life who, sadly, from the start, from their earliest years, through external circumstances, are faulted, then it is not for us to relieve them of their private neurotic traits by condoning their transferring them to the public domain; that is one step too far in de-privatisation.

The cynical, the excessively worldly-wise, and the well-intentioned faint-hearted will certainly affirm that whatever may have been the psychodynamic or psychopathology that brought him to his leadership, Blair's hijacking of the Labour Party is complete and irrevocable; and that those engaged in subversion – as is the declared intention of this book – are foolishly nostalgic and out of kilter with the times. As disenchantment spreads, I am no longer as unfashionable as I was when the first edition of this book was published in 1996; but in any event, being unfashionable is a condition to which I am no stranger; enduring the opprobrium attached to expounding initially unfashionable minority causes was a pre-condition to achieving the social reforming legislation with which I am associated, and which in my old age now comforts me for all the years I gave to the House of Commons.

When, these days, we sluggishly approach the polling-booths, we do not go with partisan rage to register our protest; nor do we go to affirm our trust; in neither despair, hate nor anger do we place the cross that once, as in a love letter, told of an affection for party, political leader or community; we go possessed only by that Cinderella of emotions: disappointment. Puny men, like Blair, now unmasked, and Iain Duncan Smith, cannot excite the grander emotions.

The dictionary definition of disappointment is an appointment cancelled. Millions of voters in the 1997 election believed that in voting for Blair they had made an appointment with a New Britain, young again; it was, of course, an impossible rendezvous, never to be kept or reached. By their very nature, strong wishes and expectations cannot be fully met; for disappointment is endemic to the human condition; the shadows of the maternal denials in our infancy, and of our boundless lustful desires are cast upon all in adulthood. We painfully learn that excitement might really be more in the anticipation; in the chase, rather than the capture; in the journey, not the arrival. The French novelist, André Gide, wrote that the first touch of the hand can be more exciting than the later sexual encounter; in public life too, the politician's promise and the electorate's wish can rarely culminate in a truly fulfilling consummation.

But there are particular reasons why the two Blair elections have resulted in an especial disappointment. All of us have dreamed the infantile dream of pure fulfilment, of a bliss that is fully uninhibited, unambivalent, untouched by elements of displeasure; the dream of transcendence, of soaring into a realm of pure pleasure is the very stuff in adult life of infatuation, the conviction which, if it does not become obsessive, temporarily affords us fantasies of omnipotence and seemingly unalloyed thrills. Only when the infatuation passes do we acknowledge our idealisations entailed a denial of complexity, and how it came about because such, in Freud's terms, is the imperishability of the infantile unconscious, that we allowed those origins to hold sway over the reality principle.

No group of politicians is more dangerous than that which infantilises its electorate; Blair, reactivating and refuelling our earliest fantasies, can certainly claim his place in the ignoble pantheon. On 2 May 1997 he announced that 'a new dawn has broken' and told us that the Millennium Dome would be a world-class symbol of Britain's rebirth and renewal. His was a political project explicitly based on the overriding value of modernisation and newness; the old was out, including Old Labour and those, like myself, who subscribed to it were 'deadwood'. Radical transformation was promised and, to the delight of so many, it was to come about without strife; Britain's metamorphosis was to be achieved painlessly; by consensus, we could bring in a pristine conflict-free world, world without end. And Middle England, which had given Blair his premiership, acclaimed his gospel with a resounding 'Amen!' Together they drifted into dream. But now, belatedly, even the deepest sleepers have been rudely awakened from that hypnotic trance; the deceptions Blair orchestrated to justify his Iraq war have left the nation, as the polls show, profoundly mistrustful of the man; he will never regain the trust so many placed in him, and because they foolishly colluded in his fantasising, they are angry with themselves, an anger that ere long will be expressed in the ballot box.

The reality, not that stuff of dreams, is of a different order and was clearly set out by the economist Will Hutton in his audacious bestseller *The State We're In* where he came to the irrefutable conclusion that without drastic change the prospect for Britain was indeed baleful; he affirmed that no state had:

ever been able to recast its economy, political structures and society to the extent that Britain must do, without suffering defeat in war, economic collapse or revolution. Only traumatic events on that scale de-legitimise the existing order to such an extent that a country concedes the case for dramatic change.

But it is certain that no catalytic event on the scale of defeat in war or total economic collapse is likely to occur. No less certain is that the needed changes eloquently categorised by Hutton will meet fierce opposition; none will be conceded voluntarily. Only a government with courage and will would be capable of ending the protection afforded to vested interests; no government led by Blair will accomplish that task.

After the pussy-footing consensus-seeking of New Labour's first four years, even the think-tank Demos, once so supportive of the Blair 'Project', acknowledged its disenchantment and bemoaned that the core issues were untouched. As 2001 arrived, Demos' director Tom Bentley pronounced that Blair had not only lost his freshness, he had too lost his intellectual nerve. Bentley's threnody is, however, off-key; the deficit from which Blair suffers, and makes us suffer, is not intellectual but emotional, and it is irremediable, for the political cowardice displayed in New Labour's years in office stems from the rigid mindset of a middle-aged man, ever fearing to attack lest he may in turn be mown down.

The resultant disappointment felt by all engaged in the political process is profound, and that felt by the electorate, although not as severe, is widespread; but it is disappointment, not despair, that is being experienced. There are countries round the world where appalling internal wars have left the national life bereft of most of its meaning and feelings. Severely depressed, we get beyond crying; but, luckily, the disappointed can still cry, for they still remember the hopes and desires once held.

The psychoanalyst tells us of patients who set up fantasies of powerful nostalgia which contrast with their current painful experiences; their fantasies are idealised memories of an imagined and glorious Idyllic Past; a past free of ambivalence, pain and uncertainty; a past in which people felt secure within themselves and within their families and communities; a past when everything was simpler and better. The infantilising political leader can woo voters by promising he will take them back to this imagined fairyland; but, paradoxically, the disappointment that must follow when the promised destination is seen to be a mirage, can, given mature political leadership, be in public life, as in private life, an aid to sustaining hopefulness and galvanising determined efforts to make things better 'again'.

In disappointment, unlike despair, hope can be reclaimed, recharged; in short, as has sometimes been suggested, disappointment can have an adaptive function. Seeking relief from current painful experiences, both individuals and society can turn to comedies, love stories and televised romantic adventures; but there are less passive ways of keeping alive hopes for the future, active ways to turn around disappointment by, with hope as the armour, living more combatively and more realistically.

Disappointment with the present political process did not begin under Blair, but it has certainly accelerated. Tom Bentley, speaking of the year 2000 and coming belatedly to note a phenomenon that has been in place in Britain for longer than he seems to have grasped, wrote:

> The most unusual politics of the year have come from the edges of the mainstream ... single issue network-based direct action politics are not restricted to the Green and anti-capitalist fringes.

Certainly the growth of lobbying and the decline of party was unequivocally expressed in 2000; yet the fuel protests, a countryside movement constructed almost overnight, and anti-GM food organisations tearing up crops were but the latest manifestations of the sea-change that has been taking place in our politics over recent decades. Blair, even with a huge parliamentary majority, is too emotionally insecure to permit dissent and so has, by every measure at his disposal, sought desperately to impose consensus by diktat; the Whips, shameless patronage, MPs panting for advancement and over-dependent upon salaries and swollen expenses which they could not reap outside Westminster, together with an Opposition that is risible, have together depreciated Parliament. It is no longer a forum where hopes can be shaped and realised – and with Parliament thus demeaned, protests by those who will not give up hope must needs become increasingly expressed, as they have, in extra-parliamentary agitation. It was not ever thus.

I can recall, when seeking to alter our divorce laws, finding that despite the oppression those laws were imposing upon so many, there was no extant organisation promoting their cause and, wanting outside support, I had to reactivate the one body formed decades earlier that had become almost totally dormant; lobbying groups in those days were sparse. Indeed it was much later when leading, together with some Nobel Peace prize-winning scientists and, less comfortably, with Arthur Scargill, Britain's first anti-civil nuclear march that I became conscious that the political parties were failing to capture the allegiances of large swathes of public opinion; the 10,000 young men and women, many with their families, that on that day I addressed from the plinths of Trafalgar Square, belonged to no party.

For me that day was the first real intimation that the established political parties – even though they were claiming to be parties of a 'broad church' – were disintegrating, and the binding forces in our society that they had hitherto provided were unlikely to endure. Now single-issue bodies proliferate as never before; some, it is true, are negative and self-interested but most, whether they protest against a bypass, a runway, a hospital closure, the rundown of the NHS, the state of our prisons, the poverty and disarray of our inner cities, the introduction of genetically manipulated foods, the desecration of the environment, the racialism and gender discriminations still prevailing – all these pressure groups are providing an opportunity for men and women to be libidinally bound together, to be part of the civilising process, as Freud has put it:

in the service of Eros whose purpose is to combine single human individuals and after that families, then races, peoples and nations, into one great unity, the unity of mankind.

Blair's incapacity to tolerate plurality is contributing to the disintegration of the party system which, in modern times, has sustained Britain's democracy; with the political parties failing us, attracting ever diminishing fealty, inspiring no common loyalty binding us to others, it is protest outside the political parties which is becoming institutionalised; and, within its organisation, men and women are seeking to recover the mutuality that is now being denied them by our depleted supra-familial collectivities; the Crown has failed us, the empty churches tell of lack of faith, and now our political parties either, like Blair's New Labour, frightened of commitment and consequent confrontation, flee from ideology or, like Iain Duncan Smith's Tory party, in a bid to stay alive, desperately voice anachronistic and xenophobic dogma which estranges all their political sophisticates.

With the political parties so discredited, the 21st century has therefore begun with the question that shocks even those with the wit and perceptiveness to ask it: Is the future Westminster or Seattle? There are those involved in single-issue lobbying, like animal-rights campaigners, who have only tunnel vision but there are many other protesters who know the specific enemy occasioning so much of the prevailing public dis-locations; and the more discerning apologists for the enemy are sensing the danger. Viewing with dismay the swamping by thousands of protesters from all over the world of the Seattle meeting of the World Trade Organisation in December 1999, The *Financial Times* complained:

The backlash against global capitalism is gaining force and power, and politicians so far have done little but sit

back and watch it happen . . . The protests have real
importance as a warning signal that public unease with
capitalism and the forces of globalisation is reaching a
worrying level.

In Seattle there had been formed the most unlikely of
coalitions: passionate environmentalists, trade union members,
church groups, and that ultimate modern political oxymoron,
organised anarchists; all took part in a demonstration telling the
world that the American mainstream political system no longer
provides any outlet for opinions which challenge the presumptions and values of global capitalism. Seattle-type events have,
since 1999, been repeated in Davos and Genoa. And here, in
London, there was an unprecedented and historic event when
one million people marched against the Iraq war, showing that
as a nation we were no longer prepared to passively accept the
political leadership of the established parties. From Seattle to
London, all the protestors were expressing their dissent with the
verve that comes from conviction and commitment.

Contrariwise, our party politics are becoming an enervating,
not an enabling, process; and, consequently, Britain's political
landscape is destined to change. To posit that Britain's lobbies
and ragged pressure groups, linked and in tune with the Seattle-
type protests, could act as a counterweight to all the formidable
minions – including our established political parties – at the disposal of global capitalism may seem extravagantly sanguine;
but there is nothing sacrosanct about our present political
parties, and their history shows that they can rise, fall and dis-
integrate; to affirm that the future may lie outside their grasp is
certainly not necessarily an expression of hope over experience.

Indeed no party could have had a more untidy and fractious
start than the Labour Party which despite, or perhaps because
of, the brevity of its periods in government was, by tempering
private greed and indifference to the disadvantaged, the single
most civilising influence enveloping Britain in the twentieth

century. Yet so ragged was its initial formation that ambiguity still prevails as to when the party can specifically be said to have come into existence; it is generally accepted that its birthday was just over a century ago – in February 1900 when, under the chairmanship of a trade union Liberal MP, 129 delegates of an extraordinary mixed tranche of interests assembled. Among them were 'Lib-Lab Possiblers', members of the Marxist Social Democratic Federation, representatives of gas workers and railway servants, radicals, and Keir Hardie of the Independent Labour Party; this somewhat motley crowd gathered together to form an alliance of mutual interests and interdependence. With bloated imperialism abroad and the Boer War raging, it was in some respects an inauspicious time – but this coming together was to prove the most fruitful of miscegenations; at the time it was little remarked upon but it was to breed the most significant political party in Britain's history, a love-in not seen before or since. A huge family of socialists and trade unionists was to come into existence with the nowadays much-mocked brothers, sisters and comrades bound together, ever quarrelling like most families, yet ever preserving a fundamental unity.

But now that family is breaking down; increasingly the estrangement between party activists and the manipulators of New Labour becomes irrevocable. With the Tories virtually written off, the activists find the enemy is within and the mood has grown, even among the most schismatic of Left groups, to find common ground. Aware of nascent fracas, Blair, ever responding to the advice of the egregious Mandelson, spon-sored in July 2003 an international conference on 'progressive governance' where, accompanied by dragooned ministers, he addressed 500 academics, think-tankers and pliant friends like Bill Clinton, and set out his stall for the next General Election; there he promised Labour Party members that the next manifesto would be written in their language and that the first priority of Labour's third term would be 'entrenching stability and spreading wealth'. That muted clarion call would have left unmoved the 500 delegates attending, in the same month, another conference held in the TUC's Congress Hall that was little noticed by the press but was probably more significant than Blair's highly publicised jamboree. With the platform draped in banners carrying portraits of Keir Hardie, Clem Attlee and John Smith, the delegates from trade union branches and constituency Labour parties were deliberating their stratagem to reclaim the Labour Party from the Blairites. The trend is clear: a new opposition is in the process of a long gestation. That conference was an intimation that, painfully, the process has begun. At some time, however long postponed, a coalescence will take place which brings together Labour Party dissidents, the protest lobbies and those coming from the Scottish and Welsh devolved bodies – each of which is likely to become a forum of discontent. Under that scenario a place will also undoubtedly be found for erstwhile Tory voters who, possessed of probity, turn away with disgust from the populism and corruptions of their party.

Such a concordance is unlikely to come into existence without the impetus of direct action; if Parliament does not supply sufficient opposition, then extra-parliamentary action becomes a coercive resource, as Thatcher found when she attempted to clamp down with the poll tax. Many wedded to our parliamentary system will recoil from such prospects but sometimes, as I have learned, there is no alternative. When a haughty Tory government was prepared to abandon the major steel-works of South Wales – as global capitalism is now doing – I participated with the intelligent moderate trade union leaders in the principality in the preparation of direct action responses; and I recall Jim Callaghan, learning of our preliminary plot to close down the Severn Bridge, asking me if I had gone mad. But the threat, and my persuasion as chairman of a select committee with a Conservative majority to have a report sent to the Commons that the government's inaction could lead to serious social disorder, brought about a volte face from a government that had lost its nerve.

Too often we can be conditioned to treat every demonstration as a 'mob'. That rare insightful Australian political scientist, Graham Little, viewing in 1999 events in nearby dictator-ridden Indonesia, pertinently wrote disparagingly of:

> the right-wing sociology defensively constructed out of 'crowd psychology' in response to revolution, especially the French Revolution in the eighteenth century and the rise of socialism in the nineteenth and twentieth. It has been a hugely successful ploy to plant in our heads an unquestioning horror of the 'mob' and of the emotional 'contagion' it is supposed to bring . . . while at the same time distracting attention from the effectiveness of orchestrated violence in crowds such as we have lately had glimpses of both in Dili and Jakarta.

Here in the West, we have seen the benign consequences of orchestrated non-violence which in Leipzig brought about the fall of the Wall, in Prague the Velvet Revolution, in Bucharest the end of Ceauşescu, and in Belgrade the end of Milosevic's dominance. Our political culture, unlike that of France, does not comfortably live in the street; but there is no room for complacency, and a belief that a *ukase* from a chief executive of a cowering legislature can suffocate all dissent in Britain has no validity in these irreverent days.

I think even my political enemies would concede that in bringing about reforms I have not lacked in parliamentarian skills; it may be wondered, therefore, that I should display such an insouciance towards the legislature, that I should prognosticate that the future may lie in extra-parliamentary action as much as within the parliamentary process. There is a particular reason why, however reluctantly, I overcome my own resistances to acknowledge the incapacities of today's parliamentary system. Serendipity occasioned me to be born a Jew, cradled in the essentially syndicalist culture of the South Walian Labour movement prevailing in the first half of the twentieth century. It can hardly be expected that a Jew whose ancestors laid down the law from Mount Sinai should feel intimidated by a parvenu legislature straining to establish its credentials – being a mere seven hundred years old. There are, or were, MPs who have fallen hopelessly in love with the institution, protecting it tenderly from any besmirching and jealous of its antiquity, its procedures and its powers; and there have been in my time splendid parliamentarians, like Michael Foot, who ever saw the Commons as the great institution which had evolved to become the bastion of all our liberties. Michael Foot once reproached me that I did not 'love' Parliament – that I only used it. Certainly I regarded it as a useful instrument to achieve reform, but I never idealised it as the gateway through which we could proceed to the Elysian fields.

Nor did the remarkable leaders of the South Wales Miners Movement, whose stances and philosophy ensured that anarcho-syndicalism, with its stresses upon direct action and disbelief in the efficacy of parliamentary democracy, became one of the most important strands of the Welsh socialism that so shaped my political thinking in my adolescence. It may seem a historical quirk that the varying anarcho-syndicalist doctrines expounded early in the twentieth century by that most original and dangerous of socialist thinkers, Georges Sorel in France, and by Daniel de Leon in the United States, should have reached and so influenced miners, all lacking formal university education, in the remote valleys of Wales; but such was the case. Indeed, in retrospect, I wonder now that as a youngster then working in a factory, I should have been made aware of Sorel through untutored miners; they, like me, were instructed by Sorel:

The most fatal of all democratic institutions are parliaments, since they depend on compromise, concessions, conciliations; even if we forget about the ruses, equivocation, hypocrisy of which syndicalists speak, political combinations are the death of all heroism, indeed of morality itself. The Member of Parliament, no matter how militant his past, is inevitably driven into peaceful association, even co-operation, with the class enemy, in committees, in lobbies, in the Chamber itself.

Such views found a strange but understandable resonance in South Wales. The essential sense of locality; the small pit or forge where all worked, when work was available; the class bonding against predatory coal-owners; the comparative isolation of valley villages or townships; the central role of the local Miners' Lodge; the cinemas and breweries owned by the miners; and the local health schemes which were to become the prototype of the National Health Service – all created a world where there was an intense loyalty to the immediate community. The commitment, however, did not end there; links were formed with syndicalists in other countries, particularly in the USA. Westminster was regarded as an irrelevance; the romantic call was an anarcho-syndicalist tinged-Marxist one: 'Workers of all lands, unite!'

This political mood was to find its fullest expression in the publication in 1912 of the pamphlet *The Miners' Next Step* by the legendary miners' leader Noah Ablett; it was the precipitate to the creation of a militant miners' union with a leadership advocating advance through what was described as 'industrial unionism', an unconventional form of syndicalism sidestepping parliamentary politics; and throughout the twentieth century, until Thatcher wiped out mining and the mining communities of Wales, this philosophy of anarcho-syndicalism in various guises continued to survive.

Some of the miners' leaders over the years, like the redoubtable Arthur J Cook and, more latterly, Dai Francis, were avowed syndicalists. Other presidents of the Miners' Union, like Arthur Horner, at whose feet when a teenager I learned so much, were card-carrying Communists; but they were of a special kind, so aberrant that Moscow could never really contain them. Although once detaining him in the USSR for many months in an attempt to 'correct' his attitudes, the Kremlin never succeeded in casting Horner, one of Britain's most significant trade unionists of the twentieth century, in the Stalinist mould. And the miner-novelist Lewis Jones, whose extraordinary oratory dazzled me when I was young, never relinquished the anarchist streak; he was the man who would attend the Comintern Conferences in Moscow and, alone of all the world-wide delegates, would refuse to stand up when Stalin arrived.

I recall these men, not out of nostalgia, nor, as a veteran parliamentarian, to proffer an apologia for viewing with equanimity the present growth of extra-parliamentary politics. Rather, I offer them as undaunted exemplars who in dark days, when Parliament had failed South Wales and left it poverty-stricken and workless, acted as inspiring and hope-carrying missionaries.

In the election year of 2001 political commentators, predicating the future on the false assumption that the existing party system is immutable, from their stale intellectual dugouts, yet again wearied us; they sought to entrap all political imagination within the confines of the existing clapped-out parties. But the clash of party, upon which contemporary parliamentary democracy has depended, has now become a charade – farcical mummery; and so it is increasingly being seen by an electorate which contemptuously dismisses the businessman's New Labour party and the Tories as indistinguishable. Blair's 'Big Tent' philosophy, large and vacuous enough to contain all, stems from an emotional, not an intellectual, disability; and, at his late age, it is irremediable. With his inclusive politics, Blair has been an incubus sucking the lifeblood out of the body politic; and it is only hope of the quality possessed by those old-timer syndicalists that will resuscitate it.

That hope is a special type of hope; not a politically zealous millenarian kind of hope but one that takes hold of the present; and it is also not a mean, private hope. For hope needs a present as well as a future; and since hope is an emotional relationship between present and future, it can only become meaningful when it is perceived as part of a web of social relations rather than the lonely inexpressive end of individualism. When hope is privatised, when a man does not link his future destiny to others but becomes an isolated stranger he, and the society in which he lives, is doomed to suffer. Pascal once wrote:

> We never take hold of the present. We anticipate the future as though it were too slow in coming and we want to hasten its arrival . . . the present never is our goal; the past and the present are our means; only the future is our end. Thus, we never live, we only hope to live; and in awaiting and preparing ourselves for happiness we inevitably never are happy.

Hope leached away from the present, as Pascal warns, indeed brings no real fulfilment; nor does hope wholly directed to personal achievement and personal fame. Hope privatised cancels itself out, leaving the bearer stricken.

Creative hope was not to be found in the party manifesto of 2001; Gordon Brown, controller of New Labour's manifesto, always boasting of his long-termism, the man who unblushingly and, indeed, with pride, eschews the needed redistribution of wealth by way of direct taxation, has told us that child poverty in Britain, the fourth wealthiest country in the world, will be conquered in the next twenty years. This is the type of promissory note that brought down the scorn of Karl Marx who, in what Isaiah Berlin has described as a most un-Marxist comment, declared: 'Whoever composes a programme for the future is a reactionary.'

Authentic, creative hope is essentially rooted in the immediate; it is an activity affect needing personal commitment. This little essay is therefore intended as an incitement and a temptation; it invites the involvement in today's politics, as well as those of tomorrow, not as a debased career choice but as a dedication. It is an invitation not necessarily confined to those within our decaying political parties; those parties, like the New Labour party, apart from subscribing millionaires purchasing peerages, only want subscriptions from passive paying members and are embarrassed by true party activists; such parties bring us no hope, for they cannot, through quiescent individual members, be journeying purveyors of hope since hope can be neither bought nor sold. Only from relatedness does hope spring.

And that authentic hope can be actualised within all those burgeoning organised groups and lobbies whose concerns, and oftimes ennobling goals, enhance both our society and their member participants. Men's and women's sexuality is a bountiful source of hope; from it can come the inhibited love, the sublimated love found within a worthy common cause; the *terroir* of such collectivities can promote growth; our stunted personal relationships and arrested societal values can, within such an environment, mature. And, if we are moved to exercise that hope, then we can have confidence that the estrangement that Blairites have caused between the parliamentary process and the electorate will not result in a gap to be filled by the detritus of Poujadists and the National Front. It is, of course, not inevitable that the envisaged concordance of dissenters, bringing with it a new political ecology, will arrive; when and if it arrives will depend upon the dynamic of historical forces as 'events, events' are so often portentously described. But it depends even more upon the living human will and, above all, upon hope.

I am already 86; my day is almost done and the future belongs to younger generations. But those who are bitterly disappointed, who lack faith in presumptuous prognostications that a new benign political configuration can come into existence, should take comfort. In the previous century we witnessed an awesome battle between those eternal adversaries governing human destiny: between Eros, the god of love, and Thanatos, the god of destruction and death; it was a century that brought terrible disasters and only by a hair's-breadth did mankind avoid self-annihilation. Yet, in the end, Eros overcame.

When colleagues suffered setbacks and disappointments, Sigmund Freud was wont to end his communications to them with the encouraging valediction: *'Corragio! Corragio!'* Following Freud's example, it is the farewell which I would make to all those disenchanted with politics. With Courage and Hope, we can still overcome.

Sources

Aberbach, D, 'Charisma and attachment theory', *International Journal of Psycho-Analysis*, vol. 76, part 4, August 1995

Abraham, K, *Selected Papers on Psychoanalysis*, Hogarth Press, 1954

Abse, D W, *Excellence and Leadership in a Democracy*, eds Stephen R Graubard & Gerald Holtom, Columbia University Press, 1962

Abse, D W, 'Charisma, Anomie and the Psychopathic Personality', address to the first International Congress on Social Psychiatry, August 1964

Abse, D W, *Hysteria* (2nd edn), Wright Bristol, 1987

Abse, L, *Private Member*, Macdonald, 1973

Abse, L, address to International Society for the History of Rhetoric, Oxford, 1985

Abse, L, *The Times*, 26 February 2003

Adcock, F, *Sunday Times*, 10 December 1995

Aldred, C, *Akhenaten: Pharaoh of Egypt*, Thames & Hudson, 1968

Anderson, B, *The Times*, 28 September 1995

'Baghdad Bounce', leader in *The Times*, 14 April 2003

Balint, M, *Thrills and Regressions*, Hogarth Press, 1959

Bentley, T, *Independent*, 26 December 2000

Berlin, I, *Against the Current: Essays in the History of Ideas*, Oxford University Press, 1981

Blair, A C L, *Let Us Face the Future*, Fabian pamphlet 571, Fabian Society

Blitz, J, *Financial Times*, 26 April 2003.

Bowlby, J, *Attachment and Loss*, Hogarth Press, 1973

Breasted, J H, 'Ikhnaton, the Religious Revolutionary', *Cambridge Ancient History*, 1st edn, vol. II, ch. 6, Cambridge, 1924

Brichto, Rabbi Dr S, *Genesis*, Sinclair-Stevenson, 2000

Burden, R, *New Statesman*, 11 August 1995

Byron, G G, *Don Juan*, canto 1

Chasseguet-Smirgel, J, *Creativity and Perversion*, Free Association Books, 1985

Chasseguet-Smirgel, J, *The Ego Ideal: The Malady of the Ideal*, Free Association Books, 1985

Demause, L, *Foundations of Psycho-History*, Creative Roots, 1982

Edmonds, J, *Tribune*, 11 August 1995

Elovitz, P, 'Clinton's Childhood, and First Year in Office', *Journal of Psycho-History*, vol. XXI, no. 3, Winter 1994

Fairbairn, W R D, *Psychoanalytical Studies of the Personality*, Routledge & Kegan Paul, 1990

Falk, A, *Herzl King of the Jews*, University Press of America, 1993

Ferenczi, S, 'On the Nosology of Male Homosexuality', *Selected Writings*, Penguin Books, 1999

Ferenczi, S, 'Psychoanalytical Observations on Tics', *Selected Writings*, Penguin Books, 1999

Flügel, J C, *The Psychoanalytic Study of the Family*, Hogarth Press, 1939

Foot, M, *Aneurin Bevan*, Davis-Poynter, 1973

Freud, S, *Leonardo da Vinci*, SE, XI, Hogarth Press

Freud, S, *Totem and Taboo*, SE, XIII, Hogarth Press

Freud, S, *On Narcissism: An Introduction*, SE, XIV, Hogarth Press

Freud, S, *Some Neurotic Mechanisms in Jealousy, Paranoia*

and Homosexuality, SE, XVIII, Hogarth Press

Freud, S, *Fetishism*, SE, XXI, Hogarth Press

Frith, S, & Goodwin, A (eds), *On Record: Rock, Pop and the Written Word*, Routledge, 1990

Gallup poll, *Daily Telegraph*, 7 February 1994

Glasser, M, 'Some Aspects of the Rôle of Aggression in the Perversions', *Sexual Deviation*, ed Ismond Rosen, Oxford University Press, 1979

Glover, E, 'Aggression and Sado-Masochism', *The Pathology and Treatment of Sexual Deviation*, ed Ismond Rosen, Oxford University Press, 1964

Griffin, R, *The Nature of Fascism*, Routledge, 1993

Grove, V, *Saga*, May 2003

Guntrip, H, *Schizoid Phenomena, Object-Relations and the Self*, Hogarth Press, 1968

Harris, R, *Sunday Times*, 31 March 1996

Harris, R, *Daily Telegraph*, 21 July 2003

Hildebrand, P, *Beyond Mid-Life Crisis*, Sheldon Press, 1995

Hoggart, S, *Guardian*, 5 July 1996

Hughes, C, *Guardian–Special Report*, 26 September 1998

Hutton, W, *The State We're In*, Jonathan Cape, 1995

Hutton, W, 'The 30 30 40 Society', *RSA Journal*, March 1996

Ingham, B, *The Wages of Spin*, John Murray, 2003

Johnson, J, *Tribune*, 31 May 1996

Jones, D, *Sunday Times*, 13 April 2003

Jung, C J, *Psychological Types*, Teigenbaur, 1923

Kahr, B, *Independent on Sunday*, 25 July 1999

Kaletsky, A, *The Times*, 9 January 1996

Kaletsky, A, *The Times*, 16 May 1996

Kaletsky, A, *The Times*, 11 July 1996

Keynes, J, M, *Essays in Persuasion*, Macmillan, 1972

Kohut, Heinz, *The Restoration of the Self*, International Universities Press, 1977

Krohn, A, *Hysteria: The Elusive Neurosis*, International Universities Press, 1978

Laplanche, J, & Pontalis, J B, *The Language of Psychoanalysis*, Hogarth Press, 1973

Laslett, P A, *Fresh Map of Life*, Weidenfeld & Nicolson, 1989

Lawson, Alvin H, 'Placental Catarrhs, Umbilical Mikes and the Maternal Rock-Beat: Verse Fantasies and Rock Music Videos', *Journal of Psycho-History*, vol. XXI, no. 3, Winter 1994

Little, G, 'Disappointment', *Sydney Morning Herald*, 8 December 1999

Loewenberg, P, 'Theodor Herzl: A Psychoanalytic Study in Charismatic Political Leadership', *The Psychoanalytic Interpretation of History*, ed Benjamin Wolman, Basic Books, 1971

Macmurray, J, *Persons in Relation*, Faber & Faber, 1961

Macmurray, J, *The Self as Agent*, Faber & Faber, 1961

Maguire, K, & White, M, 'Document re-ignites Labour rift', *Guardian*, 7 June 2003

Mandelson, P, & Liddle, R, *The Blair Revolution: Can New Labour Deliver?*, Faber & Faber, 1996

Mandelson, P, 'I never lied – Downing Street sentenced me', *Sunday Times*, 28 January 2001

Margolick, D, *Vanity Fair*, June 2003

McSmith, A, *John Smith: A Life 1938–1994*, Mandarin Paperbacks, 1994

Morgan, O, *Keir Hardie*, Weidenfeld & Nicolson, 1975

MORI poll, *The Times*, 31 March 1994

MORI poll, *The Times*, 29 April 1994

Namier, L, *Personalities and Power*, Hamish Hamilton, 1955

Parris, M, *The Times*, 2 June 1995

Pincus, L, & Dare, C, *Secrets in the Family*, Faber & Faber, 1978

Plato, 'Symposium', trans. Walter Hamilton, *The Penguin Book of International Gay Writing*, Viking, 1995

Platt, S, *Guardian*, 29 September 1995

Plumb, J, *The Death of the Past*, Macmillan, 1978

Poirot-Delpech, B, *Le Monde*, April 1995

Pollock, G, 'Ageing or Aged: Development or Pathology', *The Course of Life*, Bethesda, NIMH, 1980

Quine, M S, *Population Politics in 20th-Century Europe*, Routledge, 1996

Raven, C, *Observer*, November 1995

Rentoul, J, *Tony Blair*, Little, Brown, 1995

Riddell, P, & Webster, P, 'United we must stand on Europe' in *The Times*, 21 May 2003

Reynolds, S, & Press, J, *The Sex Revolts: Gender Rebellion and Rock 'n' Roll*, Serpent's Tail, 1995

Routledge, P, *Mandy: The Unauthorised Biography of Peter Mandelson*, Simon & Schuster UK Ltd, 1999

Rycroft, C, *A Critical Dictionary of Psychoanalysis*, Yelson, 1968

Schafer, R, 'Disappointment and the Disappointed Left', *International Journal of Psychoanalysis*, vol. 80, 1999

Selbourne, D, *New Statesman*, 11 August 1995

Short, C, 'Why did he do it?' in the *Guardian*, 7 June 2003

Simpson, M, *Independent*, 6 March 1996

Sinason, V, *Mental Handicap and the Human Condition: New Approaches from the Tavistock*, Free Association Books, 1992

Skidelsky, R, 'Language and Politics', *Spectator*, 18 June 1977

Smith, D, *Aneurin Bevan and the World of South Wales*, University of Wales Press, 1994

Smith, D, *Sunday Times*, 24 September 1995

Sopel, J, *Tony Blair the Moderniser*, Michael Joseph, 1995

Steiner, G, *In Bluebeard's Castle*, Faber & Faber, 1971

Steiner, R, 'Hermeneutics or Hermes-mess?', *International Journal of Psychoanalysis*, vol. 76, part 3, June 1995

Tait, N, address to the Cambridge Institute of Education, May 1995

Taylor, A J P (ed), *Churchill: Four Faces of the Man*, Penguin, 1973

Townsend, P, *Independent on Sunday*, 14 January 1996

Trilling, L, *Sincerity and Authenticity*, Oxford University Press, 1974

Weber, M, 'Law in Economy and Society', *Twentieth-Century Legal Philosophies Series*, ed. Rheinstein, M, vol. VI, Harvard University Press, 1954

Weber, M, *The Theory of Social and Economic Organisation*, chap. 3, translated by Henderson, A M, & Parsons, T, Oxford University Press, New York, 1947

Webster, P, *The Times*, 3 May 2003

Wegg-Prosser, B, *Guardian*, 25 January 2001

Wills, G, *Certain Trumpets*, Simon & Schuster, 1995

Winnicott, D W, *The Maturational Processes and the Facilitating Environment*, Karnac Books, 1990

Winnicott, D W, *Through Paediatrics to Psychoanalysis*, Karnac Books, 1992

Woolf, E S, *Treating the Self: Elements of Clinical Psychology*, Ilford Press, 1988

Young, H, *Guardian*, 3 October 1995

Young, H, *Guardian*, June 2003

Index

marriage and birth programmes
191–3
sibling rivalry 261–2
traditional 166–7
traumatic 132–60
fascism 180–1, 191–2
fathers
adolescent boys 157
daughters 148
Ferenczi, Sandor 276–7, 283
fetishism 218–21
Fettes College 105, 109
Fischer, Joschka 242–3
foetus, rock music 168–73
folie à deux 150
Foot, Michael 49–50, 51, 176, 314
Foundation Hospitals 107, 284
Francis, Dai 315
Freud, Otto Bauer 189
Freud, Sigmund 218–20
Akhenaten 200
anal erotogenic zone 285
body language 76
crime 227
death wishes 138
disavowal (*Verleugnung*) 108
dissatisfaction 8–9
Eucharist 150
fetishism 218–19
gambling 267–8
heritage of emotion 141
homosexuality 40, 278
hope 319
Leonardo da Vinci 204–5
narcissism 154
perversion 206
sibling rivalry 261–2
unity 308–9
friendship, John Macmurray 119–20, 294
Frith, Simon 174
Frohlich's syndrome 200–1

Gabriel, Peter 172

Gaitskell, Hugh 11–12, 15–26, 48, 70
gambling 266–8
Gandhi, Mahatma 18
Garrick, David 88
gender tourism 164
General Election 1959 26
General Election 1997
disappointment 304
narcissism 51
Peter Thomson 293
polls 11
Road to the Manifesto 299–301
pin 296–7, 298–301
General Election 2001
apathy 130–1, 159–60, 295
Campbell 288–94
control of shortlists 214
crime 223
manifesto 317–18
palingenetic myth 193–4
Germany, Balkans 241–3
Gide, André 304
Gladstone, William 46
Glasser, Mervin 206–7, 210–11, 226–7
Global Ethics Foundation 156
Glover, Edward 207–8, 261, 278
Government Information Service (GIS) 290
Great Exhibition 195
Griffin, Roger 177–8, 180
Griffiths, James 66, 98
Groddeck, George 63
guilt 138–9, 224–6, 267–70
guitars 170–1
Guntrip, Harry 122

Hague, William 85, 260
handicapped smile 104–5
Hardie, Keir 179–80, 311
Harris, Robert 215, 280–1, 293
Hattersley, Roy 70, 217–18
Hendrix, Jimi 171
heritage of emotion 141–3

Marx, Karl 117–18, 299, 317–18
Marxism 113–14
masochism 225–6, 243, 266, 266–70
Matrimonial and Family Proceedings
    Bill (1984) 73–9, 84–6
Maudling, Reggie 266
Members of Parliament 50–1, 259–63
merging, perversion 206–7, 216–18
Messiah, palingenetic myth 179, 182
Milburn, Alan 284
Millennium Dome 129, 305
Milosevic, Slobodan 239–40, 243–4
mirroring 93–6
misogyny, rock music 163–5
Mittal, Lakshmi 291
Mitterand, Francois 49
mixture 216–18
modernisation
    disappointment 305
    false consensus 82–3
    language 42–6
    palingenetic myth 187–8
Monks, John 127
Moore, Suzanne 163–4
Morris, Bill 292
Morris, William 87
Morrison, Herbert 94–5
Moses 201, 216
Mosley, Oswald 180–91
mothers
    child's capacity to be alone 95–6
    creation of identity 121–22
    development of perversion
        209–11, 212, 218–21
    disavowals 108–9
    exhibitionism 91–3
    Labour Party as 31–32
    rock music 168–70
    Wales 33–4, 66–7
mourning liberation process 196–7
Mussolini, Benito 191

Namier, Sir Lewis 272–3, 274
Napoleon Bonaparte 101

narcissism 99
    ageism 183, 185–6
    charismatic leadership 51
    Cherie Blair 146, 147
    dyadic couples 150–1, 153–6, 159
    exhibitionism 91–2, 108–9
    of the mother 210–11, 212, 221
    mourning liberation process 196
    rivalry 260
    shadow cabinet vote 1996 301–2
national insurance 66
NATO 240, 242–3, 244–5, 246, 258
Nazis 181, 182, 183, 191–2, 243
New Labour
    Bill Clinton 235
    fulture 296
    intra-party rivalry 258–63
    language 42–46
    palingenetic myth 178–98
    sleaze 293
    union funding 128
New Party 180
New Statesman 214–15
Nirvana 168–9
Nixon, Richard 15
nostalgia 162, 306–7

Oborne, Peter 279
Observer 213–14
Oedipal complex
    adolescence 157–8
    ageism 183
    Aneurin Bevan 34–5
    gambling 267–8
    George Thomas 65–6, 69
    Hugh Gaitskell 22
    Jacob 251–3
    perversion 218–21
    Tony Blair 85–6, 138–9
Old Labour
    alienation 106–7
    Bill Clinton 235
    consensus politics 215
    crime and penal legislation 228–9